New Security Challenges Series

General Editor: **Stuart Croft**, Professor of International Security in the Department of Politics and International Studies at the University of Warwick, UK, and Director of the ESRC's New Security Challenges Programme.

The last decade demonstrated that threats to security vary greatly in their causes and manifestations, and that they invite interest and demand responses from the social sciences, civil society and a very broad policy community. In the past, the avoidance of war was the primary objective, but with the end of the Cold War the retention of military defence as the centrepiece of international security agenda became untenable. There has been, therefore, a significant shift in emphasis away from traditional approaches to security to a new agenda that talks of the softer side of security, in terms of human security, economic security and environmantal security. The topical *New Security Challenges series* reflects this pressing political and research agenda.

Titles include:

Jon Coaffee, David Murakami Wood and Peter Rogers
THE EVERYDAY RESILIENCE OF THE CITY
How Cities Respond to Terrorism and Disaster

Christopher Farrington (*editor*)
GLOBAL CHANGE, CIVIL SOCIETY AND THE NORTHERN IRELAND PEACE PROCESS
Implementing the Political Settlement

Kevin Gillan, Jenny Pickerill and Frank Webster
ANTI-WAR ACTIVISM
New Media and Protest in the Information Age

Andrew Hill
RE-IMAGINING THE WAR ON TERROR
Seeing, Waiting, Travelling

Andrew Hoskins and Ben O'Loughlin
TELEVISION AND TERROR
Conflicting Times and the Crisis of News Discourse

Janne Haaland Matlary
EUROPEAN UNION SECURITY DYNAMICS
In the New National Interest

Michael Pugh, Neil Cooper and Mandy Turner (*editors*)
CRITICAL PERSPECTIVES ON THE POLITICAL ECONOMY OF PEACEBUILDING

Brian Rappert
BIOTECHNOLOGY, SECURITY AND THE SEARCH FOR LIMITS
An Inquiry into Research and Methods

Brian Rappert (*editor*)
TECHNOLOGY AND SECURITY
Governing Threats

New Security Challenges Series
Series Standing Order ISBN-978–0–230–00216–6 (hardback) and
ISBN-978–0–230–00217–3 (paperback)

You can receive future titles in this series as they are published by placing a standing order. Please contact your bookseller or, in case of difficulty, write to us at the address below with your name and address, the title of the series and the ISBN quoted above.

Customer Services Department, Macmillan Distribution Ltd, Houndmills, Basingstoke, Hampshire RG21 6XS, England

Television and Terror

Conflicting Times and the Crisis of News Discourse

Andrew Hoskins

Associate Professor of Sociology,
University of Warwick, UK

and

Ben O'Loughlin

Lecturer in International Relations,
Department of Politics and International Relations,
Royal Holloway, University of London, UK

South Essex College

Further & Higher Education, Southend Campus
Luker Road Southend-on-Sea Essex SS1 1ND
Tel: 01702 220400 Fax: 01702 432320
Minicom: 01702 220642

palgrave
macmillan

First published in hardcover 2007
First published in paperback 2009 by
PALGRAVE MACMILLAN

Palgrave Macmillan in the UK is an imprint of Macmillan Publishers Limited, registered in England, company number 785998, of Houndmills, Basingstoke, Hampshire RG21 6XS.

Palgrave Macmillan in the US is a division of St Martin's Press LLC, 175 Fifth Avenue, New York, NY 10010.

Palgrave Macmillan is the global academic imprint of the above companies and has companies and representatives throughout the world.

Palgrave® and Macmillan® are registered trademarks in the United States, the United Kingdom, Europe and other countries.

ISBN-13: 978–0–230–00231–9 hardback
ISBN-10: 0–230–00231–5 hardback
ISBN-13: 978–0–230–22902–0 paperback
ISBN-10: 0–230–22902–6 paperback

This book is printed on paper suitable for recycling and made from fully managed and sustained forest sources. Logging, pulping and manufacturing processes are expected to conform to the environmental regulations of the country of origin.

A catalogue record for this book is available from the British Library.

A catalog record for this book is available from the Library of Congress.

10   9   8   7   6   5   4   3   2   1
18   17   16   15   14   13   12   11   10   09

Printed and bound in Great Britain by
CPI Antony Rowe, Chippenham and Eastbourne

For Marie Gillespie

Contents

List of Figures and Tables

Figures

Tables

Acknowledgements

This book emerges from research funded by the Economic and Social Research Council (ESRC) New Security Challenges programme: *Shifting Securities: News Cultures Before and Beyond the Iraq Crisis 2003* (Award no. RES-223-25-0063, see www.mediatingsecurity.com). We are indebted to the project's Principal Investigator, Marie Gillespie, who has proved an inspiration throughout. Thanks are also due to James Gow. We would also like to thank those participating in the study for their time and trust (and for phrases such as 'thousand pinpricks of insecurity').

We are very grateful to Stuart Croft, the New Security Challenges' director, for leading a programme that demanded genuinely innovative, interdisciplinary and rigorous investigations, and understandings of the transforming security environment in which we all live and work. As editor of this book series, we are also grateful for his support and highly constructive feedback. We also wish to thank Amy Lankester-Owen and Gemma d' Arcy Hughes at Palgrave Macmillan, and to the anonymous reviewers for their very helpful and positive remarks.

We are indebted to Mostyn Jones for his technical expertise and incredible patience, to the good people at Transana (www.transana.org) for their innovation and support, and to Giles Moss for allowing insights from his forthcoming paper with O'Loughlin to be included in Chapter 8.

Thanks are also due to: Philip Seib and Barry Richards through collaboration on the journal of *Media, War & Conflict* (mwc.sagepub.com); Gillian Youngs for her interest in our work through her leading of the ESRC Seminar Series: Ethics and the War on Terror: Politics, Multiculturalism & Media. And for their support along the way, we are grateful to: Andreas Antoniades, Claudia Aradau, David Berry, Andrew Chadwick, Charlotte Epstein, Habiba Noor, David Smith, Jacob Eriksson, Oliver Oldfield, Sarah Pickwick, Anna Veretelnikova, Sophie West, Ivan Zvezhanovski, Jonathan Nicholson, Alison Jones, Rob John, Martin Jarvis, Beth Linklater, William Merrin and Lena Munday.

Preface to the Paperback Edition

In *Television and Terror* we argue that there is a contradictory dynamic in media coverage of war, conflict and terrorism. Television news *modulates* between bringing the world's wars and catastrophes into the West's horizon of responsibility, and yet also diminishes our consciousness of such events. While actual deaths and injuries multiply in Lebanon, Gaza and Mumbai, for example, their filtering through the prisms of Western news ultimately renders them sanitized, no matter how shocking the initial images consumed by Western publics may be. Followed by *Diffused War* (Polity, 2009) and *Media & Radicalisation* (Routledge, 2010), *Television & Terror* is the first in a series of studies by the authors of the ethical and professional dilemmas inherent in the process of representing contemporary conflict and catastrophe and the implications for audiences, journalists, media regulators and the protagonists of violence themselves.

Many journalists, editors and other news-workers seek to provide a more immediate, proximate and sometimes intimate representation of the events upon which they report, yet they do not want to be used to manipulate publics and confer legitimacy on one side or the other by granting free publicity to terrorists or fawning coverage to militaries. This book presents the resulting crisis through a series of cases that demonstrate how news has become a daily discourse structured around showing and hiding, amplifying and diminishing, remembering and forgetting. The exceptions to prove this rule were Fox News' coverage of Hurricane Katrina in 2005 and, to a lesser extent, media coverage of the Asian tsunami of late 2004. These events appeared to take government and news editors off guard, giving reporters greater freedom to represent events and capture more of the human dimensions of the catastrophes. Instead of the usual stage-managed, scrupulously edited version of events Western audiences have grown accustomed to, in each case the viewer was presented – for a few days at least – with real immediacy (rather than just the standard, dramatized 'liveness') and perhaps greater authenticity amid the chaos.

Since the hardback edition of this volume was published in late 2007 we have witnessed major terrorist attacks in India and Pakistan, a short war between Georgia and Russia, continued conflicts in Iraq and Afghanistan, and – as we write this foreword – the killing of many innocent civilians because of violent military exchanges between Israel and Hamas. Were terrorists in Mumbai using Twitter to update the world on their progress, for instance, at the same time that they and their associates used live television news reports to aid the management of their terror campaign? Yet alongside these developments, attempts by the Israeli state to limit journalists' access to and reporting from Gaza suggests traditional news control can still be achieved. All these technologies – this informational infrastructure – constitute a new media ecology that is the primary condition for terror today.

Prologue: The (Terrorised) State We're in

'Post 9/11'. This has become the principal marker of terror and insecurity today. It remains to be seen whether the terrorist attacks on the United States on 11 September 2001 have permanently disrupted the notions and structures of security the West had settled upon after the Cold War or whether they contribute to a continuity, one link in a chain of terror events enabled and executed through 'our' media. What is beyond doubt, however, is that television has been unable to prevent itself elevating and supporting a mantra. *Nothing can be the same, the world has changed.* Post 9/11, we become aware of the compression and entanglement of environmental, economic, and ontological insecurities. Out of a single discursive order are generated a thousand pinpricks of insecurity.

Central to this, terror and terrorism have acquired an extensity and mobility that is accelerated primarily by mass media, which become the terrorists' weapon of choice. Terror is the dynamic that courses readily through those intensive modes of representation that underlie what we understand as 'news'. It is on and through television that terror infuses and catalyses speculative discourses alongside, or at the expense of, proportionate, substantiated, and contextualised reporting. The medium pulls events increasingly into an anticipated, often-dreaded future as it dwells on the catastrophes and near-calamities of the past. And the 'enemy', constructed by and through this discursive crisis of our times, is all that is and which becomes 'post 9/11'.

And yet, television, as it delivers daily the spectre of endless terror and violence from places far and near, also rescues us from the brink of chaos. The unimaginable is rendered familiar and terror is harnessed in the frames, rituals, and routines of the major medium of our age. And it is this entanglement of television and terror that is pivotal in both the spinning and containing of the discourses of insecurity that appear already to mark the mediatised experience of the twenty-first century.

1
Introduction

Origins

This book presents research from a project conceived in 2003 to investigate the security environment in Britain in the aftermath of the Cold
War, 9/11,[1] and the Coalition intervention in Iraq in 2003. The emergence of an apparently new world of insecurities prompted a number
of questions. How would governments and military policymakers try to
manage security problems? How would media represent security problems? And how would audiences and publics perceive these security
problems – as representations *and* as issues potentially impacting upon
their lives? The project, *Shifting Securities*, ran from 2004 to 2006, a period
in which security problems seemed to proliferate.[2] Alongside relentless
but low-lying anxieties about environmental threats and health hazards,
terror threats, and unending wars, the period was also characterised
by unforeseen catastrophes such as the 2004 Asian tsunami, Hurricane
Katrina in 2005, and fairly regular terrorist incidents often connected to
Al-Qaeda. We were living in conflicting times.

The *Shifting Securities* project involved three strands of empirical
research. The first was an *audience ethnography*, in which researchers
carried out regular interviews and focus groups with families and individuals around Britain to map how perceptions of security events and
political responses shifted during this period of conflict and catastrophe.
The 200 or so people interviewed in the research were of a considerable
demographic mix – on axes of ethnicity, religion, language, class, gender,
and age. This allowed for an examination of questions of multiculturalism, national and transnational news consumption, and relations
between citizenship and security. The second strand of research was an
analysis of news media over the period. The particular focus was television

news coverage of major security events: the outbreak and aftermath of the 2003 Iraq war, Hurricane Katrina, and the 2005 7/7 London bombings. It is this strand of research that is primarily presented in this book. Finally, in a third strand, researchers carried out *elite interviews* with policymakers in government and the military, with news journalists, editors, and producers and with 'experts' who appear in news media whenever a security catastrophe or controversy occurs. These individuals were faced with responsibilities for conducting state and media responses to critical security problems, while achieving consent and legitimacy from a British citizenry often hotly divided about the nature of security problems and the desirability of possible solutions.

The three strands of research were intimately connected and mutually shaping. For instance, findings from audiences' interviews about what citizens felt to be key stories fed into choices about news media analysed, while findings from such analyses of news was used to frame questions for the elite interviews. The *Shifting Securities* project therefore moved iteratively, to illuminate how perceptions of security among different groups of policymakers and news publics were triggered, altered, or reinforced by security events as they occurred. In addition, the project was resolutely interdisciplinary, with researchers coming from sociology, political science, and security studies, such that the tools of each discipline could be applied where applicable to the complex 'objects' of study. The process of working with researchers from other disciplines forced our assumptions and categories to be questioned and addressed more critically than might have been the case in a single discipline project. Methods had to be justified and concepts such as 'security', 'public', 'legitimacy', and 'influence/effect' had to be reconsidered and defined afresh.

In this book, we present and use our findings from the project's second strand, an analysis of news media, to advance an argument about news coverage of security events in this period of conflict and insecurity. We also make use of the audiences research to shed some light on the relation between news production and consumption, between news content and its use by audiences. But before we introduce our argument, we will provide the reader with a brief summary of our approach, method and data.

Our approach, method, and data

We experience today a new media 'ecology' (Cottle, 2006) or media 'surround' that scholars and analysts increasingly characterise using terms such as connectivity, saturation, and immediacy. Many have hypothesised that people, events, and news media have become increasingly connected and interpenetrated, thanks to developing technologies, all part of 'time–space compression', the collapse of distance, and the availability of information immediately. The empirical foundation for such claims may be uneven, but few would deny that qualitative changes have occurred in the production and consumption of media in the last decade, altering the relation of media to politics and security matters. In the audiences ethnography strand of *Shifting Securities*, for instance, an interview with London schoolchildren in 2004 found them talking about downloading beheading videos to their mobile phones in the school playground. The possibility of children (happily) plugging into globally available footage of distant atrocities seems to exemplify the connectivity, saturation, and immediacy produced by media technologies today.

Since satellite television and then the Internet became publicly available, it is not so much that events are straightforwardly *mediated* by media to audiences; rather, media have entered into the production of events to such an unprecedented extent those events are *mediatised* (Cottle, 2006). Media are built into the design of any political event, war, or terror attack, while even when something unexpected happens, citizens may have camera phones such that the unexpected can be instantly recorded and transmitted beyond those immediately witnessing it. Hence, what becomes interesting, we suggest, is how media enter into the constitution of events.

Certain research questions follow from this. How do those attempting to direct the conduct of the 'War on Terror' use the media to advance their goals? How do the news management strategies of governments, militaries, or indeed terrorist groups contribute to what appears in the news media? How do the characteristics of particular media shape how political discourses are represented on-screen? For instance, how does the sheer *televisuality* of television – the particular modes of integrating moving images, sounds, and verbal representations – affect whether news legitimates certain actors or policies on any given day? These research questions are distinct from those studies of news media that aim simply to map the content of news over time. We have in mind here the more conventional content analysis approaches that ask only what words or images are present in media, how words cluster together, produce systematic analyses and comparisons, and make inferences from this positive data. We contend that claims generated by such systematic analyses are problematised by conditions of connectivity, saturation, and immediacy. Comparisons of the content of media over time are undermined by the changing relationship between news media and the events being reported. It is not that the content of news media has become unimportant, but that such an approach risks obscuring what is interesting and important about the changing relations of media, politics, and security. We feel that in a period when events are often mediatised – when media enter into the very 'happening' of catastrophes and controversies such that those events are to a large extent *constituted by* media – it becomes more valuable to focus research questions not just on what the content is but on *how* this content is produced *in any specific instance.*

Our approach partially falls within the ethnomethodological tradition of social research, in which the primary question applied to all social life is, how is that organised? How do television programmes come to be? How did those people in that company create that new product at that moment? How did those laws come to be applied in that way in that context? Ethnomethodologists such as Harold Garfinkel (1967, 2002) explore how people account for their actions as they do things, in particular contexts. They often go into the context itself, crossing the line from disembedded researcher to participant, working in firms, scientific laboratories, or schools, in order to discern the regularities and principles guiding practices and the meanings these practices hold for participants. Although this investigation is not based on, for example, participant observation, the principles of ethnomethodology nonetheless can be applied to textual analysis (Jalbert, 1999). One can discern the principles or logics that guide the production of television news. For instance, in what we call the 'economy of liveness', stories offering live footage have greater news value than old footage or non-visual stories. A live story may take precedence on the running order of a news bulletin, implying what is considered 'newsworthy' in the practice of news production. Of great interest in ethnomethodological textual analysis are the slips and errors made by a broadcaster, for it is in the slip and the reflexive attempt to remedy the slip that we see what norms and standards are guiding the broadcaster (Goffman, 1981). It is often in the disorderly moments of a television broadcast that we see how orderliness could ever be achieved. We hope our analyses of breaking and rolling news coverage of critical security events demonstrate this insight.

The emphasis on meaning further distinguishes our approach from many studies of media, politics, and security. Unlike some other recent analyses of media and political texts in the War on Terror, our objective is not to 'expose' or contest any particular political strategy at work (cf. Jackson, 2005; Lewis, 2005). Our interest is in establishing the properties of texts that *could* be taken to mean X or Y and that *could* be interpreted as biased. For one exponent of this approach, Paul Jalbert, such 'meanings can be logically argued to inhere in actual texts in virtue of their organization etc.; the issue is what is available to be grasped from them' (Jalbert, 1999: 32). We identify what grammatical, iconographic, lexical, and other properties are *organised into* television broadcasts. To this end, we borrow from the *multimodal* approach to textual analysis devised by Kress and van Leeuwen (2001) (see also application by Chouliaraki, 2006), in which the analyst examines how verbal, visual, and aural aspects of television content come together on a moment-by-moment basis, allowing for inference regarding how different sensoral modes in a text are combined by producers in order to establish intended meanings. For instance, a news producer of a report on the commemoration of the 9/11 attacks may use sombre music to create 'mourning', or a silent, lingering close-up on a firefighter, or footage of people jumping out of the twin towers to achieve a visceral shock. Each mode targets the audiences' senses differently to achieve a particular meaning.

A final, related approach to inform our analysis is that of John Caldwell's (1995) *Televisuality*. Caldwell argues that the way in which television brings together different modes is qualitatively different to other media and so can be analysed on its own terms. For instance, news on the radio is intensely about sound, and the lack of visuality forces audiences to imagine the visual aspect of what is reported. Think of radio news broadcasts on the day of the 7/7 London bombings or the attacks of 9/11, hearing the attacks only through the voices of eyewitnesses and reporters and the sound of sirens from the emergency services. Compare this to the experience of learning of the bombings by watching television – the flashing graphics, the oversized captions, the white faces, the blood and bodies and wreckage. Both multimodal and televisual approaches to textual analysis raise questions of coherence. Coherence applies both to the simultaneous verbal, visual, and aural aspects of a news broadcast and to the micro- and macro-aspects of texts: The set of propositions or points made in a news broadcast may be unified by a headline, striking image, or concluding verbal proposition (van Dijk, 1997). The absence of coherence and orderliness will reveal the ordering principles.

Following the principles of ethnomethodology, guided by its problematic – how is anything achieved? – we hope to offer a valid and illuminating analysis of television news coverage of key security events. Informed too by multimodal and televisuality approaches, the research presented in this book is not straightforwardly ethnomethodological. Consequently, it is more eclectic and 'messy' (Law, 2005) than many empirical studies of media, politics, and/or security. But we argue this messiness is necessary. The traditional categories applied in studies in this field, categories such as 'public', 'effect', 'national', and indeed the very boundaries of different media, offer an uncertain analytical grasp of what is happening today. We are forced to take a focused, second-by-second, frame-by-frame analysis of television news in order to begin to establish the principles, logics, and mechanisms by which television, alongside and in combination with other media, now conveys security events.

We do not offer a systematic comparison of news over the 2004–2006 period, but an analysis of 'perspicuous instances' of television news and security events intersecting in ways that exemplify or point towards regularities that characterise contemporary dynamics of news and security (Jalbert, 1999: 41).[3] We conducted ethnomethodologically informed analyses of recent key security events. We took eight hours of television footage for three events: the opening strike of the 2003 Iraq war, Hurricane Katrina, and the 7/7 London bombings.[4] The footage was digitised, transcribed, coded, and stored using *Transana*[5] software. The categorisations informing our coding were based around core thematics addressed throughout the book, such as security, legitimacy, and identity, as well as televisuality, sanitisation, and technology – and, of course, terror. *Transana* then enabled the comparison of instances of a particular code (e.g. a sanitised depiction of dead bodies) both within the eight-hour footage of an event and across events. This core analysis was bolstered by analysis of other security-salient stories in the 2004–2006 period, such as television footage of 9/11, of the Israel–Lebanon war, and images from Abu Ghraib prison.

We paid particular attention to events that arose in the interviews in the first strand of the project, the audiences ethnography; that is, to stories citizens took note of. Such research is comparable with the work of the Glasgow Media Group. For instance, in *Bad News From Israel*, Greg Philo and Mike Berry (2004) analyse the verbal and visual contents of British mainstream television news coverage of the Israel–Palestinian conflict and in particular the second Intifada in 2000 and moments of intensified conflict in 2001 and 2002. They then assessed audiences' perceptions of this news content by conducting focus groups and questionnaires with viewers around Britain. Finally, the researchers spoke to journalists about their own practices of news production and their assumptions about audiences' political and media literacy. But where Philo and Berry studied news of one (long-running) story, the Israel–Palestinian conflict, our conclusions about a crisis of news discourse and the shifting nature of a 'news culture' are based on analysis of many stories and draws on a more long-term, intensive audiences' study. It is our intention therefore to characterise and explicate the main dynamics of a period – the conflicting times and 'new' security environment that has spanned the vistas of Afghanistan and Iraq, European train stations, and downtown Manhattan and sites as disparate as Bali, Chechnya, and New Orleans, and also the living rooms and locales of television audiences and citizens whose interest in security matters may differ considerably from journalists and policymakers.

Here, in sum, are the aims and objectives of this book:

Aims:

- Address the intersection of media and security in the post-Cold War, post-9/11 context;
- Elucidate the nature of the contemporary crisis of news discourse;
- Clarify this crisis through two concepts, the 'modulation of terror' and 'renewed media';
- Demonstrate the value of an ethnomethodologically informed approach to the analysis of news media.

Objectives:

- Present new data as a contribution to the wider current reassessment of relations of media, politics, and security;
- Present analysis of two major recent security events: the 2003 Iraq war and Hurricane Katrina;
- Articulate relationships between news texts, the practices of news production, and the social, political, and economic contexts within which news production occurs;
- Articulate relationships between news production and news consumption by situating analysis of news media content with analysis of audiences data.

In the next section we offer working definitions of the concepts 'security', 'terror', and 'discourse' that are integral to our analysis, before we outline the argument of this book.

Concepts: security, terror, and discourse

'Thinking about the nature of security, insecurity, who is secure, from whom or what, when, where, and how' was part of the remit for our project (http://www.newsecurity.bham.ac.uk/). Through discussions with the 40 or so other projects in the ESRC's New Security Challenges programme, we are regularly reminded of the different meanings and uses of the terms 'security' and indeed 'terror' taken by researchers and policy practitioners according to their political, disciplinary, and pragmatic purposes. For instance, not only are there competing definitions of 'security' but there is no agreement that security is necessarily a good; for some, forms of insecurity are desirable in some instances (think of Western governments' attempts since the mid-1990s to improve the lives of unemployed people by removing their social security such that in the long term this insecurity forces them to find jobs and economic security). Security can be understood simply as freedom from some danger or terror or as that which provides that freedom from danger or terror.[6] In this book we write of human, environmental, and economic security, and for each the double sense applies: human security as freedom from that which makes insecure and as that which provides human security. Most of the book is given over to issues of human security, but our study of Hurricane Katrina in Chapter 3 examines the televised coverage of an environmental security catastrophe that resulted in economic insecurity for many American citizens, while in our presentation of data from a study of audiences' perceptions of security in Chapter 8, we find individuals perceive a panoply of differing insecurities – locally, at work or walking down the street, and global environmental or terrorism-related insecurities. We also write of ontological security, by which we mean our familiarity and trust with the world around us, formed by acting in and upon that world in our daily routines and social life (Giddens, 1984). Through our interactions we can create a degree of order such that the ambiguity, complexity, and risk of social life are rendered manageable. We explore the relation between individuals' ontological security and media and political discourses that represents imminent security catastrophes, for it is by no means guaranteed that individuals will take note of these more pessimistic discourses, should it disrupt their routine, ontological security.

No concept has been more contested in recent years than 'terror' and its relations 'terrorism', 'terrorist', and 'terrorised'. It has been used to refer to state and non-state acts designed to induce terror in a population, whether terror is defined as outright fear or relentless low-level anxiety (see Bourke, 2004). But as Carr (2006: 6) notes, terrorism is defined not by who is carrying out the action but simply as a technique: 'The essence of this technique is the use of violence against symbolic targets in order to achieve a political rather than a military victory over a particular government or regime.' Symbolic targets may be civilians, officials, and leaders, or infrastructure. It is this technique that has defined terrorism from the French Revolution and its Reign of Terror in 1793–1794 to the actions of Al-Qaeda today. Terrorism is a communicative act, therefore (Nacos, 2002; Barnett, 2003; Devji, 2005), intended to induce a response from a target population. As Kepel (2004) has documented, the history of Al-Qaeda is a history of trying to communicate to non-pious Muslims, first in the Middle East and more recently in Europe and wider afield, the need to reject aspects of modernity and accept a particular doctrine propounded by Al-Qaeda's intellectual vanguard. Terrorism is a performance intended to evoke a response from audiences (Layoun, 2006), audiences who witness the event either first hand or via news media. That terrorism is a communicative act is reinforced by the political communication techniques used by terrorists in recent years, such as the hostage video or the recording of 'martyr tapes' in which political or religious justifications are offered for acts about to be committed. Hence, on many occasions, television and terror are interwoven, part of the same communicative phenomenon.

In arguing there is a crisis of news discourse, what do we mean by news discourse? Discourse is a term used loosely in public debates and is defined and treated differently in different theories of the social sciences (Howarth, 2000). For positivists, discourses are treated as cognitive schemata – mental maps – that people hold intersubjectively. That is, discourse is an instrument for shared understanding and cooperation (Denzau and North, 1994; Braun and Busch, 1999). For realists, the social world contains objects independent of us, and discourses are one such object. Discourses are objects or systems that have relations to other objects or systems, such as the economy or the state. Discourses can therefore be caused by objective political or economic processes (Bhaskar, 1978, 1989). For post-structuralists, everything is discourse: nothing has meaning outside discourse, and therefore, discourse comes to constitute all subjects and objects, though at the same time discourse is always incomplete and ambiguous (Derrida, 1978; Laclau and Mouffe, 1985; cf. Wittgenstein, 2001). Finally, critical discourse analysts posit a duality between social structure and human agency such that while discourses can be treated as structuring and giving meaning to social life, the analyst must examine how (powerful) social actors seek to sustain particular discourses in order to dominate a society (Fairclough, 1992; Howarth, 1995; Weiss and Wodak, 2003). In our view, critical discourse analysis provides a relevant and useful framework, insofar as it links texts, practices, and social context such that none is analysed in isolation. For example, in his critical discourse analysis of the representation of Islam in British newspapers, John Richardson (2004) attempted to draw connections between racism in Britain per se (based on official studies), the financial, organisational, and occupational pressures on journalists that lead to certain practices of (mis)representation, and the actual newspaper texts. We suggest that this approach to media analysis is consistent with our ethnomethodological approach to television news. Any examination of how a piece of news comes to be must entail exploring the connection between the news clip as text, the practices of journalism and news production, and the social and political context within which the text is broadcast and the practices operate. For example, in our analysis of CNN's coverage of the opening of the 2003 Iraq war presented in Chapter 4, through the connection of CNN's programme content with the practices of journalists trying to produce a 'media event' and the social context of a nation about to go to war, it becomes possible to identify how it is that this particular news text is accomplished in *that* way and not another.

The influence of Foucault on critical discourse analysis cannot be overstated, and it is helpful to briefly summarise the conceptions of discourse Foucault proposed because it helps us see how it is possible to distinguish 'discourse' per se from 'news discourse' as well as 'media discourse' and 'political discourse'. In *The Archaelogy of Knowledge* (1972) [1989] Foucault characterises discourse as a system of statements that constitute bodies of knowledge (e.g. scientific knowledge). Such a system acts as a containing 'discursive formation' within which only certain things can be said and in which statements have meaning relationally rather than as isolated speech acts. The analyst's task is to describe the system of statements produced within a discursive formation in order to arrive at the *rules* of formation that structure such discursive practice. Additionally, not only are discursive formations constitutive of objects, insofar as the meaning of any object is only generated within the discursive practice, but so too are subject positions constituted in this way; Foucault argues that *roles* or 'enunciative modalities' are produced and meaningful within a discursive formation. All of this may appear extremely relevant for defining and analysing 'news discourse'.

News has all the features of a discourse described by Foucault. It is a system of statements in which some things can be said and others cannot – norms about what counts as news, what counts as fact, what is litigious, and so on. News as a discourse produces roles – anchor, reporter, expert, and witness.[7] News as discourse produces objects too. In coverage of the 2003 Iraq war, Western television news referred to the 1991 Gulf War. The latter was, as we shall argue later, an object created through the practices of television; that is, in parallel with the military's conduct of the actual war, CNN's rolling twenty-four-hour news coverage of the 1991 Gulf war helped constitute the war as an object for viewers and citizens. That object can now be retrieved, discussed, and used for comparison. News contains many such objects: a 'breaking news event', a commemoration, or a keynote political address. Finally, while Foucault's definition of 'rules' was vague, in our analysis of television news, we identify economies, logics, and grammars followed and sustained by those producing news. These may not become codified as rules, but can be considered rules insofar as news producers and journalists feel compelled to follow them, use them to justify their actions, and which may occasionally be broken or not followed. For instance, we identify an 'economy of liveness' in which the value of a news story depends on whether it is live and immediately accessible; or the grammar of breaking news, featuring cycles beginning with a report, interviews with witnesses, then studio analysis with in-house or external 'experts', before returning to the report.

This *archaeological* approach to discourse was not without problems, in particular the notion of treating a discourse as a coherent entity or *episteme* analysable as a single structure. In his later *genealogical* writings, Foucault broadened his analytical horizon (Foucault, 1978, 1980, 1985, 1986). Instead of analysing discourse as an exploration of what could be said within a particular discursive formation, he paid attention to the power relations that form discourses in the first place. That is, the focus now is on the mutual relation between power and knowledge. In identifying contemporary discourses he deemed oppressive (around sexuality, for instance), the question became: How did this discourse ever come to be? What role did state and church play in forming and institutionalising these discourses, and to what extent did citizens themselves become self-regulating in a manner that sustained the discourses? Discourse is taken as shaped by social practices and broad political, economic, and social processes, yet can be considered to shape social practices and process too. This takes us to the work of Fairclough and other critical discourse analysts (e.g. Howarth et al., 2000; Richardson, 2004) who explore the connections between texts, practices, and broader contexts. It provides a model of discourse analysis in which we can identify how, for instance, economics and politics, market pressures and pressures from government and military, bear upon journalistic practices and the news texts produced.

In this way, we can distinguish news discourse from other discourses (media discourse, political discourse) by reference to its internal rules, roles, and particular specifications of what is 'say-able', and carry out close analysis of news texts to see what news discourse produces on a moment-by-moment basis. Yet we can also locate news discourse within broader social, political, and economic relations to see how news discourse is shaped by and shapes those broader relations. Finally, where Foucault paid little attention to the actual texts, assuming their content to be determined by macro-discursive structures (Fairclough, 1992: 57), our ethnomethodological approach will highlight any variety, mess, and error in television news; that is, where the following of rules is not achieved.

But what of political discourses? Our enquiry explores the relation of televisual news discourse to political discourses that attempt to frame issues surrounding terror and insecurity. It follows that political discourses can also be understood in the terms set out above: a political discourse contains rules, roles, and things 'say-able' which together will constitute subjects (vigilant citizens, terrorists, strong leaders) and objects (the World Trade Centre, the statue of Saddam Hussein pulled down in 2003), such that social life and events become meaningful in particular ways. A political discourse shapes and is shaped by other political, economic, and social processes, and the analyst must identify the 'articulations' produced in this relation. Where a news discourse relates to the production of news, political discourse relates to attempts to produce political outcomes: to define problems in such a way as to legitimate particular solutions that serve certain interests (Howarth et al., 2000). To return to our analysis of CNN's coverage of the opening phase of the 2003 Iraq war, for instance, we highlight two political discourses vying for dominance in the framing of the war. The first is 'democratic imperialism', the political discourse of the Coalition leaders and their supporters who sought to create democracy overseas in order to safeguard homeland security. The second is 'assertive multilateralism', the political discourse of those seeking to identify and address problems in international society through multilateral institutions such as the UN and NATO. We argue in Chapter 4 that the norms and practices of television news discourse, such as reliance on officials and the need for a dramatic media event, operated in this instance to elevate the democratic imperialist discourse and discount assertive multilateralism. Multilateralists such as Hans Blix, the UN weapons inspector, appeared on CNN to contest the definition of the problem as 'Saddam Hussein defies weapons inspectors'. For him it was not so straightforward a case. But this did not fit the narrative of a media event that CNN was organising and the interviewer dismisses his point of view as irrelevant.[8] Thus, a news discourse reinforced one political discourse at the expense of another.

To summarise, we have introduced working definitions of security, terror, and discourse that will inform our analysis. We have emphasised the different types of security, the communicative nature of terrorism, and specified how we can distinguish between different types of discourse. It is now time to lay out our main argument.

Our Argument: modulation plus renewal equals crisis

If, following Cottle (2006), news is mediatised, with media built into and constitutive of terror events such that the events cannot be considered to exist without their media dimension, then ontologically speaking, we can point to an *interaction order* composed of both what appears in news media and what happens beyond the media text – 'out there' in the world. What happens on-screen is inseparable from off-screen events, but more and more, it is the case that off-screen events become inseparable from media representations of those events.

We borrow the concept of 'interaction order' from that developed by Erving Goffman (1971/1972: 15) for whom it concerns, 'the conditions and constraints placed upon the manner in which ends are sought or activity carried out and with patterned adaptions associated with these pursuings' rather than 'the choice of ends or the manner in which these ends may be integrated into a single system of activity'. The micro-social or interaction order that is the principal domain investigated in what follows is television news. It is this that constitutes our unit of analysis.

Developments in this interaction order point to a crisis of news discourse. By crisis we refer at a most basic level to a situation in which news fails to deliver on its promise to provide credible, reliable information about security events (in particular). Nowhere is this better exemplified than by the collective self-examination by US journalists in the wake of the 2003 Iraq war and the lack of WMD in Iraq (Massing, 2004; Fenton, 2005), and comparisons with the reporting of US journalists to those in other countries (*Columbia Journalism Review*, 2004; Lehman, 2004). Questions were raised concerning journalists' failure to scrutinise the Bush Administration's case for war and justifications based on the threat of Saddam Hussein using WMD or offering WMD to terrorists. Most notable was the *New York Times* reporter Judith Miller's reliance on dubious sources for information about Saddam Hussein's regime.

But there is nothing new in pointing out that journalists sometimes fail to provide accurate or reliable information or fail to elucidate a story's context or examine the motives and history of its participants (cf. Philo and Berry, 2004; Wolfsfeld, 2004). We intend to draw attention to a more profound crisis, woven through news content, journalistic practices, and, critically, the very 'new' security environment that appears increasingly to define politics and society in these conflicting times. With the evaporation of the Cold War frame for reporting world politics and the emergence of the 'War on Terror' frame, Davis writes, 'the United States has once again started a grand fight against its own worst enemy – its future' (Davis, 2006: 13). Behind this sweeping statement lurks a whole set of problems that revolve around issues of temporality, uncertainty, and credible journalism, problems that run together throughout this book.

We propose two concepts that give us analytical leverage to understand this crisis. The first is the *modulation of terror*. News modulates terror by often simultaneously *amplifying* and *containing* representations of threat. News amplifies by inflating the seriousness of threats, by connecting a single threat to others, or by representing threats in vague, indefinite terms through speculation, linguistic imprecision, or loose use of numerical, quantitative indicators of 'terror'. Yet news also contains, by fitting new and breaking stories within prior narratives or by sanitising graphic and disturbing images of violence, bodily injury and death – where disturbing refers to the perceptions, accurate or otherwise, of the tolerance of a presumed audiences by programme editors and managers.

Let us take an example of modulation. Containment as a news strategy became firmly established in the wake of the television coverage of the attacks of 11 September 2001 and their aftermath. The live, simultaneous, and unrelenting television coverage of that which the same media institutionalised as '9/11' had an effect similar to that of holding a magnifying glass up to the sun. The news media's mass-amplification of this event, the extent of whose impact was dependent upon that same amplification, shaped how 'terror' was conceived in news and political discourses. The medium of television has oriented itself around these conceptions ever since: many stories can be reported and analysed according to assumptions and concepts emanating in the news media's coverage of 9/11. Having amplified, the news media has modulated back towards a containment strategy (deliberately or otherwise). However, the new significance of new terror events for news media is not a drive to match the newsworthiness of 9/11, should a similar catastrophe ever be played out live, globally, on screens again. Rather, as Richard Grusin argues, there is a desire to prevent a recurrence of television's culpability for a terror event of this magnitude, in a comparable way to the US media's determination to prevent television journalism's implication again in the failure of a US military campaign that emerged following the Vietnam War, and which resulted in the general acquiescence of the same media in the face of the 1991 Gulf War. Grusin, for example, argues that partly in response to 9/11, there has occurred a shift in the cultural and media dominant from 'remediation'[9] to that of 'premediation':

> 9/11 can be seen to have marked an end to (or at least a repression or sublimation of) the U.S. cultural desire for immediacy fuelled by the dot.com hysteria of the 1990s and to have replaced it with a desire for a world in which the immediacy of the catastrophe, the immediacy of disaster, could not happen again – because it would always already have been premediated.
>
> (2004: 21)

The shock of 9/11 was amplified as television news. That news was used explicitly as a terrorist weapon, and news was ultimately *unable to contain its own hijacking* in this way. There was little opportunity for Americans and many others to escape from the immediacy of the coverage, nor for television programming to deliver any alternative. The compulsion for immediacy, developed and honed by broadcast news over many years (and accelerated during the 1990s), and the compelling fascination with the 'mediated immediacy' of the unfolding event,[10] enabled the terror of 9/11 to penetrate deep into both the psyche of the United States and into that of its media. Immediacy and its corollaries – simultaneity and proximity, the central components of the relationship between television and terror – ensured a prolonged satiation of horror on a cinematic scale.

Indeed, for many months the US media could not ease back from their saturation coverage of 9/11 and its aftermath. Uncertainty surrounded the adequacy of political and military responses to the terrorist attacks of 9/11, for what could be an 'adequate' response to 'unknown unknowns'? This also extended to a new insecurity within journalism, unsure how to act as a buffer between terror events and its intimately connected audiences, while being the chief conduit for those terror events. Patricia Mellencamp writes of the experience of watching a breaking news catastrophe:

> Simply put, TV causes anxiety (obsessive thought), which necessitates more TV viewing (compulsion), which raises the ante of fear – a loop of viewing triggering anxiety/anxiety triggering viewing, an interchangeability of cause and effect.
>
> (Mellencamp, 2006: 127)

As a consequence of this double bind, television news offers a modulation between insecurity and security: television news swings back and forth along an axis of terror between amplification and containment. This mitigates against proportionate, substantiated, and contextualised reporting and contributes to the possibility that journalists do terrorists' work. If terrorism is, as we suggest, a communicative act, then television becomes weaponised.

The second important concept for analysing the crisis of news discourse is *renewal*. Far from spelling the death of mainstream news and television news in particular, technological developments such as the Internet, blogging, YouTube, cameraphones, and citizen journalism have become integrated into mainstream news. Now, there can be no doubt that the media–terror relationship is being transformed by the proliferation of news sources and discussion forums on the web. The apparent splintering of news providers and news sources available to audiences offers the potential for fragmentation of news consumption too. The post-9/11 environment has even woken up Media Sociology from its 1980s slumber and at last there is a sense of a paradigmatic shift as the field attempts to make sense of these transformations. For example: in *Mediatized Conflict*, Simon Cottle (2006: 51) maps a complex 'new media ecology' of 'public sphere(s) and public screens'. Meanwhile, on journalism, Brian McNair posits a 'cultural chaos' paradigm, as a 'necessary response to what is emerging as a period of political, economic, ideological and cultural dissolution and realignment, unfolding globally across a range of axes and dimensions' (2006: 4). However, television is still a mass vehicle for and organiser of the millions of messages thrown out by the new digital and diffused media. The sometimes random and chaotic scraps of images become substantive and influential on a wide scale only when acknowledged by what Dan Gillmor (2006) calls 'Big Media', be they carried on the picture wires or as part of 'image clusters' whereby very similar images of the same event are mediated by a whole array of different mediums and news organisations. So, even extraordinary and shocking stories and images are translated into 'stock' narratives as they are mediatised and remediatised through the televisual-driven regime of news. Television is thus a renewed medium, renewed by the so-called new media.

In contradistinction to McNair's 'cultural chaos' position, we argue that television is not merely part of a random mass-mediated entanglement with our everyday lives. Rather, television news and current affairs constitute a highly ordered regime, a regime that still directs, shapes, and controls meaning among, and even because of, the flux of the new media forms and texts. The exception proves the rule: it is rare in the extreme for citizen journalists or bloggers to initiate a major news story or set the news agenda (Francoli, 2007). What has emerged, and that which we elucidate in what follows, is an interaction order in which television news is the key mechanism through which conflicts and catastrophes – which seemingly saturate our twenty-first-century-mediatised surround – are rendered ordered and familiar.

At times of breaking news, the televisual interaction order is supplemented, rather than disrupted, by the explosion of new media sources. For instance, the proliferation of remote and mobile audiovisual recording devices and the mass availability of amateur or 'bystander' photographs and video add to a growing 'surveillance culture' which shapes news narratives in sometimes unpredictable and random ways. To take two examples, the amateur footage of the police capture of the suspects of the attempted 21 July 2005 London bombings on a West London balcony and the mobile video of the police raid in Forest Gate in the summer of 2006 (both scooped by ITV News) were used to shape the news narratives of 'reasonable' and 'excessive' force deployed by the police, respectively. Mobile phone photographs and video recorded by members of the public are now routinely requested by news organisations at times of the breaking of catastrophic news stories and other events. Despite the presentation of these as a 'democratisation' of the mass media (i.e. 'citizen journalism'), we argue that these function as a significant new legitimation device for the construction of particular (and still highly selective) news narratives. Although they do add to the immediacy, proximity, and intimacy of the televisual representation of terror and trauma, the potential for offering a new array of perspectives is not realised. The unprecedented range of material is still incorporated into highly conventionalised news frames and templates. Hence, renewal is part of the crisis of news discourse because of the failure to date to fully capitalise on the potential offered by technological advances for a more dynamic and democratised regime.

Summary of chapters

In Chapter 2, next, we show how television's modulation of terror is made possible through its relationship with time. Television stands in relation to our 'clock time' as a regulating device in our everyday lives such that our experience of time is, to a varying extent, inseparable from our experience of media. How television constructs and plays with time is critical to its capacity to present events and address audiences.

In television news, an 'economy of liveness' defines the values of newsworthiness, placing a premium of significance on the immediate, 'nowness' of breaking events. This renders television news highly vulnerable to the amplification of terror. The chaos and uncertainty that characterise breaking news coverage open a space for unsubstantiated facts and speculation. We examine how news producers attempt to counter this problem, for instance through repetition or through managed 'media events' that could contain the unexpected and the excessive that can occur in live news.

Chapters 3 and 4 illustrate our argument through analyses of two live news events. In Chapter 3, we analyse Fox News' coverage of Hurricane Katrina's devastation of New Orleans and the surrounding area. The catastrophe raised questions concerning whether media can have 'effects' such as prompting public and governmental humanitarian responses. We use this chapter to differentiate our ethnomethodologically informed 'anatomy' of a news event to the 'CNN effect' models that characterise some political science approaches since the mid-1990s. Our analysis demonstrates that once we take note of the chaotic, fragmented messages produced in breaking news coverage, the notion of a coherent, discrete message that might 'effect' policymakers is problematic. In addition, we suggest that this messy, chaotic coverage creates uncertainty about the event being reported and that Fox News' coverage amplified terror by offering representations of connections between Hurricane Katrina and terrorism, economic insecurity, and health hazards.

Chapter 4 offers an analysis of CNN's coverage of the opening phase of the 2003 Iraq war. The analysis raises questions concerning how news discourse can reproduce political discourse. If 9/11 and other terrorist attacks show how television can become hijacked by terrorists, then our analysis of CNN's coverage of the 2003 Iraq war demonstrates how television coverage can act to reproduce the framing and assumptions of political discourses advanced by elected officials, in this case lending legitimacy to the 'democratic imperialist' discourse advanced by the Bush administration. CNN's coverage was in effect hijacked by its own demand for a predictable, manageable but exciting media event, the need for a coherent narrative that precludes or de-legitimates alternative perspectives, and by a reliance on the administration and military for information about what was happening in Iraq. Moreover, by offering simultaneous footage of events in Iraq and the US 'homeland' and by giving a platform to 'experts' who possessed little concrete information but many pessimistic hypotheses, CNN amplified terror and legitimated the democratic imperialist assertion of a link between Saddam Hussein and terrorists intent on attacking the United States. Yet as with Fox News' coverage of Hurricane Katrina, attention to the multimodal, tele-visual aspects of CNN's footage allows us to consider the complex rela-tion between the footage and audiences. The green, murky footage of air strikes over the Baghdad skyline appeared to create distance between event and viewer, containing the terror of the event. Yet the incom-pleteness of the visuals and the reporter's voiceover invited audiences to imagine, to 'do work'; one audiences member in our analysis wondered if she was, in effect, witnessing Iraqis being killed, live.

Having examined how television news represents current and future threats, in Chapter 5, we turn to demonstrate television's reliance upon history and the past in constructing these presents. Television employs its archival resources more immediately than any other medium, inter-weaving an array of texts from the past in its presentation of current events and in projecting its reflexive speculation on the future. The history of the medium itself can be mapped onto the events on which television news reports, shapes, and appropriates as constitutive of its own 'memory', as though its claims to authorship enhance its own cred-ibility and legitimacy as an actor in those events. We consider the func-tion of 'media templates',[11] namely the principal mechanism of instant comparison and contrast that television news employs to reinforce or reshape past events and also to interpret and direct those unfolding through its archival prism. We argue that the some of the most powerful media narratives of the modern age are multimodal, layering and fusing an array of textual stimulants within the televisual environment, and imposing sequential and serial connections on disparate terror events and the War on Terror. We conclude this chapter by examining the relev-ance and the endurance of the Vietnam War template in the context of the 'quagmire' of the aftermath of the 2003 Iraq war.

Representations of the injured, captured, or dead human body are of paramount importance in news coverage of conflict. In Chapter 6, we explore the moral crisis this presents for journalists. We identify a 'body paradox': while television per se is far from squeamish with regard to showing sex, violence, and other matters of contested 'taste and decency', television news is subject to intense debates concerning the depiction of graphic scenes from human conflict. Little wonder, however: Military and terrorist forces can be said to hijack or 'weaponise' news reports if they achieve the widespread depiction (or re-mediation) of images of bodies as trophies of war or as evidence of the barbarity of their opponents. Sanitisation is one means of limiting this. Yet far from containing the terror of war, we contend that sanitised footage has the potential for instilling greater anxiety and fear in viewers. Just as murky coverage of the air campaign in Iraq simultaneously distanced viewers yet drew them in, so sanitised footage of conflict invites audiences to imagine what is unseen. Finally, we explore the relation between the new 'ecology of images' of conflict and bodies in the 2003 Iraq war 'aftermath' or 'civil war' and their relation to body counts – quantitative representations of the dead and injured. We argue that despite sanitised footage, despite poor journalistic access to life in Iraq, and despite the horror of war being portrayed as much by statistics as by images, it is ultimately the relentless daily representation of suffering, injury, and death in Iraq that renders the situation a 'success' or otherwise for Coalition forces.

Drama and documentary representations of security events tell us a great deal about the crisis of news discourse. In Chapter 7, we argue that dramas such as 24 and *Spooks*,[12] which portray contemporary issues of terrorism and conflict in a curious parallel to news coverage, prioritise immediacy and excitement over comprehension or reflection. Thereby, like televised news, they may serve to reinforce certain assumptions about terrorist threats advanced in contemporary political discourses. Yet these assumptions have been powerfully criticised in recent documentaries. The BBC's *The Power of Nightmares* provided a historiography of Al-Qaeda and neoconservatism in order to provide information about the key actors in the 'War on Terror' that news had failed to provide. The documentary argued that notions of 'terror threat' presented by politicians and media are vastly exaggerated or amplified, and indeed that it was in their interests to inflate such threats. Finally, Channel 4's documentary 'Iraq: The Hidden Story' argued that television news failed to provide accurate or credible reporting from Iraq, due to the sheer chaos and risk to journalists. In different ways, then, both documentaries, as well as 24 and *Spooks*, direct attention to the often dubious 'reality' television news provides and proffer reasons for the apparently irresolute nature of the crisis of news discourse.

In Chapter 8, we explore in some detail the relation between the 'reality' of terror presented by politicians and media and the experience and perceptions of security of citizens in Britain. We contend that citizens confront political, media, and experiential 'discursive realities' that may overlap but may not, such that political or media representations of terror may seem disconnected from the local reality of citizens' experiences. We provide a series of pen portraits of individuals, families, and groups around Britain to suggest how perceptions of security have (or have not) shifted since the 2003 Iraq war. If television constructs temporalities such as live-ness and the media event and constructs distance and proximity through various televisual devices, then so citizens have their own tempos (the new security policy was 'unexpected') and their own spatialities. Moreover, just as television modulates terror, oscillating between amplification and containment, so audiences modulate their consumption of terror-related news. For instance, a tension exists between the duty some citizens feel to stay informed of current affairs and the need for ontological security or peace of mind. Political and media discourses of terror may not be useful in the course of trying to manage work and family life each day. But we conclude the chapter by considering the prospects for democratic engagement during these conflicting times. We suggest, cautiously, that just as television news has been renewed by the more chaotic production and consumption patterns of recent years, so democratic life may be renewed around the contestation of security issues. The diverse discursive realities of citizens and indeed journalists and policy-makers do not preclude the existence of shared matters of concern, but it remains to be seen whether political and media portrayals of these matters will foster or hinder what would be a slow, patient constructive process.

We conclude *Television and Terror* by further highlighting the contradictions contributing to the crisis of television news discourses. We ask whether the medium's modulations between amplification and containment, its aggregation and disaggregation of responses to events that it incorporates and presents as news, and its appropriation and celebration of the excesses and surfeit of information and images, have resulted in a set of irresolvable problems for television.

2
Television and Time

> When weather information is absolutely crucial, count on
> CNN's global weather team. Armed with the latest technology,
> real time weather reports and satellite images from around the
> planet, why depend on anyone else? CNN's forecasters draw
> from an extensive database to help put today's weather into
> historical perspective. This means forecasts that are accurate,
> clear and dependable. And if you can't tune in, log on to
> CNN.com/weather for all the information you need at your
> fingertips. So no matter where you are in the world, the CNN
> weather team has you covered. When it comes to weather, be
> prepared, be the first to know.
>
> (CNN, 19 March 2003, commercial broadcast
> minutes before the Iraq war begins)

Time is at the centre of our understanding of the relationship between
television news, television per se, and the culture within which television content is produced. In the weather commercial above, CNN
appeals to viewers with reference to different temporalities. It offers 'real-
time' weather reports, 'historical perspective', and 'forecasts' of weather
to come. Moreover, bringing to bear the present, past, and future
upon weather is a service framed as integral to the viewer's security –
enabling them to be informed and prepared, we might infer, *for the
worst*. CNN promises a premediation of potential weather catastrophes,
reminding us of the potential for catastrophe while rendering the notion
contained by CNN's own capacity to prepare us. In this chapter, we
explore the principles underlying the CNN weather broadcast as they
apply to television and television news in particular. We outline the
'economy of liveness' underlying television broadcasting. This forms

the basis for a medium-specific alternative to Johan Galtung and Mari Holmboe Ruge's (1965) 'news values' paradigm which has endured in much media analysis to this day.

In Chapter 1, we argued that the concept 'modulation of terror' is important for analysing the nature of the relationship between television news and terror. Through exploring television news' amplification and containment of terror, we highlighted a contradiction that leaves television's relation to terror problematic. On the one hand, news practices afford value to the terrible and the catastrophic, the reporting of terror events being in part determined by the passing of certain thresholds in respect of the numbers of injured or dead, and the potential for, as well as actual, death and destruction (see Chapter 6). On the other hand, the presentation of unadulterated horror and boundless threats and the consequential provocation of fear and panic could, if pushed to its limit, alienate viewers and end the television news business. As we have seen, the 9/11 terrorists pushed television towards this latter end of the spectrum and into a new age, not least through the medium's appropriation or hijacking in what we call the weaponisation of television.

Critical to television's modulation of terror is its appropriation and mixing of time. Television news seizes and plays with time; it is at the very heart of its capacity to represent and re-represent events, its modes of address, and its mirroring and manipulating of the everyday passage of 'clock time'.[1] In later chapters, we develop the role of television news and the significance of time to account for the so-called CNN effect, in the reshaping of the past and its uses to frame the terror present, and in the interplay between the temporal registers of 'urgency' and 'patience' in democratic decision-making. First, though, we provide an overview of the relevant approaches to time and temporality in media sociology, and the inherent and constructed 'liveness' of television news. In keeping with the methodology as outlined in our Introduction, we move in this chapter between the culture within which news is produced, the practices of news production, and examination of news texts.

Flow, liveness, and modulation

The media's treatment of terror is underpinned by transformations in the temporality and spatiality of television. It is the medium's construction of contiguity both with events being reported and with audiences that is central to its modulation between the amplification and the containment of terror. This involves what we might call a contradictory television news culture that seeks out and seizes upon catastrophe and disorder and affords value to stories which promote proximity, discontinuity, terror, and insecurity (amplification) and yet inevitably applies visual and narrative frames which impose coherence, continuity, order, and distance (containment). In addition to the filters and frames displayed on-screen (which we consider below), the television *news studio itself* signifies its temporal and spatial connections through the incoming and outgoing news feeds routinely arranged on rows of monitors. The studio becomes the omniscient hub of the network. The convergence of disparate and simultaneous times and places is displayed in this way as though to assert the studio's totalising control over events. Samuel Weber, for example, argues that CNN conceives of itself as a 'model for totalization' proposing an 'all-encompassing unity' in an era that lacks a 'unifying, totalizing worldly instance' (1996: 126). However, Weber also indicts television as a source of the very same problem that it seeks to remedy: 'The more the medium tends to unsettle, the more powerfully it presents itself as the antidote to the disorder to which it contributes (ibid.).' The televisual news machine is the harbinger of (selective) atrocities but also seeks to deliver us from them.

Television news achieves this disruption and resolution chiefly through its economy of liveness. Time is the driving organisational principle of television news, and to understand the relationship between television and the matters upon which it reports, the temporalities of the medium need to be fully explored. One aspect of this principle is the medium's capacity to impose a temporal ordering on events so that they mirror the continuities of what can be described as every day or 'clock-time'. For audiences, it might be suggested, the threat of terror events raised by television news needs to be neutralised to ensure the security of continued viewing (though as we show in Chapter 8, this process is not so straightforward), and the regularity or 'flow' of television news offers, paradoxically, a reassurance.

Pioneering and prophetic in defining television news in relation to its imposition of a temporal flow was Raymond Williams. Writing in the pre-24/7 news age, he argues that in respect of a newscast: 'the kind of flow which it embodies is determined by a deliberate use of the medium rather than by the nature of the material being dealt with' (1974: 115). With the technological transformations noted earlier, the trend in determining television's 'flow' has in many ways moved much further in respect of the former (the medium), over the latter (content),

than even Williams might have imagined. A key example is the establishment of liveness as the mode underlying the way in which our world
is constructed as 'news' by and through television. Liveness entails the
decreasing of the temporal distance between event, recording, transmission, and reception. Often these moments become simultaneous. Immediacy is thus institutionalised into news discourses (constructed and
enhanced through camerawork, visual graphics and icons, and broadcast
talk, for example). So, there is an interplay between the technological
facilitation of liveness and its appropriation and mimicking by news
workers. Jeffrey Sconce, for instance, writes: 'Broadcasters create and
exploit the medium's illusion of simultaneity and its sense of unending
flow through many strategies, hoping to craft the impression of immediate, intimate, and continuous contact with another world (2000: 174).'
But what are the consequences of these shifts on the nature of terror and,
relatedly, the opportunities for terrorists? If the continuity constructed
by television news has become part of a 'comfort zone' of the status quo
(even when television is switched off, alike other 'renewed'[2] media, it is
always 'on') does this diminish the potential impact of the terror event?
How successful is television in attempting to construct a totalising view
of events, and how does this tension or modulation play out?

The medium's investment in immediacy and liveness does make it
vulnerable to exploitation as a tool of terrorism (the second plane hitting
into the World Trade Center on 9/11 after the first pulled in global
real-time coverage). Yet, television could also be considered as the antidote to the shocking, penetrating real-timeness of these images. Even
initially very shocking images can eventually be effectively neutralised
and historicised through their continuous repetition and recycling (we
explore these issues in detail in Chapter 6).

The function of television in accentuating and assuaging terror is
inextricable from its wholesale consumption and construction of time(s)
and we set out this relationship in what follows. It is important to begin,
however, by stepping back to provide an overview of the significance of
time in media, and media in time.

Time and value

Time is a central phenomenon of human existence. Our daily lives, our
relations with others, our concepts of work and leisure – all are measured
by and understood through our experience of time. Indeed, as Barbara
Adam (1995: 19–20) observes, time is the most widely used noun in the
English language and:

It is not surprising, therefore, that our everyday communications are full of references to it: we speak of clock time and winter time, of opening times and bad times, of the right time for action and the timing of an interaction. We refer to the time of things and processes, to a time that flies and a time that takes its toll. We move freely between all these senses of time and know them intimately without giving much thought to their differences.

Our individual consciousness of time does not appear to match its significance in these terms. Adam argues that we need to address some of the complexities of our relations to time to reveal how it structures and governs our lives, notably through the influence of clock time. And yet, we cannot *see* time but have to rely on viewing it through various indicators (Urry, 2000). Think, for example, how the passage of time is made visible, measured, and recorded through the use of clocks, watches, diaries, calendars, schedules, and deadlines. Our day-to-day existence is considerably ordered through these different impositions of clock time.

Time (and particularly clock time) provides us with a temporal framework through which we assign different *values* to different segments of our day, week, and lives. For example, in modern societies, a premium has been placed on our possession of time, so that we speak of saving time, having 'time out', or seeking 'quality time'. Financiers complain of being money-rich, time-poor. Contemporary living is often characterised with reference to a speeding-up and also a shortage of time (and we return to consider issues of pace and speed below). What, though, have been the influences that have shaped our contemporary experience and evaluation of time in this way? Central to this is the relationship of communications technologies and mass media to the changes in our perception and organisation of time, the central organising mechanism of television, and we explore the consequences that flow from this through news discourse today. Firstly though, we map a brief history of, and examine some of the influences on, the relationship between time and news culture.

Early times

The following is taken from a description of events in the composing room of a one-off edition of the *Daily News* newspaper being used to train early students of print-journalism in Chicago, 1905:

At midnight the climax approached. The telegraph editor was working at top speed. He turned a mass of items concerning federal affairs into a special correspondent's Washington letter – what are the principles and policy in a crisis such as this? – and dictated to a stenographer, provided for an emergency, a clear condensation under a St. Petersburg dateline of telegrams from Moscow and other Russian cities, at the same time skilfully weaving in the chief facts as to the Zemstvos situation, and other related items...the foreman...'lifted' this story and substituted that in order to secure symmetry and balance of heads, to recognize news values, and to meet the exigencies [demand] of space. The fourth page was locked up, the third was on the point of being closed, when in rushed the telegraph editor with a fresh war bulletin. It must go at the head of the first page war story.

(George E. Vincent, 1905: 307)

In this account, the then latest communications technology is central to determining what stories are included or omitted at the last minute in the *Daily News*. That is, most of the action in the final editing of the paper revolves around the medium of the telegraph. Space is found for the 'fresh' war bulletin, but only at the expense of a (less recent) front-page telegram, which is moved inside the paper to page three where it displaces another (even less recent) news item. Hence, a hierarchy of recency is developed in ordering news items beginning with the front page. Another issue for the trainee journalists working at this time was the shelf life of stories in the newspaper once it has been published. For instance, earlier in the *Daily News* article above, the author outlines the concern of the team to avoid including articles that 'would be covered by the afternoon papers, and would therefore lose much of their news value' (1905: 306). When a story is 'updated' by another newspaper this serves to devalue existing reports – they simply become older news. So, news content in 1905 and the so-called news values, from this perspective, are clearly conditioned by an environment governed by time – and the immediacy of the telegraph is a key determinant in this respect.

Vincent's article appeared in an academic journal – the *American Journal of Sociology* – in 1905, the same year as the newspaper editing he describes. His discussion around news values is significant as this period marked the beginnings of the academic study of journalism. This sought to demonstrate for students the decision-making processes behind the production of news and to describe that which journalists often refer to as their 'instinct' for putting together a story. This is not remarkable in itself, given the tradition of the study of journalism that developed and much later the growth in media and communication studies. However, given that time is a defining feature of the above account, it is surprising that the temporalities of the production of news have not been more of a concern – and perhaps even dominant – in the development of the early academic writing in this field. More remarkable is that Johan Galtung and Mari Holmboe Ruge's benchmark model of news values (which we consider below) has endured in these disciplines today yet was devised some forty years ago, and that the (Norwegian) press is perhaps an unlikely medium as a model of news values applicable to others today. Although Stuart Allan (1999: 63) acknowledges that news values 'are always changing over time and are inflected differently from one news organization to the next'; he nonetheless claims that these have remained as 'relatively consistent criteria'. Significantly, it is precisely this point that has remained relatively unchallenged.

In using a modified version of Galtung and Ruge, Allan (1999) and others tend not to be medium-specific. And yet, the transformations in the temporalities of the electronic media – and notably that of television as *the* medium of time – require, firstly, some shift in academic accounts to address this fact and, secondly, and more generally, that a medium-specific approach is called for. In this way, the characteristics of a given medium can affect greatly the news values that operate in that environment. So, unlike many other so-called news values, time or temporality is a property that extends beyond the news story itself.

Cultures of immediacy

The proliferation of communication technologies and the electronic media has enabled a more continuous connectivity between people and across vast distances. We simply live a more connected existence than ever before, in which clock time is increasingly being 'squeezed'. For example, previous segments of the day allocated for eating, working, sleeping, and leisure have been transformed in the so-called 24-hour society,[3] where immediacy – an ability or desire for having or doing things now – has become a more significant force in modern living.

The consumption of popular culture in Western society[4] has been marked by a shortening of temporal horizons (living for now) and a critique of our diminishing attention spans. For example, a 'three-minute culture' is seen as driven increasingly by a demand of and for the moment, producing (or produced by) distracted channel-hopping audiences. Fashions, pop stars, hit movies, and celebrities move in and out of extreme exposure with increasing velocity. We live in an age characterised by a 'transformation of visibility' (John B. Thomson, 2000: 33) in Western politics, history, and popular culture. Reality (and often real time) based television programmes have been successfully constructed on this premise. In *Big Brother* and *Pop Idol*, instant celebrity is the format's compulsion and guarantor.

The trend towards what appears as less-demanding (or just more time-squeezed) consumption of the media, and popular culture more widely, can be traced over some time. Todd Gitlin (2001), for example, examined trends in popular American fiction and found that the average sentence length fell by 43 per cent and the number of punctuation marks fell by 32 per cent over the past fifty years (the latter taken as a measure of the complexity of sentence structure). He also looked at the proportion of dialogue in popular novels to discover if these had become to resemble television screenplays. Although Gitlin adopted a very crude methodology and drew on a small sample,[5] his findings are nonetheless very interesting in the historical mapping he produces:

	Sentence length (average number of words)	Punctuation marks (average number per sentence)	Dialogue (as percentage of all sentences)
1936	22.8	2.2	25
1956	17.8	1.5	28
1976	13.6	0.9	33
1996	16.6	1.0	35
2001	13.1	1.5	25

(Gitlin, 2002: 99)

Gitlin equates the changes outlined in the period 1936–1976[6] with the rise of television in national culture and argues 'popular fiction has gotten stripped down and now looks more like television. It goes down easier and makes fewer demands' (2002: 101). Gitlin implies that television increasingly downgraded attention spans and shaped lower consumer expectations. Television's cultural function, of course, provides an easy target for sceptics. As Jeffrey Shandler argues, 'many regard television in general as a destructive presence that diminishes or distorts the quality of modern life' (Shandler, 1999: xv–xvi). However, one of the attractions of television is its ease of viewing, which is associated with its flow or liveness. TV's language and its whole mode of address is part of its 'presence' (destructive or otherwise). In one way, we can equate the ephemerality of the medium of television (and particularly the TV image) with the increased brevity in fictional language identified by Gitlin.

These trends are of course evident in advances in other communications technologies. Text messaging is based on the brevity of language – or even a 'new' language – developed to minimise the space of and maximise the speed of transmission of the message in accordance with the technology of a new medium. This demand is partly about an apparent need for a simultaneity, of contact, of connection – a desire and expectation of a continuous updating of relations, football scores, financial markets, and so on. Nicholas Abercrombie and Brian Longhurst's (1998) notion of 'diffused audiences' is a useful model in capturing our 'time-shifted' experience of everyday media and communication. In this way, television provides merely one of numerous flows of media content that simultaneously pervade the modern world.

Under these conditions, the nature of news, how and when it is gathered, assembled, broadcast, and consumed, has fundamentally changed. How events come to be defined as 'news' in the first place is part of a long-standing debate about the criteria that effect journalistic selections and reselections. Such criteria shape assumptions about the existence of 'news values' or 'newsworthiness'. As journalists become increasingly mobile and able to report in real time, the reduction in time between an event occurring and its public dissemination is fundamental in shaping the content of news today. While 'time is the scaffolding on which [news] stories are hung' (Schudson, 1987: 97), television as *the* medium of time is simply able to deliver stories and images more immediately to mass audiences than any other medium, and so has dominated the communication of contemporary events. It is to these issues we now turn to address through evaluating the relevance and significance of news values in a world that is represented to us as news in seemingly ever more intense, immediate, and intimate ways.

Goodbye news values

We turn now from the culture within which news is produced to the practices of news production. The production of news occurs within an interaction order; journalists and other newsmakers make (implicit or explicit) judgements about what constitutes 'news' through their interaction with other newsmakers, the news environment, and audiences. Thus, news results from a complex set of interrelationships between events, people, institutions, and technology. These relations help to shape largely unwritten criteria by which judgments are made about what is selected, framed, and produced as news. However, there is a long history of media, communication, and journalism studies that has attempted to identify and describe these criteria – to state the reasoning behind newsmakers' choices. Most often, this has been done with reference to a set or framework of criteria called news values. Chibnall (1977), for example, defines news values as 'professional imperatives which act as implicit guides to the construction of news stories'. In this way, news values are seen as embodied in newsmakers and something which the journalist carries around with him or her.

If we consider some of the factors that are said to shape news values – newsmakers, audiences, technology, and markets, for example – it is apparent that all have undergone very significant transformations over the past forty years (notably since the establishment of television as a mass medium). Given the context of this historical period, with deregulation, the invention and proliferation of the TV news network, the shift to real time, on location, globally mediated reporting, and the emergence of new media forms, an important question is, *have news values also been transformed?* The answer, at least from academic writing on news values, can be seen as an emphatic 'no'. In fact, one of the most consistently and widely cited models employed in the study of news is on 'news criteria', namely that by Galtung and Ruge and first published in 1965. A simple Google™ search for 'news values', reveals how influential Galtung and Ruge's work is in the literature on news and particularly on media and communication programmes of study around the globe.

The development of this model as a benchmark has led to a reliance on a framework of news values in accounting for 'how events become news'. The actual list of news values does alter to some extent in different interpretations since 1965, although there has been a general failing in discipline to actually think outside of this framework or to comprehensively challenge it, and the list of news criteria that they provide is often reproduced without the context and other important observations they make elsewhere in their original article, and in particular what they term the 'frequency' of an event which relates specifically to temporality.

Technological advances have ushered in temporal and spatial transformations that have changed the very nature of news. For example, the availability of visual images and a correspondent being close or at the location of an event are key factors in determining the form and extent of television news coverage. Live visuals are in themselves sometimes sufficient for extended continuous television news coverage, even when very little is happening or can be seen to be happening. A good example of this occurred during the Israel–Hezbollah war in the summer of 2006.

Six flashes of rockets launched by Hezbollah militia from southern Lebanon towards Israeli towns briefly illuminated the dull-pink sky over the border. These low-tech weapons (Hezbollah's Katyusha rockets were first developed during the Second World War) were wreaking terror against a comparatively hi-tech Israeli army. Speculating that the rockets caught on film might have been those that found their target – the Israeli port of Haifa and its third largest city – many Western global television news networks incorporated this few-second footage into their near-continuous coverage of 'Day 26' (6 August) of the 2006 Middle East crisis. Sky News ran this clip through the day, with the shot panning across the horizon, following the rocket trails, and then jump-cutting back to the start. At one point, the news network played this video 11 times in a disorienting continuous loop, fixated by the spectacle. Later, the same day, CNN International (CNNI), feeding from its US domestic channel, also ran and re-ran the same footage, although slowed down, as an alternative means of 'extending the present' (to borrow from Helga Nowotny's (1994) idea of an 'extended present'[7]). Both network treatments of these images are indicative of twenty-four-hour television news' need to fill time, the trend to linger on the dramatic and the visual (at the expense of the context and the detail), and the compulsion to repeat.

These transformations in broadcast news became firmly established during the 1990s, a period Martin Bell described as the 'decade of the dish'. It is this era and the advent of more mobile communications in the twenty-first century that have revolutionised the news business of 'breaking news'. Of course, Galtung and Ruge could hardly have foreseen these developments, but they do consider the potential influence of temporality relative to a specific news medium. They clearly relate the frequency of the event (when/how often it occurs) to the times of the publication or broadcast of the medium and argue, '*the more similar the frequency of the event is to the frequency of the news medium, the more probable that it will be recorded as news by that news medium*' (1970: 262, their italics). In this way, the medium, in terms of its cycle of distribution or broadcast of news, will be more receptive to events occurring or reported at certain times of the day than others. Thus politicians and others attempting to gain maximum exposure will stage events or release information to news organisations at optimum times (e.g. in time for the evening news broadcasts, which, despite 24/7 news channels, still attract a greater audiences share of news programming).

What has in actual fact happened in the years post-Galtung and Ruge is that news values have been literally time-shifted. Broadcast news, for example, relies upon factors relating to temporality to such an extent that it is hard to imagine a set of news values where time does not predominate. Although timeliness or immediacy is present in more recent and more useful expositions of news values and narratives (e.g. Allan, 1999; Johnson-Cartee, 2005), the multiple influences of temporality on news have been understated. Instead, it is important to implicate time as a significant dynamic in television news, as well as a constant influence in the work of journalists. Furthermore, today, amidst the prevalence of reality television programming in the schedules, immediacy is the dominant presentational mode of news that audiences have reflexively come to expect.

These shifts involve everyday life being increasingly embedded in the mediascape conjoining with processes of social change. This is not just a question of the ubiquity of renewed media, insofar as that today we can observe the satiation of electronic media (images, sounds, and events) as our surround, but that there is a self-reflexive and self-accumulative media logic. As the presentational modes and production routines of the media shift, an awareness of the perceived impact of these (upon audiences' consciousness-in-the-world) feeds back to affirm and/or to develop these modes and routines.

Television, for instance, has for a long 'time' been considered to shape and reflect the daily temporal rhythms and routines as in the viewing habits of audiences, as with radio. The evening news or nightly bulletins are examples from a programming genre that is particularly cognisant with a particular (twenty-four-hour) temporal cycle (in terms of news gathering, editing, and broadcast). Stages in the enmeshing of the electronic media with our contemporary temporalities include the advent of electronic news gathering in the 1970s followed by satellite news gathering from the 1980s. A pivotal point in this process is that which CNN is practically synonymous with the round-the-clock television coverage of the 1991 Gulf War, remediated via local and national networks around the world. This apparent global simultaneity – the feeling that previously disparate audiences were unified in time and global space with the event – the Gulf War – unfolding as it was being watched (by audiences, the White House, and Saddam Hussein), ushered in a new and compelling mediatised axis of audiences–broadcasters event. However, this compulsion for the (potential) drama of the temporally connected places of the same event was thereafter pursued through the presentational modes and production routines of the electronic media. It is this that demonstrates the mediatisation of time and what today we have set out as part of an economy of time. To an unprecedented degree, the logic of the media is triumphant.

Many commentators characterise the experience of time as accelerated by the mass media. It is argued that an intensification of our experience of the present, through the simultaneity afforded by the so-called network society, promotes a heightened state of immediacy that impacts upon the nature of our relationship with the past and with the future. For instance, Franco Ferrarotti argues that 'The problem is how to exit from the labyrinth of the instant. For we are what we are and know we are that only in the moment of reflection' (1990: 28). If we accept this point of the primacy of the instant, then the hijacking of the modern present by the media affords that media tremendous power. Some commentators argue that a modern malady – the inability to relate to the past – is caused by a schizophrenic present that disconnects us from what went before and intensifies our immediate relations. Todd Gitlin, for example, argues, 'the experience of immediacy is what media immersion is largely for: to swell up the present, to give us a sense of connection to others through an experience we share' (2001: 128). This is not simply about an intensification of a culture of immediate gratification but a growing simultaneity of places, events, and experiences that appear to literally consume, fill, and perhaps even obliterate our temporal horizons.

However, as we argue below with reference to media events, television news performs another modulation: between (i) a compression of time in a frantic crowding and crowding-out of the present with multiple feeds connecting disparate times and places and (ii) a decompression of time through the maintenance of live continuous coverage when nothing is transpiring. Television speeds up and slows down the pace of events through its technological connectivity and its different modes of representation or 'frames'. It constructs times. A key mode of this actual and pseudo-connectivity and immediacy is often theorised as 'liveness' and it is to a more fuller exploration of this concept that we now turn.

A taxonomy of liveness

The dominant mode of orientation by broadcast news to events, to its overhearing viewers, and to itself is liveness. In its simplest form, liveness refers to the time elapsing between an event, its capturing or recording, its transmission, and its reception by audiences (real or presumed), being reduced to nothing, or almost nothing. This simultaneity of seeing or experiencing events as they unfold in 'real time' is essentially facilitated through the technological connections of the broadcast medium. Liveness is part of television's ontological make-up. However, the apparent or presumed impact of liveness (by programme makers, editors, etc.) on audiences, driven by the increased value afforded to immediacy, has established a pervasive culture of liveness across broadcast media and which is absolutely defining of the very substance of news today. The term is now in widespread usage in accounting for the nature and impact of television news, and we argue that liveness is a key shaper of the relationship between television and terror. Firstly, however, we set out a taxonomy of this phenomenon in more detail. We outline the overlapping aspects of liveness and some of the key contributors to the theoretical evolution of the concept.

The medium is the message

Television is ontologically live, that is to say it is part of its defining character, for it is broadcast and received in the same moment and so always appears as 'immediate' (see Feuer, 1983: 13; Ellis, 1992: 132; Marriott, 1996). The immediacy of the medium is perpetual as it is partly conveyed through its electronic presence, its here-and-nowness, and its continuousness. Television has a cycle of self-renewal that is inherent in its form, a point made by early scholars of the then 'new' medium, most persuasively by Marshall McLuhan: 'The elementary and basic fact about the TV image is that it is a mosaic or mesh, continuously in a state of formation by the "scanning finger". Such mosaic involves the viewer in a perpetual act of participation and completion' (1987/1962: 286). Television then is always a medium 'of the moment', emanating a connectedness through its electronic presence.

Continuousness

24-Hour programming and particularly rolling news networks' perpetual broadcast effect a permanent presence. As noted earlier, television is always 'on' and has been seen as a form of company for the lonely and those confined to their home. In one way, it has become more like radio being used as 'background noise' and reassurance. Often television is left on when there is no one watching or even no one in the room.

Mixing times and simultaneity

Television is temporally messy.[8] News environments mix multiple feeds from different times (and so different contexts) into a broadcast present creating a high degree of temporal disorder (see Hoskins, 2001: 216). Conversely, we can say that television news imposes its own temporal order through combining these times into a single unfolding 'here and now'. Not only is recorded footage mixed on our screens with that unfolding as we watch but different time zones from around the globe, night and day, are juxtaposed before our eyes. Television enables audiences to feel simultaneously connected to different and faraway places, where aspects of the same story are unfolding in numerous occasions at the same time. The multi-screen news format has been mimicked by film and other television programmes, for instance in the US drama series *24*. This unfolds in apparently real time on screen and so closely resembles aspects of the temporality of television news.

Many commentators cite the 1991 Gulf War as a landmark in television simultaneity with scenes of Coalition attacks over Baghdad, air raid warnings and panic over Israel as Saddam Hussein launched Scud missiles, and responses from citizens in the United States and elsewhere in the world, all unfolding continuously and witnessed by a global audience tuned into CNN.

The mixing of simultaneous times of the same story (unfolding in different places) on the TV screen at the same time can be seen as an extension of what the more traditional news bulletin has always done – notably the successive mix of sometimes very different stories within the same programme. Whereas newspapers and magazines juxtapose stories in print, television news enables a rapid succession of stories and images which critics claim actually inhibit audiences' understanding. Think of an evening news bulletin, for example. What connection is there between the news items, and how much or little time is or should be devoted to each story? Neil Postman famously critiqued these defining aspects of American television news of the 1980s:

> We are now so thoroughly adjusted to the 'Now... this' world of news – a world of fragments, where events stand alone, stripped of any connection to the past, or to the future, or to other events – that all assumptions of coherence have vanished. And so, perforce, has contradiction. In the context of *no context*, so to speak, it simply disappears.
>
> (Postman, 1986: 112, emphasis in original)

Even with the transformation of news gathering and delivery since this period and the advent of twenty-four-hour news programming, which allows for continuous live coverage of events, most of the time news items are extraordinarily structured and packaged into fifteen-minute or half-hour segments. Most of the time, mainstream television news delivers a rapid succession of stories, events, and images – there is little 'time out'.

Equivalency

In addition to the irreverent juxtaposing of news items in different media, imminence and immediacy blanket television news production to the extent that an equal import is structurally attributed to all news pieces. This contributes to the totalising flow of programming, as noted above, on one level, even though 24/7 news is highly segmented and ordered around clock time and genres of news, on another.

Extended present[9] and continuity

Television news also mixes past, present, and future times, continuously summarising what has happened while feeding audiences' expectations of future developments, in an ongoing present. Television is significantly geared for the promise of what-is-yet-to-happen, for it is the medium most prone to audiences switching, zapping, and surfing channels. This is achieved both verbally and visually. Reporters often use the present or future tense to convey a sense of immediacy – that events are happening now or are about to happen. Allan Bell, writing on print media, draws an important distinction in this respect: '*Immediacy* is a wider concept than recency, since it encompasses the future as well as the past. Most news covers the past, and therefore immediacy is equivalent to recency. However, some news deals with the future, where immediacy means imminence' (Bell, 1995: 326).

Imminence on television is also increasingly conveyed visually as well as in broadcast talk across programming genres. Increasingly, the *next* event is depicted visually in another window on screen; for example, the preparations for a news conference with journalists milling around and cameras and sound equipment being put into position. This contributes to the effect of liveness in two ways: through providing simultaneity (as above) and conveying a sense of imminence.

More generally, the continuity announcer has shifted from the spaces between programmes to within the shows themselves, acknowledging the impatience of audiences and the temptation to switch channels as the credits roll. In the United Kingdom, Chris Tarrant is probably the most visible of these as he attempts to persuade the *Who Wants To Be A Millionaire* audiences to stick around for the news, or maybe switch over to ITV2. The repeats of *Inspector Morse* running on ITV, for example, have had their end credits truncated and windowed to allow audiences to hear a preview of the latest atrocity story from Baghdad that follows. This device is also used by twenty-four-hour music video channels such as MTV. A small window frame is opened over a music video being shown which plays in miniature (and without sound) an excerpt of the video that follows in the hope that it meets with the approval of the audiences currently watching. Thus the logic of the extended present exists on television generally, not just in television news.

The CNN effect

Much of our explanation and critique of the CNN effect is the subject of Chapter 3. However, given its centrality to the development and institutionalisation of liveness, it is important for us to introduce it here.

The most immediate form of liveness occurs when the time of the news event, its broadcast, and its reception are simultaneous[10]; events are experienced by the viewer in real time. This is probably the most simple and most commented-upon aspect of liveness in terms of the acclaimed effects of television reporting on events as they unfold live on location, not just on audiences comprised of you and me but on those who are actually portrayed on the news. The journalist Nik Gowing has written widely on this subject in terms of the impact of the rise of real-time news reporting of conflict on political decision-makers. In his 1994 thesis,[11] he concluded that real-time reporting only exceptionally altered the policy of presidents and governments, but it more often affected presentation of those policies and political discourse. Thus, at times of terror events and warfare, for example, time is of more consequence than it is in the coverage of other events: audiences responses to real-time images, and the action or inaction of politicians and military leaders, may save or end lives. So, the impact of this aspect of television's liveness is often articulated with reference to the medium's reflexivity – that is to say, its ability to feed in to and shape the event being covered by news programming – the so-called CNN effect. This phenomenon has been defined with reference to the words of Benjamin Netanyahu (then Israeli Deputy Foreign Minister) commenting on the unfolding of the 1991 Gulf War on television:

> What we are facing now is political communication. As we speak it may be that in a bunker in Baghdad, they listen to us. In fact, I'll

delete the 'maybe' – I'm sure they listen to us. They are listening to us in Moscow, in Washington and everywhere else. So that the impact of what is seen and said on television is an integral part of the – of the war effort on both sides ... television is no longer a spectator.

You know, in physics – in subatomic physics – there's something called the Heisenburg Principle, which basically says that if you observe a phenomenon you actually change it. Well, now we have the Heisenburg Principle of politics: If you observe a phenomenon with television instantaneously you modify it.

(CNN: *Larry King Live*, 17 January 1991[12])

Notably, though, the reflexivity of television is greatest during these kinds of media events (war and catastrophe). Such events afford a more intensive and extensive environment for the media to consciously reflect upon their role as news-makers – to often insert themselves into the news frame itself.

Performing liveness

There are a number of ways television constructs and performs liveness – what Jérôme Bourdon calls 'textual indices of liveness' (2000: 53). These include aspects of televisuality and, notably, broadcast talk, which is a live narrative all of its own; often it is the manner of telling that further dramatises news stories. Changes in pace, tone, and fluency of talk, for example, all contribute to the immediacy and urgency of reporting. It is in this respect that one can identify liveness as increasingly the predominant mode of broadcast television news. CNN's weather commercial that opened this chapter exemplifies this.

Co-presence

Time is often coupled with space in broadcast talk and visually on screen; news presenters often implicate a shared sense of the here-and-now or 'co-presence', consciously addressing an overhearing audiences. In the study of linguistics, for example, the use of words relating to the time and place of utterance is known as *deixis*. And the deictics of news talk are fundamental to constructing a shared here-and-now of speaker and viewer; the discourse of presenters and journalists attempts to carry audiences with them literally into the place and time, event and story.

This taxonomy of liveness reveals some of the complexities in television's orientation to and management of time and informs our analysis in subsequent chapters. Talk, as we have suggested, is a key conveyor of liveness, and we now develop this aspect in more detail.

Time and talk

It can be said that all print media inhabit and convey an essential 'pastness' in their very form. Newspapers and magazines crumple and deteriorate as they are folded and read, and re-read. Their use and replacement is most often fixed by the temporal cycle of the day, week, or month. Newspapers and other printed news matter carry an inevitable obsolescence in their materiality; if they are not discarded, they increasingly reveal signs of their age, of the past; they fade, they yellow. The reading of printed news stories is always a past event, with the time lag between narrator and audiences extended by the mechanics of production, distribution, and sale. Time zero (the actual time and date of the event being reported) is always in the past in relation to the act of reading a newspaper, even though it is written as present.

However, television narrative, on one level at least, is timeless. For, as we consider in the first element of our definition of liveness above ('the medium is the message'), television inhabits a cycle of self-renewal that is inherent in its form. The temporal (and also spatial) intensity of the medium, however, is further enhanced in broadcast news by the embodiment of a present tense through the narration of the reporter or anchor. Time zero in broadcast news is one that is constantly shifting, for it is sustained in the flow of talk and forever present in and of the moment. The situating of past and present is continually shared between speaker and viewer, for instance, as Marriott (1997: 184) observes:

> Every utterance, whether composed of a sentence produced many times before or of an entirely novel string, is delivered into a fresh moment of time, a now-moment which has never occurred before and which can never occur again.

This 'once-through' quality is one that we can recognise from daily life and attracts the interest of sociologists (Boden and Hoskins, 1995). There is a unique quality to broadcast liveness, precisely because it intensifies the experience of the present moment – turn away from the screen or switch channel, and you might miss something. Yet, the intensifying of the present in broadcast news does not just involve news talk focusing upon the now – on time zero; liveness also involves emphasising what has *just* occurred and the promise of what is to come. For television then, we need to include in our definition of discourse structure, its inherent temporal and spatial dimensions and complexities. This is not to say that broadcast talk (and particularly unscripted talk) does not possess a discourse structure, but, rather, it conforms to different principles and to different patterns in different moments.

Significantly, in broadcast talk, present tense is embodied in the talk of the reporter or anchor; time zero, rather than just being a property of the story, is constantly shifting, for it is sustained in the flow of talk and forever present in and of the moment. Spoken narrative is in this way tied up with deixis, and often in highly complex ways as multiple times and distant places are connected in the televisual frame.

The tense of choice for broadcast news talk is the present. This is not a new phenomenon, as Bell (1991: 210) points out, 'Broadcast copy editors regularly convert past tense in agency stories to present'. News stories are thus rewritten to correspond to a perception of the temporality of the medium (in this case, Bell is referring to radio). As noted earlier, the 1991 Gulf War is defining of the genre of media events with highly extended live on-location talk. Three of CNN's correspondents dominated the opening global news coverage of this event by being the only journalists with access to a satellite phone, holed up in a hotel room in the four-teenth floor of the al-Rashid Hotel, Baghdad, as the then Coalition begun their bombing of Iraq. Their initial exclusive access to live commentary of events ensured that CNN prioritised this coverage and often went 'live to Baghdad' when there was little new to report. Another defining aspect of this reporting over the 16–17 January 1991 was that it was (unusually for television by this time) extended commentary without live visuals,[13] and thus more characteristic of the rich description more often associated with radio talk. For example, Figure 2.1 relates to the handover from CNN's Atlanta studio-based anchor, Catherine Crier, to John Holliman and colleagues in the al-Rashid hotel.

Holliman's talk revolves around mostly present-tense expressions and is typical of live unscripted commentary and that which Marriott (1995: 351) defines as 'an "experiential" mode of description, which is used to talk about events or processes that are occurring at or around the moment of utterance (with events presented either as if they have just occurred or as if they are occurring now)'. It is characteristically disfluent – note the recycled phrases and the general disruption to Holliman's report as he tries to comment in real time when there is very little news to add.

Moreover, his talk is actually quite 'compressed' in time and space, referring to little outside of his field of vision and mostly to the time frame of their reporting of the opening of the Gulf War a few days earlier. And, to draw on Marriott again, in this form of commentary there is

1	**Full screen shot of anchor Catherine Crier in Atlanta studio**
2	**CC**: describing the bombing raids throughout the evening . throughout the <u>early</u>
3	morning hours in baghdad three cnn correspondents . bernie shaw.
4	**cut to full screen map of the region marked 'Baghdad, Iraq' with three inset**
5	**photographs of the three correspondents**
6	peter arnett and john holliman .live at the al-rashid hotel john holliman is standing
7	by . john

8	**JH**: (2.5) catherine . hello to you I'm going to go back over to the window because
9	dawn is broken here bernie shaw is with me . we're gonna look out and uh . and tell
10	you if <u>we</u> can see any signs of er of any
11	**cut to full screen shot of map of wider Middle East region**
12	da↑mage after what happened here . in the hours er . preceding er the sun's coming
13	up here this morning . and I will be honest with you I <u>don't</u> see any sign . but I do
14	smell something there's an acrid smell in the a:ir that er . that wasn't here yesterday
15	or the morning's before this to my knowledge it's er . as we look out we can see the
16	early morning Baghdad fog perhaps not as thick as it has bin in . ye- er er it was
17	yesterday or the day before . you can still see the . baghdad tomb of the unknown
18	soldier their memorial to their war dead from previous battles . um we can still see
19	a- an oil refinery off in the distance where we thought we saw a bomb go off earlier
20	. and um . we can still see a tower from a a broadcast tra:nsmitter . which er was
21	another thing that we thought er you kno- might possible be a target but apparently
22	was <u>not</u>

Figure 2.1   Extract from CNN Live, 17 January 1991.

relatively little 'displacement' (1995: 351), that is, reference to anything outside of the immediate situation. One can also suggest that this compressing of time (over a number of successive reports over successive days) affords a certain claustrophobia to the news. For instance, being bound to the same event there is little time out or relief that the usual juxtaposition of disconnected and multi-genre news stories (print and broadcast) provides.

With CNN's 1991 Gulf War coverage, the media event came of age and produced a successful model for the appropriation of liveness as the standard for sustaining breaking news. We now turn to address the modes of liveness employed in today's more graphically sophisticated renewed television news environment.

Temporality or televisuality?

A key consequence of television news' attempts to 'totalise' events through the imposition of liveness is the production of a disjuncture between the *requirement* to maintain an output of a continuous flow of images and sound and the *actual* intermittent images and sound available to programme editors. In rolling and breaking news, this disjuncture is resolved through the devices of speculation and repetition, to the extent that these devices shape news content. Moreover, these devices – speculation and repetition – roughly equate to the amplification and containment of events, respectively. Indeed, it appears that the devices themselves (if not their consequences) are so obvious and familiar that the televisual news culture of liveness is a subject of popular satire as well as critique. For instance, the UK BBC2 satirical sketch show *Broken News* is founded upon sending up the artifice and banality of mostly UK and US televisual news style, i.e. television driven by liveness. Figure 2.2 is a transcript of a spoof television breaking news of a plane hijack taken from this comedy programme.

In the extract shown in Figure 2.2, the immediacy and imminence of events and prospective events (or rather merely information about those events) are carried simultaneously in the 'anchor' talk and by the content of the news ticker as well as by its actual presence. Rolling text affords an on-screen movement that has inherent immediacy, and the 'newsbar' has become a standard feature of many 24/7 news networks over the past decade. MB's contribution (especially lines 22–26) satirises repetition and speculation as dominant features of the breaking of news stories, both driven by, and communicative of, very minimal information. 24/7 networks treat and throw out the barest scraps of information as 'breaking news', many of which are later discarded and which are not included in the condensed prime-time evening news bulletins, exposing the intrinsic value of immediacy and its instant obsolescence.

The *Breaking News* sketch is loosely based on ITV and Sky News' near cinematic backdrops, whose studio set-length videowall transforms the scale of news images so that they tower larger than life over the presenters. On screen, brevity and movement have become key-framing devices as television news has become a concatenation of the tabloid front-page headline and by-line, and a busy computer desktop. For instance, in recent years, BBC News 24's banners have grown larger and brighter as they adopted the tabloid-top red of Sky News and have gradually incorporated the rolling news bar into their standard presentation. The huge headline banner, the breaking news icon, and the five- or six-word by-line summary – all diminish the news to instant visual fragments. In Figure 2.2, for example, *Breaking News* reduces the by-line summary to a near meaningless one word: 'PASSENGERS', and then 'INCIDENT'. However, perhaps an acknowledgment of a limit to the competition in tabloid visuals is the calmer look of CNN International

	Studio talk	Visuals
1 2 3	**RP**: Still to come. **KT**: This is ESN News with Katie Tate and Richard Pritchard.	Close-up of anchors sat at desk with studio as backdrop including videowall (VW).
4 5 6 7	**RP**: Stay with us for a reminder of the top stories still to come tonight. That's coming up next, but later.	*ESN NEWS* logo top-left of screen. Scrolling 'ticker' news bar with text from right to left along the bottom.
8 9 10 11 12	**KT**: All that, still to come. But first, now. And whilst we've been on air tonight reports have been coming in of an incident on board a Union Air passenger aircraft bound for Amsterdam from Chicago.	Close-up of KT. 'BREAKING DRAMA' icon and one-word subtitle 'PASSENGERS' above news ticker.
13 14 15 16 17 18 19	**RP**: Details are still emerging, but for the latest we can cross now live to our standing colleague Melanie Bellamy who has the latest. Melanie, where are you?	Close-up of RP. 'BREAKING NEWS' banner scrolling across VW from left to right. Medium shot of anchors and MB standing with clipboard at in front of videowall.
20 21 22 23 24 25 26 27 28 29 30 31	**MB**: Yes Richard, I'm over here. Now as Richard was saying there just a moment ago details are still very sketchy. The plane a Union Air 747 en route from Chicago to Amsterdam apparently on its way to Amsterdam from Chicago is on its way to Amsterdam from Chicago and may have up to 387 unconfirmed passengers and crew on board although how many people there are actually on board isn't yet clear. Suggestions that there may have been a mid-air explosion of terrorists on the aircraft have so far yet to emerge. Richard.	MB walking back-and-for and up and down some steps in front of VW. 'BREAKING NEWS' banner and image of a Union Air plane montage scrolling across VW. On-screen subtitle changes to 'INCIDENT'. Medium studio shot.
32 33 34	**RP**: Melanie. Thank you. Coming up. Obviously we'll keep you up to date with that story the moment we have some.	Close-up of anchors.
35 36	**KT**: All that still to happen. But first, a look now at a reminder of our round-up so far.	Close-up of KT.

Contributors: RP: 'Richard Pritchard', co-anchor; KT: 'Katie Tate', co-anchor; MB: 'Melanie Bellamy', reporter.

Figure 2.2   Extract from *Broken News*, BBC2.

introduced in 2006. CNNI has exchanged the bright reds for less shouty yellows and then black-and-white and lowercase captions. The ticker has been replaced by what has been called a 'flipper' – an information bar which displays whole sentences at a time rather than the more frantic movement of breaking news captions commonplace among its rivals and its sister channel CNN domestic.

The development of on-screen and in-studio aesthetics in shaping news is part of a phenomenon John Thornton Caldwell (1995) identifies as 'televisuality'. He dismisses what he calls an 'ideology of liveness myth'. He claims that television theorists of the 1980s significantly overestimated the importance of liveness: 'Television now defines itself less by its inherent temporality and presentness than by pleasure, style, and commodity' (1995: 30). Caldwell's critique is based on a number of programming genres (rather than focusing on news) and is founded in the economic and cultural specifics of US television news in response to accounts of the era in which he was writing. As we argue here, since the 1990s, temporality has become more influential in shaping news content, but not necessarily at the expense of TV's self-conscious aesthetic style. Rather, the latter is an important signifier of the former.

Media events

For our purposes, liveness is an essential factor in mapping the relationship between television and terror, and, as Caldwell (1995: 31) acknowledges, it is often considered in relation to the coverage of catastrophe.[14] He writes: 'Liveness, at least when linked to death and disaster, is textually disruptive but ultimately pleasurable since its coverage works to assure domestic viewers that the catastrophe is not happening to them' (ibid.). This may apply to particular types of events represented as news that possess a certain degree of distance and also closure. That is to say, even catastrophic events that do not project new or potentially open or unlimited risks into the future of viewers can reinforce a degree of ontological security, notably through mediatised separation from the threat posed. Furthermore, the repetition in rolling and breaking news leaches out the impact and the textual disruption of even the initially most shocking of events. Roger Silverstone (2002: 10), for example, argues in a post-9/11 context:

> The representational tools are ready and waiting to be mobilised in the containment of the catastrophic. Their renaturalisation in the endless repetition of image and the reiteration and reinforcement of narrative cements a version of the world which moves imperceptibly but entirely into the familiar and unexceptional. Our lives go on, as the spatial, temporal and representational distancing necessary for the threats of chaos to be repressed work its magic.

Although the stasis of repetition and 'reinforcement' provides a reassuring familiarity, a corollary of this expansion of news time is the speculation about anything and everything that is deemed even tangentially related to the dominant news agenda of the age, usually catastrophe and war – and notably terrorism in the twenty-first century. This is not just a matter of a rapid succession of terror events but, rather, the connections that are made between them by news correspondents and anchors, politicians, and 'expert' commentators in the studio. These multi-layered discourses produce a web of insecurity and security. This becomes clear in Chapter 8, when we analyse how audiences have responded to recent security events and 'terror' threats. The totalising regime of television news facilitates discursive and temporal linkages between disparate and different events and threats. One of its key-linking mechanisms in this regard is the routine use of 'media templates' (detailed in Chapter 5) in stitching together video extracts of coverage of terror events which have occurred over months, years, or even decades into a totalising and compressed visual narrative to impose on the latest atrocity and to speculate as to the potential threat of the next in this imaginary 'series'.

The other key temporal containing device, particularly in television news, is the media event. The origins of this idea tend to support a thesis of television as a totalising medium, premised upon a mass spectacle and assumptions about a watching audience, unified through their collective experience of an unfolding event. Daniel Dayan and Elihu Katz (1992: 1), who are synonymous with the concept, mostly emphasise the functional characteristics of what they call 'the festive viewing of television'. Media events such as the Olympics, state weddings and funerals, and the moon landing are the ultimate media frame, being based around a particular (mostly televisual) discourse that reflexively situates the medium, newsmakers, and audiences in the production of an unfolding event. Dayan and Katz argue that these constitute 'a new narrative genre that employs the unique potential of the electronic media to command attention universally and simultaneously in order to tell a primordial story about current events' (ibid.). However, this influential model is restricted to their classification of three types of events, namely 'contests', 'conquests', and 'coronations', and on the celebratory and ceremonial unifying of audiences on such occasions.

James Friedman (2002) provides a model of events based on a 'continuum of liveness' and identifies four categories in this respect, incorporating Dayan and Katz's model under 'ceremony'. The other three categories Friedman defines are 'unstructured events', typical of spontaneous news coverage of crises and catastrophes where there is (at least initially, we would argue) a relative lack of 'narrative containment'; 'unscripted events', for instance live talk shows and sporting occasions; and, finally, '(re)presentation', which refers to the mixing of live inter-actions between anchors and reporters with recorded reports. The latter is scripted and ordered and includes the now standard live on-location book-ending of taped reports (known in the United States as 'donuts').

For Friedman, it appears that (re)presentation coverage is the most effective means of the containing of events: 'This temporal and spatial distancing serves to spare the viewer – in a physical, emotional, and psychological sense – from both *response and responsibility* in relation to the tragedies and atrocities that take place in our world' (2002: 144, original italics). However, although Friedman's audiences oscillate from being subject of, to participating in, news discourses, according to their experience along a spectrum of liveness, he is ultimately generous in his according of 'participatory space' for viewers (Friedman, 2002: 147). Instead, the projection of inclusiveness by television that once may have appeared to enfranchise the masses and delivered Dayan and Katz's 'neo-Durkheimian spirit' (Dayan and Katz, 1992: viii) has been frac-tured in our digital age. Of course television news still welcomes us and invites us in to share the experience that it provides. It still projects an imaginary collective, but today that collective (if one can even use the term) can hardly be assumed. The opening phase of the 2003 Iraq war was undoubtedly a media event, yet it provided an opportunity for citizens around the world, and within each national collective, to focus upon the same phenomenon, the same matter-of-concern, and recon-firm their political disagreement about what was happening.[15] Regarding the Hizbullah–Israeli conflict we considered earlier, for example, audi-ences and policymakers in the United Kingdom and the United States witnessed quite different televisual events,[16] while depictions from Fox News and Al-Jazeera regularly offer purposefully different perspectives of the same event. In an age of transnational television, the Internet, and a series of conflicts and terrors, media events today may trigger conflict rather than social integration.

Proximity

In addition to the temporal conditions outlined here, television news has also accelerated the transformation of our experience of space, prox-imity and distance, and as Roger Friedland and Deirdre Boden (1994: 7) write, 'The experiential here and now of modernity is...in a real sense nowhere yet everywhere'. Specifically, one of the key perception-shifting mechanisms of television news in modulating terror is its capacity to obliterate time and space through intimately connecting disparate people, places, and events into a simultaneous frame. This includes managing that which Marriott (2001: 727) calls 'the tension between co-presence and omnipresence'. That is to say, media events are constructed by and connected through multiple live cameras and reporters on-location, individually privileging an often intimate proximity to events, but also combining to create a pseudo-ubiquitous view.

In respect of terror events, which are already geographically prox-imate and/or affect a sense of personal or national security, the presence of a familiar television reporter can function as a 'buffer', mitigating that which we noted earlier as the 'penetration' of the event into the collective psyche. For instance, the aftermath of 9/11 was reported by some news programme anchors sat outside with the smouldering New York skyline in place of their studio set.[17] Their on-location presence was thus doubly reassuring as part of a near-continuous vigil over the site of the terrorist attacks and also in expressing a form of intimate solidarity with the wounded city.

On 6 August 2006, when news broke of the UK–US air terror plot, by the evening, all the major British television news bulletins (BBC1, ITV1 and Channel 4) and even some American programmes (NBC *Nightly News*) were being anchored from London's Heathrow Airport. The familiar figures of the news anchors on-location and the sight and sound of planes still taking off safely provided continuity and reassur-ance in the face of potential terror, had the plot succeeded. In this way, news reporters and particularly anchors are instrumental in the ritual organisation of events by television. This is particularly evident in their absence: For instance, the remoteness and the devastation wreaked by the 2004 Boxing Day Tsunami made access difficult for relief and news organisations. The initial news reports of the terrible destruction itself were heavily reliant upon amateur footage and photographs, captured by those caught up in the tsunami. Although these images provided compelling viewing, the coverage initially lacked the co-presence of the familiar correspondents whose audiences were accustomed to their narrating, contextualising, and ultimately mitigating unfolding terror events. The BBC even received complaints via one of its television viewer feedback shows: 'Where is *John Simpson*'? one viewer demanded.

The televising of terror is partly effected through news correspond-ents being routinely inserted into the news frame of stories to be seen as 'witnesses', producing personal and intimate connections between events and the overhearing/viewing audiences. Their more frequent and faster proximity to events has been facilitated through the availability and portability of audiovisual recording devices, with the 'videophone' now standard equipment in live reporting from remote and also from dangerous locations. In this way, the mediation of proximity by television coverage of war and terror events has been significantly enhanced by this greater mobility and simultaneity of vision. As noted above, viewers are privileged with a sometimes dizzying multiplicity of viewpoints and temporalities. However, the presence of multiple cameras positioned across the 'field' of the unfolding event does not necessarily produce an informed or coherent picture. For instance, the multiple 'embedded' views stitched together in news coverage of the Iraq war resulted in visually compelling, immediate, and sanitised snapshots of rather random locales. Yet this offered only a pseudo-ubiquity and did little to enhance viewers' knowledge of the nature of the most consequential battles of the war nor their wider human cost.

The multiple and simultaneous viewpoints facilitated by the advanced mobility and ubiquity of television journalism enable highly reflexive and proximate views of fast unfolding events. To return to the example, we opened this chapter with, the 2006 Israeli–Hezbollah conflict: Interspersed with the spectacle of the Hezbollah rockets, the news networks (including *Sky*, CNNI, and BBC *News 24*) broadcast (also repeatedly) a street-long view in Haifa of a convoy of emergency service vehicles, all responding to attend to the real and lethal endpoint of the spectacle. From the distant spectacle to the 'signs' of the terror (the emergency vehicles), the Western televisual view eventually arrived in proximity to the houses hit in central Haifa. For example, the BBC's Humphrey Hawksley reported amid the aftermath of the rocket attack in front of partially destroyed houses, carefully avoiding being precise about the exact location of the 'hit' 'because of censorship rules' (BBC *News 24*, 6 August 2006), that is to say, not to assist Hezbollah in pinpointing the accuracy of their rockets. In this instance, as with much of the coverage of the Israeli–Hezbollah conflict, television effected a shifting representation between war as spectacle and the actuality and the victims of war in terms of the depiction of the wounded and the dead.

As noted earlier, the media–terror relationship has intensified with the growth in niche news channels and organisations. For instance, Fox News Channel in the United States, renown for their gung-ho (and ratings-winning) coverage of the Iraq war, frequently reported on Israeli casualties (rather than Lebanese) and focused upon the impact of Hezbollah rocket strikes: 'Think Katyusha rockets are not a problem? Think terror doesn't rain on the north of Israel? We'll take you to an apartment complex and you'll see, in vivid colour' (Shepard Smith, 'Studio B', *Fox News*, 11 August 2006). This heavily trailed report involved Smith providing a continuous commentary while following a civilian woman who is covered from head to toe in blood, as she is taken away by medics.

However, few televised conflicts in recent history have produced such an extensive and vociferous discourse over the media coverage itself, and particularly in relation to accusations of both pro- and anti-Israeli bias levelled, for example, at the BBC by newspaper columnists, academics, and by bloggers.[18] The conflict and the media war reached a peak on 31 July when Israeli air strikes in southern Lebanon killed 28 Lebanese and 16 children in the town of Qana. Footage of the bodies being carried from the rubble was carried by media around the globe and provoked the storming of the UN building in Beirut by protestors angered by the scenes of death and at the paralysis of the international community to intervene. The mediated disjuncture between the extensive coverage of the Israeli–Hezbollah conflict and the stasis of the West (principally the United States) in supporting a UN-negotiated ceasefire provoked intense debate and commentary on television, in print, and online.

The greater proximity and immediacy to sites of death and destruction produced by the televising of terror appear to radicalise responses in this way. Enhanced virtual proximity to sites of catastrophe produces both 'powerful' and 'powerless' positions. This is achieved through a ubiquity of multiple camera positions that afford an array and simultaneity of viewpoints not available to the co-present witness on the ground and through a particularity of connection with the victims of terror, once known that cannot be unknown. John Ellis (2002: 11), for example, argues that the 'seeing' invokes a particular connection with television events:

> by the very act of looking, individuals in the witnessing audience become accomplices in the events they see. Events on a screen make a mute appeal: 'You cannot say you did not know'.[19] The double negative captures the nature of the experience of witness. At once distanced and involving, it implies a necessary relationship with what is seen.

However, the rise of niche satellite channels and programmes in affording so-called viewer choice, mitigates against the obligation of the vicarious witness at an editorial level, shifting the balance from powerless to powerful viewer positions in pursuing the politics of their presumed audiences and of 'selective witnessing'.

Conclusion

The spectacle of global terror has been temporally and spatially expanded by the proliferation of round-the-clock, regional, and round-the-world news networks. Conflicts and catastrophes occurring anywhere on earth are immediately and repeatedly broadcast to us, wherever we are. This is not to equate broadcast time or programme reach with actual audience numbers but to point to the transformed global news cultures that 24/7 television news has ushered in. A significant phase in this development was the creation of a fast-developed aural and visual style of news programming that refracted and embellished these temporal and spatial connections. This development, enabled by improved satellite technologies, encompassed global audiences through the momentous events of 1989–1991 (in China, Eastern Europe, and the Middle East). At the time, these revolutions and conflicts were among the most intensively recorded and extensively observed collective moments in human history. Furthermore, there was a real sense that the pace, speed, and extent of the television coverage during this period actually shaped the events themselves, feeding back in a reflexive global loop, and we consider in detail the genealogy of and critique what became known as the 'CNN phenomenon' (Boden and Hoskins, 1995) or 'CNN effect' (Livingston, 1997; Volkmer, 1999; Robinson, 2002) as we explore in Chapter 3.

Reflecting on this period of rapid representational and perceptual change (and notably following from the 1991 Gulf War), McKenzie Wark developed Paul Virilio's notion of a 'vector' to explore the shifts and disruptions in news narratives:

> As the volume, velocity, and flexibility of the media vector proliferate, events appear more suddenly and connect quite disparate sites together in a tightly coupled form ... The more quickly the media get to the scene of an event and the more rapidly they transmit information about it to the rest of the world, the more impossible it becomes to disentangle the conjuncture itself from the vectors into which it is inexorably drawn.
>
> (1994: 22)

This vector 'entanglement' was certainly a characteristic of the Israel–Hezbollah war of 2006, which sucked in the world's media machine overnight, instantly accessing the frontlines and rendering transparent much of the entire field of conflict. Furthermore, as we consider below, the Western televising of this war was some of the most contested (in and by the media) coverage of conflict in the current era.

However, in the twenty-first century, the dimensions of the media vector(s) have multiplied with the explosion of information and news sources and providers, enabling an array of niche channels and organisations to radically affect and alter the media–terror relationship. The mono-global empire of CNN (which is now mostly split into the niche channel CNN US domestic and its liberal international sister – CNNI) has been effectively dismantled along with a number of previous models of media influence which had been founded upon a perceived influence of CNN and/or the nature of 'media events'. And it is to these highly influential models and debates that we now turn to address.

3
Hurricane Katrina and the Failure of the 'CNN Effect'

Introduction

The purpose of this chapter is to offer an alternative understanding of media–policy relations or the 'CNN effect' to that which has dominated existing political science approaches. In doing so, we show how our alternative ethnomethodological approach can shed more light on the original matter of concern. Hence, before we analyse media events, we must take a step back into sociological method. Through our ethnomethodological analysis of one case study – Fox News' coverage of Hurricane Katrina – we examine how the television coverage was achieved. We explore the televisual construction of the event. It becomes clear how messy the coverage is, and therefore how any attempt to map out causal relations between ontologically discrete units, 'media coverage' and 'policy decisions', is problematic. In addition, we suggest that this messy, chaotic coverage creates uncertainty about what was happening and that terror was amplified by Fox News offering representations of connections between Hurricane Katrina and terrorism, economic insecurity, and health hazards.

The notion that television news can change government policy is one that has excited journalists, frightened policymakers, and brought research funding to media scholars. By the late 1980s, a coming together of new technologies, growing international television stations, and sudden political upheavals suddenly offered the opportunity for the communication of dramatic footage *instantly* and *constantly* into households anywhere on the planet. In May 1989, global audiences could view live images from Tien-an-Men Square. By November that year, MTV images of the fall of the Berlin Wall announced the end of the Cold War. Critically, the broadcasting of these images actually *shaped events* on both sides of the wall that night (Boden, 1991). From that point, the mediation of present history in the present shaped that present and thus the future trajectory of history. Hence, Cottle (2006) refers to the mediatisation of conflict rather than direct mediation. As we discussed in Chapter 2, on 17 January 1991, following the first night of the bombing of Baghdad, the then Israeli Deputy Foreign Minister summarised this new phenomenon:

> the impact of what is seen and said on television is an integral part of the war effort on both sides...television is not a spectator. [Furthermore] if you observe a phenomenon with television instantaneously you modify it.
>
> (CNN: Larry King Live, 17 January 1991[1])

The live, near-monopoly coverage of the 1991 Gulf War by CNN and the widespread realisation that, from then on, live, twenty-four-hour global television would affect the events it covered sparked an enormous amount of interest from policymakers, journalists, and academics about what became known as the 'CNN effect'. It is important that changes in the media landscape coincided with the end of the Cold War, which for so long had defined and structured so much of international politics. World politics was suddenly unstructured, and as the US President called for a 'New World Order', CNN became a 'significant actor in international relations' (Gilboa, 2005: 325). As foreign policy became mediatised, this gave greater scope for news media to contest the legitimacy and direction of policy. Famously, the CNN reporter Christine Amanpour challenged US President Bill Clinton in 1994 so vigorously that it seemed accurate to consider CNN as one actor among others trying to influence Western foreign policy. Amanpour said to Clinton:

> As a leader of the free world, as leader of the only superpower, why has it taken you, the United States, so long to articulate a policy on Bosnia? Why, in the absence of policy, have you allowed the U.S. and the West to be held hostage to those who do have a clear policy, the Bosnian Serbs? And do you not think the constant flip-flop of your administration on the issue of Bosnia sets a very dangerous precedent and would lead people such as Kim Il Sung or other strong people to take you less seriously than you would like to be taken?
>
> (Quoted in Ricchiardi, 1996: 25)

Given this apparent power and momentary confidence, it is understandable why the *phenomenon* in question – global real-time television affecting the events it televises – was rendered the CNN *effect*. Policymakers wanted to know how to manage the effect and perhaps use it to their advantage. Journalists considered the ethics of their apparent new-found power, for surely it was only their job to report events, not influence them? Scholars sought to deploy their methods to theorise and model the phenomenon so as to predict when the effects might occur, perhaps helping the policymakers and journalists fulfil their roles along the way. At some point, then, the object of analysis became slightly different from what it might have been. The CNN effect was understood as a theory about a relationship between television news and policy, particularly foreign policy. Scholars constructed models that might validate the theory. They defined key variables, providing taxonomies of types of effects, types of policies, and types of roles that television news plays. These scholars suggested that if we could identify these types and their relations over time, we could arrive at 'causal' links between television news and policy decisions. That is, we might identify when and how CNN, or other global television stations, affected policy.

In a review of this academic literature a decade on, Gilboa (2005: 325) concludes that of these studies, 'none has contributed significantly to resolving the issue'. The debates offered more heat than light, more confusion than insight. Effects had been exaggerated. Other questions about communications in international politics had been sidelined. Yet Gilboa's own conclusion appears to reproduce the problem: no studies had *resolved the issue*? No studies had produced the final valid and reliable theory about how and when global television would affect policy? We contend that the CNN phenomenon, as it originally was, is not an issue to be resolved or a problem to be solved.

We must understand the CNN phenomenon not as a question of who has control and influence in a historical situation, as though media–politics relations were about the interaction of defined actors with defined interests within a given context. Instead, we understand televised history as a moment-by-moment production of events within which it is thereby implicated:

> television has entered into the actual production of the events it records, in that process altering the moment by moment trajectory of events. In this way, the medium is not only the message but also enters into the constitution of society itself.
>
> (Boden and Hoskins, 1995: 2)

This constituting role includes creating a sense of space and proximity, for instance, through split-screen reporting in which a synchronic connection is drawn between events in several geographical locations. And the role includes creating diachronic connections through recursive remediation of past events in the coverage of current actions, through the depiction of the present as a continuous, ever-extending present, and, consequently, the foreclosure of imagining the future as very different from today's extended present (Grusin, 2004).

This chapter sets out an alternative approach to studying the CNN phenomenon; we aim to provide an anatomy of a news event. If it is the speed of coverage that produces an effect on government, forcing the pace of decision-making, then we must find ways of *seeing* liveness. If television draws public attention to distant disasters, we must find methods to *see* the representation of proximity and distance. We apply the approach outlined in our Introduction, drawing upon the ethnomethodological question of 'how is this piece of everyday life achieved' as well as multimodality and televisuality approaches. We carry out an analysis of Fox News's coverage of Hurricane Katrina. We offer an anatomy of this news event, laying bare the second-by-second portrayal of the aftermath of the Hurricane. It becomes clear that any small segment of breaking news contains several, often contradictory or ambiguous meanings. Televisual devices such as the split screen, the reporter roving un-directed in the field, and the relentless barrage of graphics, captions, and ticker tape text may present a range of conflicting messages, simultaneously. When we examine television coverage in this way, we see how problematic it is to speak of 'effects'. There is no unified message 'transmitted' by any television broadcast. That is not the relation between television and the ongoing history of the present.

In fact, the coverage of Hurricane Katrina by US television networks may – more than any other event – exemplify the crisis of news discourse that characterises today's television news media.

Ontology: what exactly is being researched?

Most scholars tackle some variant of the question: How and when does news media influence the policymaking process and policy decisions? Different scholars will read this question differently depending on their disciplinary focus. Media and communication theorists are interested in, What is it about the media (content, mode of communication) that results in it influencing or affecting political decisions? Political scientists have asked, What factors influence policy decisions? When do news media have more influence than other factors (e.g. strategic interests, economic pressures, democratic pressures), or how do they combine with those other factors? All of these questions entail some ontological commitment to the nature and boundaries of such analytical units as 'the media', the 'policymaking process', and the 'policy decision'. To operationalise a hypothesis such as the 'CNN effect', it helps to define the entities being studied so scholars can attempt to see clearly which actor is affecting what. It is important to quickly summarise how scholars have devised their units of analysis, as this allows us later to distinguish our approach from the mainstream 'CNN effect' literature.[2]

Three units of analysis recur: 'policy', 'the media', and 'effect' (the type of relation between the first two units) (Table 3.1).

In discussions of policy, there is a common distinction between who is making policy and the nature of the policymaking process. Two bodies of research maintain that the key determinants of policy are the influence of certain groups of people. In the manufacturing consent approach, government maintains hegemony through control of information and restriction of democratic debate (Herman and Chomsky, 1988). For indexing models, the media 'index' their coverage to the level of elite dissensus, whereby the media only influence policy in the event of a polarised debate (Bennett, 1990; Hallin, 1993; Mermin, 1999). In both cases, our analytical attention is focused on *who* thinks what. It is important for these studies to define who are these 'elites' and who exactly is 'government'. In contrast, other studies give priority to the *type of policy decision*. As Livingston (1997: 1, italics in original) writes, '*different foreign policy objectives will present different*

Table 3.1 Units analysed in existing 'CNN effect' studies

Unit	How the unit has been unpacked
Policy	Policymaking actors The nature of the policy process The type of policy decision
'The' media	Frames used Sources used Production practices
Effect	Strong Weak

types and levels of sensitivity to different types of media'. That is, the 'effect' of media will depend on the nature of the policy. For example, in conventional warfare, news media might act as an accelerant to policy action due to their reliance on military information; or as an impediment to policy by, conversely, trying to maintain professional journalistic independence and finding information that contradicts the military line. Peacekeeping operations are less likely to attract any media attention, but imposed humanitarian interventions may attract more interest as 'our' troops are in action – television pictures of dead US troops in Somalia are a potential case for media having an 'effect' (though there is much evidence to the contrary (Livingston, 1997; Robinson, 2001a)). In this case, rather than posit a direct media–policy relation, we must consider the indirect relation whereby media coverage of an event affects public opinion. As public opinion is a condition for certain policy options, altered public opinion may bring an alteration in policy. These relations are represented in Figure 3.1.

Scholars have also unpacked 'the media' in such a way as to discern what it is about media coverage that might have an 'effect'. For example, the presence of *frames* is integral to Entman's (2004) study of US political–media relations. He defines the process of framing a news story as:

> *selecting and highlighting some facets of events or issues, and making connections among them so as to promote a particular interpretation, evaluation, and/or solution.*
>
> (Entman, 2004: 5, italics in original)

Entman distinguishes substantive frames, which define problems, causes, and solutions, from procedural frames, which evaluate how

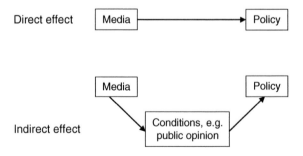

Figure 3.1   The ontology of mainstream CNN effect studies.

well or badly political actors are 'playing the game', so to speak. For instance, 'this war is morally wrong' is a substantive frame, whereas 'the President has no mandate for this war' is procedural. Robinson (2002) distinguishes between news stories that frame an issue as distant, or of no relevance to viewers (e.g. a distant conflict is merely the inevitable replaying of 'ancient hatreds'), and those stories that frame issues to elicit a sense of proximity and possibly sympathy for victims. Robinson mobilises the concept 'frame' by counting keywords that reflect these distancing or sympathetic frames. Other scholars have focused on the *sources* a news story cites or allows to speak (Livingston and Eachus, 1995). Who is interviewed, which reports are mentioned, which official statements are ignored? Choice of sources is part of the framing of an issue, but it is also part of broader news *production practices*. The indexing and manufacturing consent scholars usefully drew attention to the fact that journalists are part of social and professional networks that include government officials, civil servants, and other policy elites. This will bear upon the news media's potential 'effect' on policy. For example, in Bennett and Paletz (1994), we see how, for reasons of cost and convenience, foreign policy journalists in the United States rely upon a 'golden triangle' of the White House, Pentagon, and State Department. Such institutions appear legitimate sources insofar as they are key sites in a democratic government, but the effect is to constrain the nature and extent of information reaching news audiences (cf. Schudson, 1990: 118).

Having differentiated these understandings of 'policy' and 'media', scholars similarly have constructed typologies of 'effect'. We have seen that Livingston (1997) distinguishes between accelerant and impediment effects of media on policy. He also points to the agenda-setting role news media can have, and at different stages of the policy process (defining the initial national interest, defining specific problems for the nation, raising awareness of particular solutions, and so on). Robinson (2002) adds to the typology. He defines a *strong* CNN effect as one in which media coverage *helps push* policymaking down a specific path (possibly in tandem with other factors) and a *weak* CNN effect as one in which 'media reports *might incline* policy-makers to act rather than create a political imperative to act' (Robinson, 2002: 39, italics added). Using these rather fuzzy definitions of 'strong' and 'weak' effects, Robinson sets out to verify the presence of these effects in various conflict situations since the end of the Cold War.

Given the construction of these variables, how do these scholars theorise the relation between them?

Causation? Attempts to model media influence

In constructing the hypothesis that media coverage of foreign affairs *influences* or *effects* policy decisions, several scholars have approached the problem by developing models of policy–media relations. In this section, we will examine how three political scientists have approached the problem.[3] In *The CNN Effect*, Robinson (2002) seeks to develop a two-way 'policy–media interaction model' to explain when it is that news media influence decisions pertaining to the conduct of US-led humanitarian interventions (see also Robinson 2001a and 2001b). His cases include the 1990s interventions – or notable non-interventions – in Somalia, Bosnia, Rwanda, and Serbia. Robinson defines the CNN effect as:

> the generic term for the ability of real-time communications techno-logy, via the news media, to provoke major responses from domestic audiences and political elites to both global and national events.
> (Robinson, 2002: 2)

However, Robinson chooses to avoid studying how the news media's provocation of audiences does or does not affect audiences' views. Instead, he assumes that policymakers pay some attention to the media's coverage of opinion poll representations of 'public opinion', but only a little. Speaking of the foreign policy 'elite':

> These groups are more attentive than the wider public to foreign affairs news and play a pivotal role in setting both the tone of the policy debate and policy options. As such the CNN effect is as much to do with the complex perceptions formed among these groups as it is to do with the immediate impact of public opinion polls.
> (Robinson, 2002: 3)

Discounting any other way, 'the public' could affect foreign policy decisions, this leaves Robinson free to construct a simple causal model between two main variables, media and policy. Robinson acknowledges the problems of speaking of causation but decides to use the term in the sense of, 'if "A" had not been present, "B" would have been unlikely to occur' (p. 4). For instance, if the media had not covered an unfolding humanitarian disaster, policymakers would not have acted. This implies a commitment to a *mechanical* metaphor structure for understanding media-policy relations: discrete, sovereign agents (akin to billiard balls) in a relationship that social scientists can observe and measure. That is, A influences B, clearly affecting B's behaviour. There is a temporal dimension to this model, as Robinson's process traces the chronology of events, news, and policymakers' decisions. In addition, in such an analysis, it follows that A and B, CNN and government, may be considered to have identifiable intentions, interests, and responsibilities.

Robinson operationalises this model through the testing of two hypotheses: (i) The greater policymakers' certainty, the less scope for media influence, and vice versa, and (ii) the framing of an issue by media will effect policy if it is critical of the policy and if it is empathetic towards victims on whose behalf humanitarian intervention would be made. His data is a mix of post hoc interviews with policymakers and textual evidence such as news reports, official documents, and published accounts of policymakers, academics, and commentators. As noted in the previous section, Robinson looks for various types of media 'effects'.

Across a series of intervention decisions, Robinson's findings support the hypothesis that policy certainty correlates with *no* CNN effect. Operation Iraqi Comfort, a policy to protect Iraqi Kurds in the aftermath of the 1991 Gulf War, was a decisive government policy driven not by media but above all by geopolitical considerations such as keeping NATO ally Turkey happy. Regarding Somalia in 1992, US officials had been intervening *before* the media began to cover the story. By the time of Rwanda in 1994, the United States had a clear non-intervention policy, and the sparse media coverage tended to use a 'distance' frame of 'ancient hatreds', thus reinforcing the existing non-intervention policy. In the case of Kosovo in 1999, there was little deviation from a policy of air strikes rather than sending in ground troops, and the media served to 'enable' the policy by considering no other options. But Robinson did find some cases that appeared to exemplify the CNN effect. First, at the time of the 1994 bombing of a Sarajevo market, the United States had no ready-made policy and was openly criticised by France among others. Media reports were critical of the US government, empathetic towards the civilians targeted, and quoted many sources in favour of intervention. Within four days, President Clinton threatened air strikes. This appears to Robinson a case of a strong CNN effect. Similarly, in 1995, the fall of the Srebrenica 'safe area' in Bosnia was followed by the fall of the Goradze 'safe area', yet allied countries were divided and the United States had no clear strategy. Media reports were again critical of Western governments and empathetic to Bosnian Serb civilians. Western credibility was made an issue both by events and by media coverage of the events. Eventually, air strikes were threatened, again suggesting a strong CNN effect.

A second model of media–policy interaction comes from Entman's (2004) *Projections of Power*. Entman sets out to explain why it seems (to him) the US media has become less deferential towards White House foreign policymaking in recent decades. He renders this problem an object of analysis by proposing that the spread of ideas and frames between policymakers, media, and public operates through a mechanism he labels 'cascading activation'. This directs us to the possibility of conflict and competition in the battle to frame news events, and the potential for challenging leaders' framing. He depicts a model akin to a waterfall, with ideas and influence flowing down – and sometimes up (Figure 3.2).

Entman acknowledges that *spreading* activation is a metaphor and that spread is not an automatic phenomenon. He suggests his model

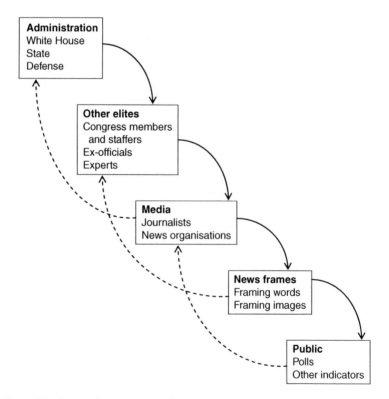

Figure 3.2 Entman's model: cascading network activism.

is rather intended to 'explain how variations in strategy, motivation, power, and cultural congruence all affect the degree to which competing ideas spread' (Entman, 2004, fn p. 172). For instance, the direction and extent of 'spread' is partly determined by the motivations of audiences, journalists, or policymakers who may instinctively feel a *pull* towards particular mental associations. Or, the strategy of policymakers or journalists may *push* frames towards audiences. He hypothesises that frames spread from leaders via media to the public most easily when frames are simple, culturally congruent, and do not require much thinking on the public's behalf ('low cognitive cost').

Entman arrives at compelling evidence for his model of cascading activation and the operation of pull/push factors. He compares the different interpretations by the US media of two near-identical events. The shooting down of a Korean airliner by the USSR that left 269 dead was framed as *murder*, whereas the shooting down of an Iranian airliner by the United States that left 290 dead was framed as a *technical glitch*.[4] The White House had easily achieved 'frame dominance' because the notion of USSR as evil 'red menace' and United States as good and benign had cultural resonance among the US public at that time, according to the opinion polls Entman cites. However, the White House achieved frame dominance less easily for its 1980s interventions in Grenada, Libya, and Panama. Media coverage favoured the Reagan Administration's framing of each problem, but coverage of each proposed solution was more critical. That critical media coverage, however, drew primarily on non-US sources that may have been less credible to US audiences. In addition, the *visual* images used to challenge White House policy could easily have been read as supportive. It was not easy to visualise international law, and it was impermissibly unpatriotic to show civilians killed by US troops. General public disinterest meant it was not worthwhile for Democrats to oppose these interventions strongly, leaving journalists alone and ineffective against White House cascading activation. Finally, the 1991 Gulf War saw further ineffective critical media coverage of the White House decision to invade Iraq. Entman's analysis demonstrates how journalists focused on the procedural aspects of going to war, rather than the substantive issues. Once President Bush began to follow expected procedures of debate and decision-making, the question of other policy options had been silenced.

All of these cases point to the importance of detailed study of media coverage of events, including visual coverage. In the 1990s, *Time* magazine argued that mistaken US interventions in the Balkans and elsewhere were the fault of media images, which had apparently stirred the emotion of policymakers and public (though *Time* continued to use such images). This contradiction points out a second important implication: journalistic practices determine what makes it to the screen, airwaves or page. Entman notes that critical media coverage in the United States was weakened by its reliance on non-US voices for criticism. In debates prior to the 1991 Gulf War, newspaper editorials were often critical of the decision to go to war, but news reports in the same newspapers framed the war positively due to reliance on military or government sources, the prioritising of 'facts' over opinion, and the frantic need to file stories every day. Entman is not the first to note how the practices of journalism lead journalists usually opposed to military actions to produce reports that endorse war. The need for simplicity, novelty, drama, and ethnocentric coverage will result in stories that amplify threats and conflict (Galtung, 1998). Here, Entman adds the concept 'calibration': journalists will report on those actors most likely to determine outcomes, so as to best inform their audiences about future events. Regarding the White House strategy to pursue war in Iraq in 2003, once it was clear Democrats would support the strategy, with war likely and media in the habit of calibrating coverage to likely events, any opposition to war became un-newsworthy.

Entman's analysis appears to illuminate the factors determining policy and the 'spread' of ideas about policy, but no more. He closes down the possibility of a rigorously causal model of media–policy relations, writing 'any effort to empirically validate causal relationships in this causal model would encounter enormous obstacles' (p. 145). For instance, if one suggested that US public outrage at the attacks of 9/11 helped determine the White House decision to invade:

> to find out more about exactly how much the public inspired the leadership behaviour, we would have to peer into the hearts and minds of leaders in ways requiring a level of cooperation, introspection, and honesty on the part of elite informants that political scientists are unlikely to receive.
>
> (Entman, 2004: 146)

Not only are 'media' and 'public' too fuzzy and complex to be rendered as coherent bounded variables that can have independent effects, but we could not know the effects anyway because we do not know how policymakers perceive matters. Yet, operating from within the boundaries of imagination common to mainstream political science, Entman gathers observable data and makes inferences concerning 'influence' from correlations between opinion polls ('the' public's view), news reports (journalists' views), and House and Senate votes (politicians' views). There is no attempt to ascertain the *meaning* of events for these interested parties.

Nevertheless, Entman's analysis alerts us to the role of visuals and images in the 'spread' of news frames and ideas about policy. Above all, his analysis highlights the importance of timing. The framing of events happens quickly, creating a trajectory of supportive or oppositional media coverage. An excellent examination of these 'waves' is provided in Wolfsfeld's (2004) *Media and the Path to Peace*. Wolfsfeld offers a third model of media–policy influence, to contrast with Robinson and Entman. His focus is on how the media can promote or retard peace processes. Wolfsfeld offers a 'political contest model' (Wolfsfeld, 2004: 1) tracing how, in a peace process situation, different groups compete to promote their messages through the media. Understanding the rules of this group competition will then enable us, Wolfsfeld argues, to understand the role the media then play. Above all, he hypothesises that news and politics interact in a cyclical manner. Changes in the political environment (P) bring changes in the media environment (M) which then reshape the political environment (P) – the P–M–P cycle. The media *never* initiate a political event or process, they only react, and so political control will yield control of news media coverage.

Wolfsfeld used this model to analyse the 1993 Oslo peace process, the 1999 Northern Ireland Good Friday Agreement, and the failure of the Barak/Arafat summit at Camp David in 2000. Unlike Entman, who dismissed the possibility of accessing the understandings and meanings held by participants, Wolfsfeld carried out in-depth interviews with political and military leaders, their advisors, news editors, and journalists. Like Entman and Robinson, he carried out content analysis of media reports. In each of his case studies, he found the political process generated 'waves' of news coverage, which then affected that same political process. In general, the frames, narratives, and general hysteria of media coverage of the initial events had a retarding effect on the prospect for conflict resolution, most clearly contributing to the collapse of the Oslo Accord. In contrast, the existence of elite consensus and the involvement of many parties and viewpoints tended to force media to cover events using positive frames.

Even in Wolfsfeld's detailed analysis of the daily interactions of politicians and media, however, the presentation to the reader of neat waves and patterns of interactions over the course of months (see for instance Wolfsfeld, 2004: 59) distracts attention from the existence of political waves within a *single morning, afternoon,* or *evening.* As Entman noted, actors seek to establish their preferred framing of an event *instantly.* Meanwhile, the frantic nature of producing news reports makes the presentation of incongruent, accidentally misleading frames, narratives, and 'facts' very likely.

To summarise, models from political scientists have offered ways of seeing the relation of media to policy but in a way that obscures what might be important. There is, of course, no need to lose sight of political, economic, technical, and other forces that may determine how a media outlet will report news events over time. But the models presented thus far do not allow us to see how *meaning* is constructed. It is not enough just see how events are represented and seek correlations with policy decisions.

Towards an anatomy of news events

Mainstream CNN effect theorists such as Robinson and Entman approached the problem by trying to model the relations between policymaking and media coverage of events relevant to those policies. From this position, we begin with a fairly clear picture of order, and the interesting thing about everyday orderly life is, who does what to whom, what causes things to happen, and what we can learn from this. But in this book, we propose an alternative approach, informed by ethnomethodological, multimodal, and televisuality studies of media. As set out in our Introduction, ethnomethodologists explore how anything is achieved in social life by following how individuals account for their actions as they go along, in specific contexts. From everyday actions, properties somehow emerge that may be common to such contexts or practices. In many respects, such an approach can fruitfully be applied to television news. How did that report come to be the way it is? How would the newscaster and reporters explain what it is they think they are doing? When they were covering that event at that moment, what information did they have, and not have? We are directed to the haecceities or 'just-thisness' of phenomena, the 'just here, just now, with just what is at hand, with just who is here' (Lemert, in Rawls (ed.), 2002: 38).

Goffman's (1981) analysis of 'radio talk' offers a good example of how the ethnomethodological approach can be applied to news broadcasts. Goffman sees talk – all talk – as a flexible series of moves, in which actors can accept, deny, or modify the previous move. Talk is open yet routinised, like dance. Talk is situated, so analysis of talk must always account for the context of the conversation. Analysis must also pay attention to all the rituals and gestures a person uses in communication. When we consider the goals and constraints governing any person's acts in that situation, we can identify their social competencies: 'the capacity to routinely accomplish a given complicated end' (Goffman, 1981: 198). How, we can ask, is the news-reader using facial expression, tone of voice, and gesture, as well as a script, to communicate a piece of news to the viewer such that it will be understood?

It is in the errors, Goffman suggests, that we can begin to learn what it is newsreaders think they are doing. In particular, we can pay close attention to how errors are avoided or remedied, such as avoiding difficult words, driving on when one knows one has made an error, or stridently correcting oneself. It is in these instances that we can begin to identify the constraints bearing upon the newsreader:

> A significant amount of speech trouble announcers get into is to be traced to such matters as transmission technology, staff division of labor, format and editing practices, sponsorship, FCC regulations, and audience reach, and cannot be analyzed without reference to the ethnographic details of the announcer's work.
>
> (Goffman, 1981: 246)

For example, a typing error in the autocue, a badly timed cutback from the field reporter to the studio, a legal restriction on which names can be spoken of, will all allow us to identify how news is produced at that moment. In this way, the broad determinants of media–policy relations in the mainstream CNN effect studies – political pressure, media regulations, ownership, available technology, professional norms, the need to gain market/audiences share, and so on – are made visible in the most exact way. We can see exactly how they are affecting news.

Our approach allows us to identify what it is about the news reports that policymakers and audiences are supposed to be being 'influenced' by, as the CNN effect theorists would tell us. That is, we can identify an anatomy of the rational and affective aspects of news, the political messages, and the sensory stimuli. For instance, in the following quote from one ethnographic interview, with an Indian person living in Britain talking about coverage of the 2003 war in Iraq, the interviewee perceives television news through a complex of sensory and political prisms (italics added):

> From my perspective, the war is not such a fair war. Therefore the BBC's coverage given the situation was completely *unbiased*. Uh…the presentation on CNN, the *colour* on CNN was much better. I don't know, maybe they have more *resources*. But off hand, I can't remember very much of what CNN did but I can look back at BBC and think of people *who were speaking* and of you know, news reporters who would impress me as news reporters. You know for instance if you look back at the Afghanistan war, and in those days we were in England, and used to watch [Indian channel] NDTV and I can clearly visualise that and picture [the presenter]. He made an impact during that war which I don't think many made…of course, [there was] that other BBC girl who speak with the *North Indian English accent* .

Studies of audiences' responses to televised political addresses support our contention that a multimodal analysis is necessary to explain putative 'effects' of television news. For instance, in the months after 9/11, an experimental study was conducted in which audiences were shown clips of negative images from the attacks followed by close-up reactions and statements by President Bush (Bucy, 2002). The sample was selected such that news images varied in their 'intensity' and the presidential reactions varied in their 'potency' (a combination of gestures and verbal cues). A key finding was that while viewers could easily distinguish between low- and high-potency presidential responses, it depended on the news image intensity shown *prior* to Bush; thus the order or grammar of a news broadcast intersected with a particular mix of presidential words and gestures to create cognitive and affective responses.

Hence, only a close, second-by-second analysis will allow us to identify and compare the very aspect of the 'CNN effect' that was originally considered to be constitutive of the phenomenon, namely liveness, the creation of spatial and temporal aspects through simultaneity and historical stock footage, and the relentless sense of breaking news that was considered to heap unprecedented pressure on policymakers to act instantly.

An anatomy of Fox News' coverage of Hurricane Katrina

In August 2005, Hurricane Katrina hit the Gulf of Mexico, creating catastrophic damage along the coastlines of Alabama, Louisiana, and

Mississippi. About 80 per cent of New Orleans was flooded as levees protecting the city from Lake Pontchartrain were breached on 29 August. Well over 1,000 people died and over 2,000 remain unaccounted for. We close this chapter by analysing Fox News' coverage of this breaking event.

Fox News' coverage offers no discernible unified message that government or audiences could interpret that might 'affect' policy. The viewer instead is presented with ambiguous and contradictory coverage. We attribute this confusion to the very liveness of the event. The reporters are forced to construct the story as they go. For example, there is a contradiction between pictures from the scene and the 'official' and repeated Fox News verdict that officials are responding well and the situation is under control. The televisual composition of the screen, then, works to undermine officials' legitimacy. In the following extract, we see how a reporter, Shepard Smith, interviews a survivor emerging from the floods and then a police officer:

> Smith: This lady has been stuck in an apartment since the storm came through and the flood waters came in after that. Now they are just trying to get her to dry land. Once she gets there is no food and water, there's no medical attention, there's no shade, there's no shelter. At least for now, just like the rest of these people who're coming up out of the water, <instructs camera> pan to the left over there...there's nowhere to go.
>
> Survivor: We need water, we need help! We really need help. There are sick people in the projects. People can't walk, people can't talk. People can't see. You know what I'm saying? They got old people on the bridge. Can't get no water or nothin'!
>
> Smith: And this is where they end up on a bridge, over the city on a ninety percent [humidity] day with no shade, no place to go to the bathroom, and no help. You can see the police cars coming through and they do from time to time but the police have no where to take people, the police have no medical assistance for them. They have no way to get them out of here, because they have no where to take them.
>
> <Smith questions police officer>
>
> Smith: What you going to do with all these people? When is help coming for these people? Is there gonna be help? I mean...they're very thirsty. Do you have any idea yet?
>
> Officer: <silence>
>
> Smith: Nothing? Officer?

<Officer walks away in silence>

Smith: The truth is the officer doesn't know either...The officer is up here with no instructions and nowhere to take them. ... *This is not to pass blame* or to be angry with anyone. Just to show you how difficult a process this is. There aren't even people up here to instruct them; much less give them food and water. This is a brand new development and a very exciting one.

Shepard Smith communicates several messages. He cultivates co-presence, the shared 'here-and-now-ness' between reporter and audiences (see taxonomy of liveness in Chapter 2). We are told this is a new, exciting development, implicitly telling the viewer to keep watching; the premium news value of 'new-ness'. Yet we are also told of, and shown, a terrible humanitarian disaster. Smith repeats that there is 'no shade, no shelter' and directs the camera to find visual evidence for this. It is suggested that the police have no more idea what is happening than the reporter or survivors, but that we the audiences should not blame them for being unable to help. Smith feels a need to speak *for* and excuse the police officer. As the day unfolds, Fox News reporters talk repeatedly of the emergency rescue operations underway, yet we never see visual evidence of these operations. Instead, we see the reporters actually intervene in the disaster by bringing food and trying to direct official figures to the location of survivors. As with the fall of the Berlin Wall and countless wars and disasters since, television news entered into and became part of the history it reported.

The differing types and sources of information on screen at any one time reinforce these contradictions. Some information is simply wrong. Announcers and reporters offer statistics, the precision and foundation of which are uncertain. This is not surprising, given the disaster is a breaking news story. With the benefit of hindsight, we can see how many of Fox News' 'facts' were wrong. But these were not politically neutral or insignificant facts. Along with other television networks, Fox overstated the extent of rape and gun violence (Mediamatters, 2005). This may have coloured audiences' responses to the ongoing humanitarian disaster, for instance, by introducing a 'distancing' frame and reducing audiences' sympathy for the populations affected. Other information was contradictory. Viewers were simultaneously offered positive and negative evaluations of the events. Graphics appear featuring positive statements such as 'Assistant Secretary of Defense: All hands are on deck'. The viewer is offered statistics on the volume of water being drained from New Orleans, reductions in the number of homes without power, and assurances that life is 'returning to normal'. Yet the rolling news tape at the bottom of the screen contradicts these positive assessments. It notes that the Senator for Louisiana has referred to the disaster as 'unprecedented'; the Mayor of New Orleans has made a 'grim assessment', and looting and shootings are reported. The use of split screen only adds to the confusion: An interview in which the Governor of Mississippi attempts to reassure viewers is contradicted as the other half of the screen shows scenes of devastation. A reporter in Biloxi, Mississippi, depicts an idyllic American town destroyed. With a graphic of a fluttering US flag imposed in the corner of the screen, the reporter points to the buildings around him:

> Reporter: … it's absolutely incredible to consider that this was a restaurant right here, and its gone. The whole first floor of that medical office building is gone. Over here was a one-storey motel that, you can see the pool, but the motel stretched all the way back that way and it's completely levelled. On the other side of that blue building which is still standing, remarkably, was a restaurant, the Bombay Bicycle Club, and that is a pile of rubble. And we're not just in this one area because this is the area that was affected; trust me when I tell you that all the way down the beach in both directions it's a similar scene.

Fox News' coverage also drew connections, unintentionally or not, between the disaster it was reporting and other global insecurities. It thereby offered both uncertainty *and* amplification of terror. As audiences were presented with the footage and captions concerning the effects of Hurricane Katrina, the rolling tape along the bottom of the screen communicated stories about bird flu, the elevation of the terrorism alert level, and a terrible stampede in Baghdad. Fox News reported a statement by President Bush in which he too connected the disaster to other, broader security issues[5]:

> The government of this nation will do its part as well. Our cities must have clear and up-to-date plans for responding to natural disasters, disease outbreaks, or terrorist attack … for evacuating large numbers of people in an emergency … and for providing the food, water, and security they would need. In a time of terror threats and weapons of mass destruction, the danger to our citizens reaches much wider than

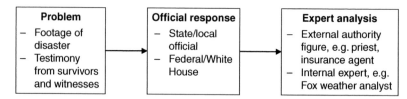

Figure 3.3 Grammatical structure of breaking news.

a fault line or a flood plain. I consider detailed emergency planning to be a national security priority.

In several ways, then, Fox News sustains a particular political inter-pretation of an interconnection of problems such as terror, global warming, and health pandemics, in which the meta-problem or unifying theme is the danger of contingency itself (Cooper, 2006; Dillon, 2007).

A final finding in our analysis of Fox News' coverage of Hurricane Katrina concerns the presence of a grammar of breaking news. The main grammatical structure is represented in Figure 3.3.

This structure is repeated on ten- to- fifteen-minute cycles, interrupted by commercial breaks and national weather reports. The structure may suggest to audiences that officials are responding to the problem, with experts helping the audiences understand and evaluate both problem and official response. But this grammar poses problems for the official responses. It creates the relentless demand to give an official account and evaluation of events, and the possibility of being contradicted by the prior footage and subsequent expert analysis. Furthermore, and as we have seen, this grammar is often ruptured. Interviews with officials are presented on half of a split screen, alongside footage of the problem and potentially contradictory graphics and captions. In this way, we see how the complex televisuality of even the smallest segment of a massive breaking news event defies attempts to ascribe coherent meanings and messages. We also see how such television defies attempts to manage the political meaning of breaking news events. Officials can easily be made to look powerless and ignorant, while even Fox News, with its clear political leanings, struggles to provide a unified framing of the event (except the proliferation of many dangerous and possibly connected contingent dangers). Reporter Shepard Smith later commented on Fox News' critical coverage of the Bush administration response, 'We were getting fed a pack of untruths and we showed the truth' (Johnson, 2006).

Conclusion

The CNN phenomenon originally referred to the manner in which global, real-time television coverage of events actually became part of the events it was televising. Events were depicted as part of an extended present, connected diachronically to past events and synchronically to other places and issues around the world. This allowed television news both to describe and to help make the history of the present; breaking news could contribute to the *constitution* of those events. Yet the appropriation of the CNN phenomenon by certain scholars, journalists, and policymakers, rendering the object of analysis the CNN *effect*, has not helped us understand the relation between television news and contemporary political developments. Attempts were made to model this relation as a mechanistic interaction of clearly definable elements such as 'media', 'policy', and 'effect'. But as Gilboa observed, a decade of research has offered very little insight. We have gone further than Gilboa, arguing that this body of research actually obscured the phenomenon of interest altogether.

In this chapter, we have set out an alternative approach, inspired by ethnomethodology's problematic: how is anything organised? We have set out the analytical horizons that will allow us to see an anatomy of a news event. This approach, we have argued, allows us to see the very elements of the CNN phenomenon that originally provoked interest, such as liveness, simultaneity, and the relentless sense that this new information is something policymakers may have to react to. Through an analysis of Fox News' coverage of Hurricane Katrina, it became clear that any split second of news can contain multiple, contradicting frames. Meaning is not clearly transmitted, but is instead constructed through a series of televisual devices, such as the split screen, the reporter in the field, the captions and rolling ticker tape, and an assortment of graphics and diagrams. This analysis has demonstrated how television news invites audiences to draw connections between one event and others, between one location and others, and between those implicated in the aftermath of Hurricane Katrina and themselves as potential victims of other security threats. Fox News' coverage of Hurricane Katrina best exemplifies the crisis of news discourse, producing news that offers uncertainty and terror amplified.

4
Talking Terror: Political Discourses and the 2003 Iraq War

Introduction

Discussions of security issues have featured notable conceptual innovation since 11 September 2001. Concepts such as 'War on Terror' and 'long war' have been created, while concepts such as 'WMD' and 'rogue states' have moved from policy discourses into the public vernacular. For nation-states, a 'new' security dilemma has replaced an old one,[1] and Islamic concepts such as 'jihad' and 'caliphate' have been the subject of increasing attention and contestation among Muslim and non-Muslim audiences.

Concepts do not emerge spontaneously, independently of social action. Language does not hold a mirror to social life. In the industrial revolution, concepts such as 'capitalism', 'socialism', and 'ideology' were devised and deployed through changing social, economic, and political practices (Hobsbawm, 1962). One could similarly offer a genealogy of the so-called information revolution of the 1990s. Computing metaphors such as 'network', 'node', and 'interface' and the ubiquitous 'e-' prefix appeared to colonise a transforming global society – but from where did they come, from who, and why? James Farr writes:

> conceptual change may be explained in terms of the attempt by political actors to solve speculative or practical problems and to resolve contradictions which . . . criticism has exposed in their beliefs, actions, and practices.

> (Farr, 1989: 36)

The evolution of language is tied intimately to social and political actions. Political actors seek to define a situation or policy in ways that warrant particular understandings and actions. They produce concepts such as 'War on Terror' or 'martyrdom operation' not just to describe or name a phenomenon but as an attempt to gain legitimacy for their strategies.

In the light of McLuhan's statement that 'the medium is the message', however, we must consider how this political, conceptual work is affected by the medium through which it is conducted. We seek to answer the following questions in this chapter: How do political discourses become represented in the medium of television under the conditions of contemporary news discourse? How does the televisuality of television news shape the presentation of political actors, processes, ideas, and events? Television's modulation of terror, its economy of time, and the simultaneous reporting from spatially disparate locations surely contribute to a particular rendering of political discourses. And in so doing, television news helps form or constitute a different interaction order for all actors – including audiences and policymakers – than if television did not exist.

We address this nexus of televised news discourse and political discourses by examining a controversial case: How American television news presented the 2003 Iraq war. The US media has been criticised for failing to interrogate the case made for war by the US and British administrations in 2003, and even engaged in a period of critical self-reflection. We will study an important slice of the overall war coverage: how CNN covered the opening phase of the war. We pay particular attention to discourses surrounding the phenomena 'terror', 'terrorism', and 'terrorist'. The 2003 Iraq war is an event that beforehand some political actors, most explicitly the US and UK administrations, suggested was linked to defeating terrorism. Additionally, the military campaign against the Iraqi regime created a degree of terror for many Iraqi civilians and increased the threat to Coalition countries. In this chapter, we provide a chronological analysis of CNN's coverage of the hours before and after the US-imposed deadline that signalled the beginning of the war. We apply the ethnomethodological, multimodal, and televisuality approaches outlined in our Introduction in order to illuminate the principles and logics at work in television news that lead to the achievement of what appears on screen.

We find that the practices intrinsic to the 'event time' of television news, evidenced in CNN's coverage in this case, lead CNN to effectively lend legitimacy to the framing and assumptions of the Bush administration's discourse and 'discount' rival interpretations. Yet we also find that, as in Chapter 3, the chaotic televisuality – with its moments of

overload broken by lulls and with its modulation between containment and amplification of terror – invites counter-interpretations. For
instance, we explore audience data that suggests viewers watching
grainy, unchanging footage of the Baghdad skyline from a hotel roof are
drawn into imagining a reality beyond that hotel roof view. But first,
we will outline the background to the event and our analysis.

The 2003 Iraq war as pre- and breaking news: background and discourses

Media coverage of the 2003 Iraq war was not without interest and
controversy. The Coalition military made great use of embedded
reporters, with major news organisations accepting that a loss of journalistic freedom was more than offset by the promise of offering audiences
a 'front row seat' in the war spectacle. Another controversy concerned
the degree to which news media had failed to interrogate the Coalition
powers' case for war prior to the invasion. The notion that news media
had become unwitting 'cheerleaders' led to a critical debate after the war
among journalists and editors. At stake in all of these controversies was
the question of legitimacy and whether news media had provided a false
legitimacy to the Coalition's actions. That Colin Powell made a case to
the UN outlining 'proof' that Iraq possessed WMD, and that Tony Blair
persuaded the United States to seek a second UN resolution endorsing
the invasion, does suggest Coalition leaders wanted legitimacy for their
actions (cf. Suskind, 2006). Yet it was never clear that the motive for
the Coalition actions was simply to remove WMD from Iraq. Another
motive was to make Iraq a democratic country, as a possible first step
or 'domino' for wider democratisation in the Middle East. In this case,
proof of WMD in Iraq was irrelevant. The political advantages of such
a diversified, clouded case for war are clear[2]; criticism of one motive
can be countered by proposing another (a critic may say the case was
slippery or hydra-headed). Or, advocates of one motive may be content
to believe theirs is the prime motive even if they disagree with the other
motives offered. As we shall see, such ambivalence was present in the
television footage analysed and noted by respondents of the audience
study we analyse more fully in Chapter 8.

If we are to discern how the medium of television shapes the presentation of political discourses, we need to clarify the political discourses in
question. In the build-up to the 2003 Iraq war, there were, at the risk of
simplification, two political discourses present in CNN broadcasts and
debates in the United States and the United Kingdom more broadly.

The first discourse was *democratic imperialism,* and this discourse encompassed the motives for war mentioned above. Daalder and Lindsay (2003) describe as democratic imperialists those policymakers and intellectuals who identify a convergence of US national interests and the interests of humanity, such that the spread of democracy will result in peaceful nation-states and contented peoples who will thereafter pose no security threat to the United States. Spreading democracy and maintaining security are separate motives that mutually reinforce one another. Leading democratic imperialists include politicians George W. Bush and Tony Blair after 9/11, and writers William Kristol and Robert Kagan before and after 9/11 (Kagan and Kristol, 1996, 2001; Kagan, 2002). Democratic imperialists are distinguishable from 'assertive nationalists' or traditional realists, the latter of whom are 'willing to use American military power to defeat threats to US security but reluctant, as a general rule, to use American primacy to remake the world in its image' (Daalder and Lindsay, 2003: 15). The division between democratic imperialists and traditional realists was evident in debates surrounding the 2003 Iraq war, with Dick Cheney, Paul Wolfowitz, and other neoconservatives who can be characterised as democratic imperialists having greater influence over the direction of US foreign policy than traditional realists such as Colin Powell, the elder President George Bush, Brent Scowcroft, and Henry Kissinger.[3] By the time of the opening phase of the 2003 Iraq war, the official discourse of the US administration was democratic imperialist, as we shall see in the analysis below.

The second political discourse present in debates at the outset of the 2003 Iraq war and CNN's coverage was *assertive multilateralism.* The term was originally used by US Secretary of State Madeline Albright to describe the foreign policy of the Clinton Administration. It entailed working through the UN, NATO, and other multilateral bodies to identify and resolve problems in international society. Though the assertiveness of US foreign policy was diminished by an aborted intervention in Somalia in 1993, the principle of assertive joint action and the enforcement of international law was upheld by NATO countries for some time (see also Gow, 2005: 101–103). By March 2003, this discourse was advocated by opponents of the war in the United States and the United Kingdom, and by the official statements of the leaders of France, Germany, and Russia. The UNSCOM weapons inspection operations led by Hans Blix were an attempt to put this discourse into practice.

Before beginning our analysis of CNN's coverage of the opening phase of the 2003 Iraq war, we present in Table 4.1 a simple timeline

Table 4.1   Timeline of opening phase of 2003 Iraq war

Eastern standard time	Iraq time	Event	CNN coverage
19:00	03:00		Our analysis begins
19:46	03:46		Interview with Hans Blix
20:00	04:00	US-imposed deadline for Saddam Hussein to leave Iraq or surrender	Journalist in Kurdish area reports 'dead silence' but spots 'what seems to be aircraft activity'
20:12	04:12		CNN's experts speculate on likely course of war
20:33	04:33		CNN reports on terror threat to Chicago and Sears Tower
21:39	05:39	Explosions heard in Baghdad after Coalition launches decapitation attempt to remove Saddam Hussein by firing Tomahawk cruise missiles at a so-called bunker	Nic Robertson reports he heard air raid sirens 2 or 3 minutes ago, then sees anti-aircraft fire
21:45	05:45	White House Press Secretary Ari Fleischer announces 'the opening stages of the disarmament of the Iraq regime have begun'	CNN anchors and reporters note the war is proceeding at a time of the President's choosing. Larry King: 'Only one sentence from Ari Fleischer – few words but great drama in what he announced, the liberation of Iraq'
22:15	06:15	President George W. Bush announces he ordered an 'attack of opportunity' and that major operations have not begun	

of the period under study. We analyse footage from 19:00EST on 19 March, one hour before the US-imposed deadline and the possible beginning of the war, to 01:00EST on 20 March. We present the analysis in chronological order.

03:46 Iraq time: the existence of WMD

A few hours before US military strikes begin, Hans Blix appears on CNN. The interview is an interesting instance of a struggle between interviewer and interviewee to define the narrative of the situation, with certain 'moves' deployed in the conversation. We see how the two journalists, Lian and Richard, introduce Blix but belittle the status of his work and his role. This is in the context of an a priori narrative of 'Saddam's defiance' that CNN reproduces. However, Blix responds by expressing the view that even if Iraq possessed WMD, there was little incentive to use them:

> Lian: Chief UN weapons inspector Hans Blix has submitted a report to the United Nations, but his insights into Iraq's alleged weapons of mass destruction may have *become moot*. Richard Roth interviews Blix as the White House moves toward war.
>
> Richard: *He was the man of the moment for four months, and now well, a little bit of a different moment here*, Chief inspector Hans Blix with me. What do you think invading forces, if there is a war, will face regarding chemical biological weapons from Iraq?
>
> Blix: Well if they have any, still, and that's a big if, I would doubt that they would use it, because a lot of countries and people in the world are negative to the idea of waging war, and if the Iraqis were to use any chemical weapons, then I think public opinion around the world would immediately turn against Iraq, and they would say that 'well, you see, the invasion was justified'.

Note the intransitive clause, Blix's insights have *become moot*. The journalist assumes Blix's insights are moot and that how they became moot – whether they were *made* moot *by* particular actors – is not for discussion. In the next extract, Blix further disrupts the narrative of 'Saddam's defiance' by depicting 'the Iraqis' (plural) as reasonable. The interviewer attempts to lure Blix into stating that the Iraqis had been uncooperative, but Blix refuses. Furthermore, he states that any evaluation of the situation requires 'a sober eye'. A boundary is present in Blix's statement, between sober multilateralists and democratic imperialists. We can infer that Blix is questioning the credibility of evaluations based on an un-sober perspective, i.e. the impatient urge for war expressed by reporters in CNN's coverage:

> Richard: What are your feelings now war is imminent, maybe just hours away, and your job has been interrupted?
> Blix: Well, it's a sad moment I think. First of all it's sad because war is horrible, and secondly because I think that we were there for three and a half months and we had better conditions for inspection than UNSCOM ever did. The Iraqis after all allowed us to get in everywhere, we were also fully occupied with destroying a lot of missiles that we had judged were violating the rules, so I think we were moving. And then of course it is rather sad to leave after such a short time.
> Richard: But you said they did not give you enough co-operation right?
> Blix: Well they gave co-operation on process, what we term process –
> Richard: But not substance?
> Blix: – access ... well, lately I would say from some time in early February they gave more co-operation on substance, they sort of showered us with letters trying to explain this or that, but as I said in the Council one has to look at these things with a sober eye, and when they analyze it they find relatively new, little new material in it.

This disconcerts the interviewer, who loses coherence. But Blix responds by offering some agreement with the need to remove Saddam Hussein:

> Richard: Did, did you, you've said I think to me, maybe others, or to yourself, that maybe Saddam Hussein and the leadership was the problem. The scientists you dealt with you thought they understood the urgency, is that correct?
> Blix: Well I think they did, but you know, there was only one truth at any given time in a country like Iraq, and that is the truth that the leader decides on. And I remember well in 1991 when I was there and I sat in a car, and the leader of their Atomic Energy Commission said to me 'Mr. Blix, we have no enrichment of uranium'. And only a month or two months later, we discovered, the IAEA that they were indeed working in several different ways of enrichment. And he was a sincere man, but if he had not took the

line that the President had set well, he wouldn't have existed any longer.

Nevertheless, the interviewer has the last word by reminding Blix that his status is now that of all other spectators:

Richard: Chief inspector Hans Blix, still chief inspector, still at your post here, watching with everyone else what is indeed going to happen either later tonight, or in the next few days to come. Thank you very much.

In this Hans Blix interview, we have identified various principles at work in CNN's coverage. Through casual use of intransitive grammar, CNN's journalist discounts the agency that made Blix's work 'moot'; both parties engage in boundary work to establish the credibility and status of 'them' and 'us'; the interviewer searches for answers that confirm CNN's narrative, which is the democratic imperialist discourse; the interview loses coherence when the discourse is challenged; and finally news affords status to those who can affect future outcomes; hence the journalists feel able to belittle Blix.

04:12 Iraq time: will Saddam use WMD? Expert opinions

In the rhythm of twenty-four-hour news, there are lulls between moments of action or the arrival of new information. These lulls are often filled by analysis and reflection, provided by 'experts'. Experts may be those with professional experience in the type of situation at hand, legislators with a brief for the issue in question, or academics, writers, and intellectuals who are motivated to enter public debate. These 'talking heads' can fill air time and provide the news channels with a hint of credibility or 'seriousness'. Experts may provide 'context', a currency valued for conferring credibility on the 'quality' or 'depth' of the news coverage. Their authority allows them to 'tell the truth' of the matter under discussion – to speak the truth of war (Foucault, 1978: 57). But when the event in question is a war, then the status of such information is both sensitive and questionable. It is sensitive because particularly well-informed experts, such as recently retired generals, may reveal tactics or plans that the enemy may overhear and take advantage of. For the very same reason, the information provided by experts is also questionable: no sensible military would release information of value to its enemy, so how much can experts really tell the audiences? For instance, CNN anchor Aaron Brown asks General Wesley Clark when the war will begin:

> Brown: General Clark, General Wesley Clark, the former supreme NATO commander, does it resonate – forgive me for that word – does it resonate to you at all that [...] having the president of the United States go on to indicate that this is on, that we still may be 24, 48 hours or so away from the shock and awe, as Pentagon planners have described it, of this war?
>
> Clark: Aaron, I think it's entirely possible that that could be the case. Again, of course, none of us have seen the operations plan. We really don't know what is going to happen, but I think it's entirely possible...

Clark cannot provide concrete information, only possibilities. The lulls in CNN's coverage are defined by speculation. Following the interview with Hans Blix (above), CNN anchor David Ensor consults more experts: Judy Yaphe (ex-CIA analyst), Lt. Gen. Dan Christman (retired), and Ken Pollack (think tank director). The experts speculate about the likely course of a war. Ensor initially defines the parameters of 'the possible' and the stakes – the lives of Americans – confirmed by Yaphe:

> David Ensor: Will Saddam Hussein fight at the border or pull back to fight in the streets of Baghdad? Will he try to survive or attack with chemical weapons and try to go down as an Arab martyr? Only he knows for sure. But former CIA analyst Judy Yaphe says one way or another the man she's analysed for so many years will try to kill a lot of Americans.
>
> Judy Yaphe: I think his theory is I will do as much as I can to make it as ugly as possible for the Americans. I still believe that they have a Vietnam syndrome lingering that once they see bodybags, 'cause they will, this is not Kuwait, this is Iraq, this is Baghdad. We Iraqis know how to fight on the streets. Those Americans can't handle this.

Ensor then cites unnamed 'military analysts' and 'some believe'. CNN's experts are offering *a sense* rather than anything factual:

> David Ensor: Military analysts say the Iraqi leader may order dams breached to flood the Tigris and Euphrates river plains. Some believe he may force thousands of Iraqi civilians, women and children, out on to the roads, creating a human buffer between the

Americans and his forces. And then wait for US troops in the streets of Baghdad and surrounding villages.

The military representative also qualifies his statement with 'I think', while Pollack draws on a Second World War template as he attempts to introduce a soundbite:

Lt. Gen. Dan Christman: I think what is of most concern to commanders though is the hunkering down in the villages and neighbourhoods themselves that will force house-to-house fighting.

Ken Pollack: And the goal, the strategy he seems to be pursuing is that he is going to create this fortress Baghdad, but I keep calling the Mesopotamian Stalingrad.

By now, the experts have collectively constructed a small narrative: Saddam Hussein will not surrender, he will create a human shield, and the US will be drawn into guerrilla battles or trenches. The experts move towards the story's end (Note again that comments are qualified by 'may' or 'my instinct is ... '):

David Ensor: Then if the end appears near military analysts fear Saddam Hussein may order the use of the very weapons of mass destruction he insists he does not have.

Lt. Gen. Dan Christman: My instinct is if he decides to use chemical weapons it will be in a last case, armageddon scenario.

David Ensor: The analysts we spoke to agreed on this: there are likely to be some surprises for American troops as well as for the Iraqis. David Ensor, CNN Washington.

The experts have agreed (definite) about what is likely (speculative), presenting a decisive form to a story whose content has no factual basis. This happens repeatedly. When asked his opinion, Senator John McCain speaks of 'the conventional wisdom' and 'it's generally believed'. Note how he mixes up 'may' and 'will', such that a series of possibilities somehow add up to something definite:

I think you *will* see ... bad things *will* happen, he *can* set the oil wells on fire, he *may* fire a Scud missile at Israel or at our troops with a chemical weapon. I mean bad things *will* happen, that's why this is the last option.

This logic is akin to the 'faith ladder' described in William James' *Some Problems of Philosophy*, summarised by Lippmann (1922, Chapter X, Pt 10): 'In the future possibilities are almost indistinguishable from probabilities and probabilities from certainties. If the future is long enough, the human will might turn what is just conceivable into what is very likely, and what is likely into what is sure to happen'. The lull in twenty-four-hour news coverage of the opening stage of a war appears a likely site for faith ladders. Given the investment by all parties in the event, the urge to know what will happen – even before it has happened – is understandable. It is perhaps the logic of the situation that experts, paid to tell the audiences the meaning of events and 'calibrate' discussion towards probable future events (see Chapter 3), will succumb to the temptation to step up the ladder from possibilities to probabilities to certainties, to tell the audiences what *will* happen.

As noted in our opening chapter, this is the logic of pre-mediation (Grusin, 2004). If re-mediation is to borrow news clips or images from other news sources to bolster a report about what has happened, then to pre-mediate is to create news clips or images in an attempt to anticipate and define the future before it has happened. Re-mediation poses a problem for political leaders, argues Grusin. Think of 9/11: the world witnessed the sudden proliferation of *very immediate* images and sounds from the actual event. But political leaders – and quite possibly audiences – may not want another rupture like that. The 9/11 footage was *too* immediate. Would not it be more comforting if we were warned of events, or if events fitted familiar storylines? Would not that afford a greater legitimacy to security policy? Grusin cites the example of the anthrax scare in the United States in 2002. He writes:

> the anthrax scare became an obsession of the media not for the damage it had done but for the damage it could do in the future, for the threat it might become. In order that the news media would not be surprised as it had been by 9/11, it was imperative that the fullest extent of the national security threat from anthrax be premediated before it had ever happened, or *even if it never did.*
>
> (Grusin, 2004: 23, italics added)

Government, media, and audiences may have wanted to know whether Saddam Hussein would use WMD and when the war would begin. But nobody could say with certainty. Indeed, CNN's experts offered scenarios such as breached dams, the use of chemical weapons, and a 'Mesopotamian Stalingrad', while earlier Hans Blix had suggested that there would be no use of WMD. An apparently full range of outcomes was anticipated. And it was not just in the use of experts that CNN's coverage offered instances of speculation, anticipation, and pre-mediation. Reporters in Iraq speculated about the likely course of war, and in particular any clash between Coalition forces and the Iraqi Republican Guard. Audiences were primed for the stage after the initial invasion, for a potentially bloody fight. The result of these practices of the organisation of news is the creation of news as extended present, as discussed in Chapter 2 (Nowotny, 1994). Reporters' anticipation of a dramatic struggle between Coalition forces and the Republican Guard may be an act of informing audiences, but it may also be an attempt to keep them watching for a few more days.

04:33 Iraq time: connecting Iraq to attacks on the homeland

Thirty minutes later, a CNN report raises the possibility of terrorist attacks in Chicago at the Sears Tower and O'Hara Airport. This suggests, implicitly, a connection between Iraq and 9/11 and draws a causal pathway from US action in Iraq to possible actions against US citizens within the United States:

> Lian Pek: We're joined now by Chicago Bureau Chief Jeff Flock who is at the Sears Tower, the tallest building in the US following the terror attacks of September 11th. Certainly stepped up security where you are.
>
> Jeff Flock: Indeed all across the US tonight Lian er ... precautions being taken particularly at perceived targets. As you point out we are at the Sears Tower tallest building in the US. Tonight er ... many people have been afraid, particularly since 9/11, that perhaps this building would er ... would er ... er ... come under a similar attack. In fact some people at work in this tower have gone so far as to purchase parachutes so that if er ... they were unable to get out any other way they could perhaps get out that way. We've got pictures of this tower in the daylight, we can tell you what they've done is erected er ... cement barricades, red, white and blue ones er ... that would er ... preclude er ... a bomb laden vehicle from perhaps being driven too close to the building.

That the US authorities had painted cement barricades red, white, and blue reminds us that discourse can be instantiated, materially, as well as spoken or written. Flock continues:

In addition, all of the shipments inside the s...the Sears Tower are now X-rayed. Anyone that walks into the Sears Tower goes through a magnetometer. And they say...they say if er...it goes to a code red in the US, er...a danger level code red, they would shut down the popular sky deck where folks can go up and take a look out over the city.

Other precautions, at the world's busiest airport, that's O'Hare Airport here in Chicago, er...[...] stepped up security at the airport as well, including we are er...being told tonight er...er...police officers being dispatched to er...streets er...beneath flight paths of airplanes so as to head of anyone who might be er...having a er...shoulder-launched missile. Er...so serious precautions all across the US particularly here in Chicago where we stand tonight. Lian back to you.

This description of precautions against shoulder-launched missiles alerts us to the instance on 12 February 2003 at London Heathrow Airport where intelligence warned security services of the likelihood of such an attack that day. It is perhaps surprising that this precedent is not mentioned, for without this contextual information these precautions seem alarming.

This emphasis on precautions taken in the United States alerts us to where, for CNN, the 'social centre' is for the society they believe they are addressing (Dayan and Katz, 1992). This is evident in the following quote, prior to the deadline:

Lian: Suzanne, all eyes are on the war, but has the White House addressed uh...the threat of terrorist reprisals, how prepared is the US for that as it moves into Iraq?

Suzanne: Well that's a very good question. Today the Secretary of Homeland Security Tom Ridge met with the President to discuss exactly that, the risk involved for terrorist attacks overseas as well as *here at home*, yes everything has been beefed up, you know our terror alert is at level orange and that we have seen bridges as well as ports, even here at the White House intense security, fortified security, protesters not allowed from like a block away from the White House, but clearly *everything is on a heightened state of alert*.

Note that Suzanne, amplifying terror, reports everything and not everyone is 'on a heightened state of alert' – a slip that suggests inanimate objects are also becoming vigilant.

A further connection between Iraq and the homeland is drawn very clearly in a speech by President Bush. Just after 6 am EDT, after the deadline has passed, CNN offers live coverage as Bush offered his explanation for the war. He defined the war as primarily *defensive*, 'to defend the world from grave danger' during a 'time of peril' against 'an outlaw regime that threatens the peace with weapons of mass murder'. The coalition forces were acting to protect an international constituency, 'our common defense', and to protect the United States. In a pivotal passage, Bush attempted to bolster the notion of a defensive war by connecting the threat posed by Iraq using WMD to 9/11:

> We will meet that threat now, with our Army, Air Force, Navy, Coast Guard and Marines, so that we do not have to meet it later with armies of fire fighters and police and doctors on the streets of our cities.

This argument – attack them over there so we do not fight them over here – makes a connection between events in Iraq and security in the United States. The argument is in fact a threat: if we do not go to war, we will suffer at home. The spatial ordering of security by a politician is reinforced by CNN's coverage of preparations for attacks on the homeland.

04:37 Iraq time: CNN equates protest with terror

Having taken the perspective of the US government and security services throughout their coverage, CNN then constructs a *logic of equivalence* in the agents these authorities face that draws together the 'threat' of Iraqi military, terrorists, and anti-war protestors.[4] Flock is still in Chicago:

> Lian Pek: You mentioned Jeff of course er…war protestors taking to the streets in LA, in New York, in Washington. How manageable was that for the security forces, certainly a very tough job here as they tried to *juggle the threat of terrorism and of course now these war demonstrations*, anti-war demonstrations?
>
> Jeff Flock: Indeed the plan is, here in Chicago as in many cities, for five o'clock on the day and the afternoon after hostilities commence that er…folks gather. Here it will be on the Federal Plaza not too

many blocks from where I stand back there behind me in the darkness. Er...a group will come er...pre-arranged to that location to
demonstrate. Er...*local authorities are prepared for that they know its
coming and they're ready for it.*

The final sentence mimics the terms in which the US military in Iraq
is described: prepared and ready to face an enemy. From this lexical
similarity, the viewer could infer that political opposition to the war is a
problem – one more problem for the authorities. Moreover, CNN reports
from the implicit perspective of the authorities.

In constructing such boundaries, several CNN correspondents report
the statements of those not supporting the United States in a manner
that 'discounts' their credibility (Potter, in Silverman (ed.) 2004). For
instance, Nic Robertson reports that 'we have heard *of course*' from
various Iraqi officials that day, and that they are all 'essentially saying
the same thing'. CNN's journalists do not use this dismissive tone
to describe the speeches of Coalition leaders. CNN's correspondent at
the United Nations, Michael Okwu, describes a speech made by Iraqi
Deputy Prime Minster Tariq Aziz at the UN as a 'speech-a-thon of sorts',
though he admits he was not present at the speech. Aaron Brown
responds:

> Brown: It was interesting, Michael, you said at the beginning that
> we expect to hear a lot of speechmaking at the United Nations. I
> think there are a whole lot of people who would say that's all we've
> heard from the United Nations over the last several months, and
> perhaps the president might agree with that. There's been a lot of
> speechmaking.

By implication, the UN is all talk, no action. And by implication,
the President's position is valid. Okwu concludes his report, 'So a lot
of angry words there in the Security Council, which is something that
we have seen quite a bit in the last two months or so – Aaron'. Such
an evaluation of the UN discounts the validity of assertive multilateralism, given that the UN is a key body for coordinating such an
approach.

05:39 Iraq time: the decapitation strike: journalists and audiences as witnesses to the sublime

At around 05:39 in Iraq, CNN correspondent Nic Robinson began to report his experience of witnessing the sound of anti-aircraft fire over Baghdad; this was an Iraqi military response to what the White House later called a decapitation strike against the Iraqi leadership. This was the first footage during the 2003 Iraq war that resembled the familiar coverage of the US air campaign in the 1991 war: dark, grainy footage of a panorama of Baghdad lit up by military fire, with a journalist voiceover attempting to bestow specific meaning on the visuals. Robinson's report is multimodal; that is, he describes experiencing the event through different senses, and the audiences are offered sights, sounds, and a verbal interpretation. Forty minutes before the US-imposed deadline, Robinson's eyes see nothing but his ears are alerted:

> Brown: What can you tell us, Nic? Nic, go ahead.
> Robertson: Well, what we heard here in Baghdad a few minutes ago were the air raid sirens going off. *We could hear in the distance* around the city the sound of antiaircraft – antiaircraft guns being fired
>
> > [...]
>
> The streets are quiet, as they have been all night. The city at this time is still a city that has all its streetlights on even though the sun is just coming up here.
>
> *As far as we can see* at the moment, the city does not appear to be under attack. But the air raid sirens did go off and Iraqi antiaircraft gun positions did fire into the air about two or three minutes ago.

About fifteen seconds later, Robinson begins to see something:

> I can hear more antiaircraft gunfire erupting across the city at this time. I don't see any tracer fire – I see tracer fire flying through the air past this hotel.
> Yes, now, heavy bursts of antiaircraft gunfire coming up from the city's... coming up from across the city.

Twenty seconds later, Robinson notes he cannot *feel* the action he is reporting:

> As I look out across the city at this time, I am not seeing any detona-
> tions. I'm not seeing any explosions impacting on the ground [...]
> and *we have not felt any detonations* on the ground. <camera shakes>

McLuhan claimed to identify a 'basic principle' in distinguishing
between different types of media. He argued, 'A hot medium is one that
extends one single sense in 'high definition'. High definition is the state
of being well filled in with data ... Hot media are, therefore, low in participation, and cool media are high in participation or completion by the
audience' (1964: 22). In this sense, radio is a hot medium and television
is cool. Nic Robertson's report begins with relayed sound, which would
invite audiences' participation to imagine the scene. We then hear the
sound of the anti-aircraft fire ourselves. Robertson then provides a visual
description and indeed we see flashes of fire on the screen. And despite
Robertson reporting he feels no detonations, we hear several 'thumps'
and the still camera shakes. The nightvision camera offers a green picture
of the Baghdad skyline, before we switch to a normal camera that shows
a dark blue sky. Yet though this is television, the medium is neither hot
nor cold in this coverage; the footage is poor quality but we see *something*. Critical is how Robertson's voiceover meshes with the visuals to
create meaning. Mellencamp (2006: 121) writes of the visuals, 'Because
they were bad and barely decipherable, we assumed they must be real –
the key attribute of catastrophe coverage's claim on reality'. But it is
more complex:

> It would appear that vision serves sound, which remains the
> dominant code of television. Sights on television are accompanied by
> varying facts and opinions, suggesting that words create the context
> that critically determine meaning. Thus, seeing is not believing.
>
> (Mellencamp, 2006: 122)

Hence the first moment of action in CNN's war coverage is visually represented by a picture of what appears to be *nothing happening* –
a deserted skyline broken only by the occasional flash of anti-aircraft
fire. As we discuss in more detail in Chapter 6, in such instances the
audiences are still invited to *imagine* the cruise missiles in the sky
and the Iraqi military firing anti-aircraft weapons, encouraged by the
voiceover. The audiences must participate and mentally complete the
coverage.

The audiences are distanced from the events, hence viewers must
imagine. How is this distancing achieved? The murky, featureless skyline

is one step. Another is the use of intransitive grammar. Transitive grammar attributes agency, such that X did Y to Z, e.g. 'the US fired missiles at Saddam Hussein'. Intransitive does not, e.g. 'missiles fell on Baghdad'. In the footage we analysed, there were 17 instances of transitive clauses related to military fire and 12 intransitive clauses. However, of those 17 transitive clauses, the objects 'hit' by the coalition were labelled 'targets', 'artillery pieces', or 'Saddam'. That is, the target was always dehumanised in CNN's reporting. Chouliaraki draws attention to another mode of distancing audiences from events in war coverage. On the BBC's coverage of the 2003 Coalition bombing campaign, she writes:

> Despite the total visibility that this point of view offers, or precisely because of this, the spectator...is simultaneously kept resolutely outside the scene of action. She is an onlooker, watching from a safe distance. The quality of proximity that this 'detached' overview provides...is cinematic, a witness position that turns the reality of the war into a spectacular panorama that fills the television screen. [The footage] does not move through the streets of Baghdad, in the homes of Iraqis or hospitals and, therefore, is unable to shift the position of the spectator from the 'detached' overview to an 'involved' observation of suffering in proximity (as for example Al Jazeera did).
>
> (Chouliaraki, 2005: 151)

Alongside this visual detachment, the reporter inserts his own sensorial experience between the event and the viewer: he refers to 'what *we* have heard', 'as far as *we* can see', and '*we* have not felt any detonations'. The past tense adds a temporal distancing too. Viewers are told of what reporters have experienced rather than directly witnessing anything specific and intelligible themselves.

The category of the *sublime* becomes important here.[5] The sublime has two related characteristics. On the one hand, it refers to something pleasurable – one can enjoy the spectacle of terror *qua* spectacular (because it is at a distance). Safe, we can feel not horror but an enthusiastic horror; not terror but an awed terror. On the other hand, the sublime can refer to the cognitive containment of excess. Beholding something awesome, we agonise momentarily as we try to comprehend it; and then – suddenly – we enjoy a moment in which the thing becomes intelligible; we amaze ourselves and enjoy a moment of self-transcendence (Crowther, 1998). Stimulated to imagine and reach a comprehension between the images of military fire and the dark, silenced city, CNN's coverage offers audiences the opportunity for a sublime experience. Viewers first witness a firework display, then may make the imaginative connection to the unseen bombed. But can they? Does shock and awe invite, paradoxically, a curiosity into what is actually being seen beyond mere spectacle? For as Chouliaraki notes, there are no pictures from street level, no pictures of Iraqis, and no mention of Coalition bombs falling on Iraqis. The Iraqi civilian is 'cancelled' from the coverage (Chouliaraki, 2005: 155). The work of imagining any suffering (or rejoicing) among Iraqi civilians is entirely in the audiences' hands, and in fact Chouliaraki argues that the aestheticised, spectacular, and distanced coverage inhibits any emotional connection to those civilians. Is this really the case?

Turning to the audience study we draw upon, we find that the green-ish nightvision camera footage of the Iraqi skyline stayed in the memories of many audiences members. When asked about the war, this was frequently the first recollection. So did viewers in Britain find coverage of the 2003 Iraq war sublime, and if so, how was that experience related to the researchers? In the following quote, mother Lynne and daughter Faye, middle-class residents in Edinburgh, were asked what images they recalled from the war:

> Lynne: Probably quite a few actually. Seeing the bombing the first night actually, the first couple of days.
>
> Faye: This sounds really stupid but it kind of looked like fireworks 'cause it showed up greeny. It looked like fireworks but you know it wasn't.
>
> Lynne: Actually I find it quite shocking in a way to watch people being bombed. I think because it was live, somehow that was worse. To watch news live and know that people were being killed I actually find quite disturbing.

Lynne found herself drawn emotionally into the situation, in contrast to Chouliaraki's thesis. The footage triggered an emotive connection as she reflected on how her experience of watching the footage coincided temporally, in real time, with people being killed. Whether Lynne was disturbed by the notion of people dying as she sat comfortably or by her powerlessness to alter the situation, she connected the news she watched with knowing people were being killed – people unseen but imagined. This is an example of co-presence and deixis, part of the taxonomy of liveness outlined in Chapter 2. In addition, we see how television coverage helps constitute an interaction order beyond the screen. This footage led Lynne to consider herself in relation to people thousands of miles away being bombed.

The next quote is taken from an exercise by the researcher Habiba Noor[6] in which a group of fifteen-year-old Bengali Muslim schoolchildren in Tower Hamlets, East London, were asked to produce their own episode of a children's news programme (like BBC's *Newsround*) using Apple's i-movie software. They picked from a range of images from the war, put them in the order they thought the war occurred, and scripted a voiceover. Here they are discussing the nightvision footage as they pick clips to put into their episode:

Mod: What about bombing?
Sha: Yeah, that's it. Show the bombing.
Interviewer: The one that looks like fireworks.
Sha: Oh...that one.
Mod: This one?
Interviewer: There's this...
Amin: Wasn't there one from the plane, like shooting people? A target bombing – killing people like ants – or something like that.
Amin: Killing people like ants.
Sha: No...for little kids that's too much. They are going to go stomping around killing ants!
Interviewer: What about if it was for adults?
Amin: That would be alright then.

The children connect the bombing to people being killed, equating Iraqi civilians with ants being crushed. It is also interesting that they raise and debate the ethics of sanitisation, with Amin concluding that adults should not be given sanitised footage. But after sympathy for people being killed like ants, Sha reverts to interpreting the footage in aesthetic terms:

Sha: <Looking at the night bombing> That looks like the alien movie <chuckle>. I like the other one with fireworks. That one looks nice actually.

Nonetheless, in deciding on a voiceover for the clip, the children are unequivocal about the need for transitive grammar and the attribution of agency:

Amin: Yeah...we should use effective bold words.
Sha: Bombs...creating...I don't know...

Mod: Bombs have landed causing destruction.
Sha: Yeah bombs sent down to cause destruction.
Sha: Landed... yeah, but how do they get there?
Mod: Kids ain't that stupid, they don't fall out of the sky bro.
Amin: Alright go on.
Amin: Is there a picture of Bush happy – he has no worries?
Amin: We should have something like that.
Mod: After that, why don't you have that smoking car and the woman crying?
Sha: That map that zooms into Fallujah – that one.

The children construct a clear causal narrative from Bush's orders, to the bombs, to destruction. They then connect the initial bombing to later conflict in Iraq, the siege of Fallujah. And bombing was given a motive: 'sent down to cause destruction'. Such extracts illuminate the manner in which audiences contest television and political discourses.

To summarise, CNN's murky footage of air strikes invited audiences to use their senses and imagine the reality of what was being partially represented on-screen. While such footage may offer a buffer, distancing audiences from events, liveness, and co-presence triggers concern as viewers overcome the televisual murk and they are effectively watching people dying live. Hence, we see how audiences 'do work' and contest news representations. We return to this theme in Chapter 6 when we consider the 'body paradox' that surrounds representations of death and injury.

05:45 Iraq time: tempo, coherence, and orderliness: a White House announcement

In CNN's Iraq war coverage, it is notable that CNN's reporting loses coherence when too much happens. There is a state of overload. This often happens when there is an official announcement, which brings new information that CNN is compelled to report, contextualise, analyse, and fit into its news discourse as rapidly as possible. For instance, just after Nic Robertson hears air raid sirens in Baghdad and sees anti-aircraft fire in the sky, coverage cuts to a more newsworthy event as White House Press Secretary Ari Fleischer announces in Washington DC:

The opening stages of the disarmament of the Iraqi regime have begun. The president will address the nation at 10:15.

After the waiting, CNN is able to offer some news at last. Having reported some military fire from Iraq, CNN find their report confirmed by the White House. Coverage noticeably speeds up and loses coherence as CNN's anchors and reporters attempt to interpret what is happening. Larry King and Aaron Brown emphasise the drama:

> King: Only one sentence from Ari Fleischer – few words but great drama in what he announced, the liberation of Iraq…
> Brown: Certainly was…
> King: …the president says, has begun.
> Brown: I heard it as the disarmament, but you may have heard it better than I.

Based on Fleischer's few words, a slightly confused conversation about the start of the war follows between anchor Aaron Brown and Jamie McIntyre, reporting from the Pentagon. There are echoes of the BBC parody *Broken News*, as introduced in Chapter 2:

> Brown: Jamie McIntyre, do you know yet where this has started?
> McIntyre: Well, Aaron, I think it's not clear exactly what's going on now. I know that it sounded pretty definitive when they said President Bush would be addressing the nation. We were told there might be something the president wanted to comment on that could possibly be less than the actual start of the war, again in the area of prepping the battlefield.
>
> I've not been able to get a clarification, but it appears that there might be some limited strikes that would be very close to Baghdad, perhaps with either planes or cruise missiles would probably be the most – the weapon of choice. This is – the timing of this just seems to be unlikely to be the full-blown start of the war. But I have to say, I have yet to get clarification.
> Brown: Right. At the same time, it's hard to – I mean, it is hard to read Ari Fleischer's words in any other way than what he said, that the disarmament of Iraq has begun.
>
> Now we can, I suppose, and will know in the next minutes or hours what precisely that means, that extent of the beginning, but there's no question that it is on. And so I guess the question is, where is it on, what is happening, in what parts of the country? And that's what I guess you and we and all of us need to find out and want to know.

Brown and McIntyre frantically try to deal with breaking news. Their task is to provide an immediate interpretation of a brief statement, an interpretation that fulfils their journalistic goal of reporting the event, that extends and fleshes out the narrative of this media event, and that keeps us watching. Their conversation is a good example of journalists attempting to impose orderliness on coverage in a situation of uncertainty, with no script and very little reliable information. Their practice becomes transparent through their informal phrases. For instance, Brown's concluding phrase, 'that's what I guess you and we and all of us need to find out and want to know', reveals his assumptions about CNN's audiences and the assumed common responsibilities and needs in the relationship between CNN and its audiences. Brown is accounting for his practice as he goes.

CNN's coverage of the opening phase of the 2003 Iraq war contrasts with Fox's coverage of Hurricane Katrina, as analysed in Chapter 3. For Katrina, Fox journalists appeared to be better informed about the disaster than officials, so there was less chance of official sources disrupting the rhythm of the news discourse. Hence, we find an opposing dynamic in different types of news events. In Iraq, CNN reported a politically managed, orderly opening phase of the war that left the orderliness of CNN's coverage exposed to the timing of official sources and decisions. For instance, following Fleischer's statement and more speculation from CNN journalists, McIntyre suggests, 'I'm not sure we'll really know precisely what's going on until we actually hear the words from the White House'. CNN's knowledge and scope for reporting from the war zone are limited. For Hurricane Katrina, Fox News was best placed of any actors involved to impose (discursive) order on the chaos.

06:35 Iraq time: did CNN accomplish a media event?

CNN's coverage contained many references to what journalists and viewers should expect from the event. CNN were presenting the beginning of a war in which they had been promised 'shock and awe' by the US military. Anticipating a spectacle, the complexity of the situation was not what CNN appeared interested in. We have seen how the perspective and insights of Hans Blix were deemed 'moot', how the words of Iraqi officials and debates at the UN were discounted, and how protesters were depicted as a problem to be dealt with. At around 22:35EST, Aaron Brown introduces a reporter, Ben Wederman, in a Kurdish area of Iraq, and in the process he suggests this night is not a time to be considering complex issues:

Brown: Ben is with Kurdish troops. This is part of the complicated ethnic and religious makeup of Iraq that, over the weeks that this war plays out, we suspect we'll spend a fair amount of time talking about, probably *not the night for it now*, but it is the time to go to Ben and see what he can tell us.

After Wederman's report, Brown reveals his expectation that at the opening of a war, life in Iraq should not appear normal. This appears to reflect Dayan and Katz's (1992) thesis that a 'media event' features a suspension of daily life:

Brown: As you look at these pictures of Iraq, of Baghdad right now, you know what has happened. You know that a dozen to two dozen cruise missiles have hit a couple of sites, one site in the city. At the same time, oddly, life has gone on. Iraqi TV has been on the air. Iraqi radio has been on the air, all of normal Thursday morning life. I think that's probably a bit of a stretch, to say normal Thursday morning life has gone on. But, in fact, life has gone on.

Did Brown expect an immediate 'Mesopotamian Stalingrad'? He continues to ask reporters for signs of normalcy and at around 23:20EST, or 07:20 in Iraq, Nic Robertson reports signs of rupture:

Robertson: It certainly is not coming alive for a normal Thursday morning. I'm on the 11th floor of a hotel...no signs of soldiers out on the streets here at this time but then no signs, no signs of normal life, the stores are closed, there are vehicles parked at the side of the road...

Nevertheless, thereafter there were no new incidents in the coverage. CNN returned to stories from earlier and attempted to construct a timeline themselves. CNN correspondent Walt Rogers interviewed US soldiers at around 00:45EDT and repeatedly asked them (seven times) whether they were surprised to have not begun their advance and surprised by the earlier decapitation attempt. One could infer that Rogers was hoping that the order to advance would have come, and he imposes his interpretation: 'The problem for [the soldiers], of course, is that the order has not come forward'. For the time being, CNN could not deliver the media event they perhaps anticipated.

Conclusion

We began this chapter asking how the relation between news discourse and political discourse might operate in this moment early in the twenty-first century when a crisis of news discourse has taken hold of television. If 9/11 and other terrorist attacks show how television can become hijacked by terrorists, then our analysis of CNN's coverage of the opening phase of the 2003 Iraq war demonstrates how television coverage can act to reproduce the framing and assumptions of political discourses advanced by elected officials. CNN's coverage lent legitimacy to the 'democratic imperialist' discourse advanced by the Bush Administration. But our analysis has highlighted how various mechanisms intrinsic to current journalistic practices led to this legitimating process. CNN's coverage was in effect hijacked by its own demand for a predictable, manageable but exciting media event, the need for a coherent narrative that precludes certain positions (Hans Blix, UN members, protesting citizens), and by a reliance on the administration and military for information about what was happening in Iraq. Moreover, by offering simultaneous footage of events in Iraq and the US 'homeland' and by giving a platform to 'experts' who possessed little concrete information but many pessimistic hypotheses, CNN amplified terror and legitimated the democratic imperialist assertion of a link between Saddam Hussein and terrorists intent on attacking the United States.

Yet the relation between news discourse and political discourse is not so straightforward. Attention to the multimodal, televisual aspects of CNN's footage allows us to consider the relation between the footage and viewers. For instance, the green, murky footage of the Baghdad skyline as air strikes were launched appears to create distance between event and viewer, containing the terror of the event. However, the incompleteness of the visuals and the reporter's voiceover invites the viewer to imagine, to 'do work'. Through the category 'the sublime' and use of audiences interview data, we have suggested how viewers are not simply distanced but can feel compelled to contest the sometimes-reductive rendering offered by television news. We shall return to the manner in which citizens themselves can modulate terror in Chapter 8. But having examined how television news represents current and future threats, we turn now to television's reliance upon history and the past in constructing these presents.

5
Television's Quagmire: The Misremembered and the Unforgotten

Introduction

Television relies upon history and the past in reporting the present. Thanks to growing archives of footage, television can mix together images and stories from the past to instantly frame the present and indeed the future. In fact, stories from *the* past are increasingly stories from *television's* past. The history of the medium itself can be mapped onto the events that television news has reported. Such appropriation becomes constitutive of television's own 'memory'. As television announces, 'remember when we brought you this', it claims authorship as if to enhance its own credibility and legitimacy as an actor in those events. Critical to these operations are 'media templates', the principal mechanism of instant comparison and contrast that television news employs to reinforce or reshape past events as well as to interpret and direct those unfolding. In this chapter, we examine how some of the most powerful media narratives of the modern age are composed through a multimodal layering and fusing of an array of textual stimulants within the televisual environment. In this way, television news imposes sequential and serial connections on disparate terror events and lends legitimacy to political discourses surrounding the War on Terror. This chapter analyses news texts from 9/11, the 7/7 London bombings, and concludes by exploring the relevance and the endurance of the Vietnam War template in the context of the 'quagmire' of the aftermath of the 2003 Iraq war.

The inescapable past

We have suggested some of the ways in which the complex temporal modulations of television news amplify and assuage the threat of terror in the new century. Principally, we have so far focused upon the medium's seizure and manipulation of present times and its projections into and onto the future. However, the same digital technologies that have enabled these transformations and which have entrenched the frames of immediacy, simultaneity, and proximity as standard in television news have also facilitated a greater and more immediate access to the archive. The medium's representation, reconstruction, and reshaping of the past have attained new levels. Partly, this is not only owing to the organisation, availability, and retrievability of digitally stored images and footage, but also owing to television's intensifying relationship to a past that it contributed to 'producing' in the first place. For instance, as White and Schwoch (1999) write, 'The medium's own mechanisms – its prevailing technologies and discourses – become the defining characteristics of modern historiography'.[1] This is part of a long trend in technological advances enhancing the imprint of the medium upon the message, and for decades television news has increasingly entwined itself with unfolding news events. In this way, it is also bound up with how such events are later selectively represented, reconstructed, or discarded. Thus, White and Schwoch argue:

> television's ideas of history are intimately bound up with the history of the medium itself (and indirectly with other audiovisual recording media), and with its abilities to record, circulate, and preserve images. In other words, the medium's representations of the past are highly dependent on events that have been recorded on film or video, such that history assumes the form of television's self-reflection.[2]

However, television's 'self-reflection' has become more defining of its treatment of its own 'past' and its application of this past in and on the present. Television news' self-referentiality and self-importance are partly constructed through its promotion of its authorial relationship to events. So, television news discourse has shifted such that the statement 'there is the world' is now replaced by 'we bring you the world' that is usually pronounced at times of crisis and catastrophe, and in the retrospective narrativising of momentous events. And in stamping its authorship on events that it initially brings to wide spectatorship, TV news weds itself to when and how (and if at all) those events are later represented, remembered, and understood.

Yet, television news' mediatising of the past is not accidental or impartial. It has a vested interest in embedding itself into the social and historical landscape; it 'brands' events through its televisual signifiers, logos, straplines, and celebratory montages of the 'history' it wants to be synonymous with. However, the tendency of television news to dwell on the extraordinary, the horrific, and the catastrophic, as delivering what is 'newsworthy', renders that news ultimately beholden to those whose interests are served by the perpetuation of insecurity. In relation to the spread of terrorism and terror in the twenty-first century, television had become weaponised. As we will demonstrate in this chapter, television history is a powerful contributor to the global War on Terror because it is so effective in maintaining the currency of past nodal terror events, using them to frame, contextualise, and even rationalise those which are occurring today. Inasmuch as the medium participated in delivering the terror of 9/11 and other atrocities, which continues to be the primary legitimising frame of the US-led War on Terror, it is also absolutely central to its continued trajectory, for the events in question are inextricably part of television history. In this chapter, we explore to what extent television as a 'global memory bank' is a potentially lethal weapon of terror. The apparent obsession of television news that the past potentially holds a redemptive retrospective security, founded on the certainties of a history of survival, is thereby unfounded.

9/11 and the War on Terror schema

In Chapter 2, we introduced the notions of mediatisation and reflexivity as processes through which television is potentially able to shape the events on which it reports in real time in its prompting or facilitating of immediate responses from actors invested in those unfolding events. Although the dramatic actual and pseudo-immediacy and proximity of television news afford terrorists the ideal instant vehicle to spread outrage, fear, and insecurity, the longue duree of television news also provides an effective structure for both the amplification and the containment of the same terror events. The interaction order of television news stitches together previous terror atrocities with each new incoming attack. The medium's capacity for producing instant and visual comparisons with previous events – media templates – is a key component in TV news' construction and reinforcement of familiar narratives. Thanks to its vast and accumulating archive, television news is able to sequence and serialise new, breaking, and often unrelated terror events, rendering them as a continuum of the War on Terror. Through immediate recourse to templates, television news has in many cases reproduced the political and military rubric of the War; indeed, sustaining this narrative or schema is pivotal to the reflexive impact of the atrocity being reported, the advancement of the notion of a homogenous enemy and support for mass military intervention (Afghanistan and Iraq), and the incitement of and cover for new terrorist atrocities in response. In this way, media templates afford an imagined trajectory to current events through the production or reinforcement of a speculative discourse on the basis of past events, events whose comparability is often contestable.

With the London bombings, the UK–US air terror plots, and the many often-unfathomable terrorist atrocities around the globe in recent years, it has become clear that the dominance of the stirring simplicities of the War on Terror narrative is indicative of the mainstream media's capitulation to both 'sides'. The business of reporting news has increasingly become entwined with an amplification of the actuality of 'terrorism'. Is there a more effective means of spreading terror than through the news media's inability or unwillingness to prevent itself from being the principal publicity of those acts it abhors but which are key to its own economy? Although the development of niche channels might have offered some way out of this paradox, they seem, instead, to have entrenched the War on Terror as the discursive status quo. The War on Terror schema not only blankets the complexities of the nature and forms of terrorist and other threats to the security of the West but also dignifies a unifying and magnifying voice to disconnected and disparate terrorists and potential terrorists. For example, Zygmunt Bauman draws upon comments from Pierre de Bousquet (director of DST, the French domestic intelligence service): the terrorist groups are 'not homogenous, but a variety of blends' – in other words they are formed ad hoc, recruited each time from different milieus, and sometimes from quarters deemed mutually incompatible. They defy all categorical reasoning – rubbing the salt of incapacitating incomprehension into the wounds inflicted by the horrific deeds, and so adding more fear to the already frightening effects of the outrages (2006: 108).

However, could the potential spread of fear and terror through the continual imposition of a War on Terror schema paradoxically be nullified by the very containment of a series of news events such a schema implies? The function of media templates in rendering terror events 'familiar and unexceptional' (Silverstone, 2002) is actually made visible in the rare occasion of their absence. 11 September 2001 was one such occasion: Notably, there was a struggle by commentators, 'experts', and politicians, via the mass media, to obtain an immediate, adequate, and consensual template through which to comprehend and also to mitigate the attacks on the WTC and the Pentagon. The Japanese bombing of

Pearl Harbor in the Second World War, and the Vietnam War, appeared to be the events of nearest sufficient magnitude in the US collective psyche at the time to employ as comparative frames. For example, Henry Kissinger, the fifty-sixth US Secretary of State (himself very much associated with traumatic histories) compared the 9/11 terrorist attacks – and the response needed – with those on Pearl Harbor, live on CNN on the afternoon of 11 September. Yet, there was a general consensus amongst commentators of the inadequacy of other nodal US catastrophes as measures against which to make sense of and to contain the shock of 9/11. As noted earlier, the default containment strategy across media appeared to be the inuring repetition of the new in the absence of the familiarity of the old. However, television news soon began to attempt to situate and rationalise the event through its visual archive. Figure 5.1, for example, is an extract from a CNN recorded package that was aired two days after the attacks on New York and Washington.

Bruce Morten's report is structured around a film montage of nodal US military interventions from the Second World War including Korea, Vietnam, and the 1991 Gulf War. The visual template for the latter is a

Main strapline: AMERICA'S NEW WAR	
Commentary	**Visuals**
1 **Bruce Morten:** World War II 2 brought Americans together. 3 Most believed that Nazi 4 Germany and Imperial Japan 5 were evil and aggressive. 6 Americans demanded victory: 7 the phrase of the day was 8 'unconditional surrender'.	Black-and-white footage of various troops being paraded and in action in World War II;
9 Korea and Vietnam contest in 10 contrast divided the country. 11	Soldiers shooting at a target out-of-shot with mountains as backdrop, presumably taken from the Korean War;
12 Vietnam in particular left 13 Americans suspicious, weary 14 of wars, and in the conflicts 15 since the model seems to have 16 been: 17 bomb all you want but we 18 can't stand American 19 casualties. 20	sepia-tinged colour film of a marked US helicopter flying overhead and a scene of anti-war protestors; Sharper colour footage of a US jet taking off from an aircraft carrier at sea (presumable from the 1991 Gulf War); Colour shot of coffin draped in Stars and Stripes on airport tarmac;
21 That seems different now.	Smoke billowing from WTC

Figure 5.1   Extract from CNN continuous coverage, 13 September 2001.

view taken through the targeting cross hairs of a jet of the trajectory and the impact of its missile, a sequence of images that became a common televisual view of war from the 1990s onwards, waged on behalf of, and sanitised for, Western audiences. The last two template images, however – footage of the arrival of the coffin of a US serviceman back on home soil and the smouldering remains of the Twin Towers – reveal the intended message of this visual narrative. Notably, the montage supports the commentary in reflexively recognising a putative shift in the imagined, collective American outlook on war, from a reluctance to sustain casualties in fighting distant wars to an acceptance of potentially greater human costs necessary in that which CNN and other US news networks almost immediately declared as 'AMERICA'S NEW WAR'.

So, media templates not only function to anchor the shock of terror events in the 'settled' history of previous conflicts but also promote a particular future course of action based on the lessons of that history – in this example, the need for unity of purpose even in the circumstances of the potential loss of US lives. It is precisely this type of reporting in the US that became a condition for what was to become established as the War on Terror schema, which would powerfully frame many terror events in the years to come. For a number of commentators, this period is marked by a capitulation of the Fourth Estate in its acquiescence to the Bush-led War on Terror. Todd Gitlin (2004), for example, writes:

> Journalists have missed the boat – amplifying disingenuous claims, downplaying doubts, belittling dissent. As it thrashed about in a state of emergency, America needed solid reporting – and solid scepticism – more than ever. Instead, large numbers of people were left believing that some of the September 11 hijackers were Iraqis, that Saddam Hussein was implicated in the terror attacks, and that the United States had actually found weapons of mass destruction in Iraq.[3]

Television news coverage on and after 9/11 helped engineer a powerful visual frame of a 'new war' and a requisite 'unified' response. At times of national and international crisis and catastrophe, the mass media are instrumental in supplying an immediate, and perhaps knee-jerk, solidarity schema. This may feature several overlapping explanations of events. The immediate impact of 9/11 was reflected not only in the searching for nodal templates sufficient to help shape public under-standing of what the attacks meant but also in the use of grand state-ments and metaphors, and some evoking memories of past public calls for international solidarity in the face of rapidly changing world events.

Even the French newspaper *Le Monde* paraphrased John F. Kennedy in Berlin in 1962 with a front-page editorial: 'We Are All Americans' (12 September 2001); Tony Blair declared that Britain stood 'shoulder to shoulder with our American friends in this hour of tragedy'[4]; and the then CBS anchorman Dan Rather appearing on the *CBS Late Show with David Letterman* soon after 9/11 declared, 'George Bush is the President, he makes the decisions, and, you know, as just one American, he wants me to line up, just tell me where'.[5] This totalising televisual discourse of shock and solidarity following 9/11 perhaps constituted the attacks as the first and last global media event of this century. Last, that is, because the notion of the 'collective' experience alluded to by Dayan and Katz (1992) and others has been undermined by the mainstream media's inability or unwillingness to challenge or critique not only the consensual solidarity schema that was forged through it but the policies that followed in Iraq and at home.

The War on Terror schema endured long after the approximate consensual solidarity in the aftermath of atrocities and other catastrophes had fractured.[6] This is partly owing to the political dominance of the Bush White House, whose discourse is echoed by the Blair Government. The dominance of the War on Terror schema in media, military, and political discourses since the turn of the new century presents several problems: firstly, it is inextricably embedded with the perceived failures of the Iraq War and, secondly, there appears little consensus around any potential replacement (schema or strategy). Nevertheless, the term may have projected a rhetorical and strategic vacuum, but there are no prospects of the War on Terror's closure or completion. For example, George Soros argues, 'The war on terror is a false metaphor that has led to counterproductive and self-defeating policies. Five years after 9/11, a misleading figure of speech applied literally has unleashed a real war fought on several fronts... But the war on terror remains the frame into which American policy has to fit'.[7] And the continuing bloody irresolution of the war in Iraq simultaneously undermines *and* reinforces the schema as it demonstrates the improbability of 'victory' but also feeds into the White House discourse of 'staying the course'.

Part of the War on Terror schema was a widespread propagation of a 'terrorist' or 'terrorism' template, which has been employed to represent disconnected groups and events as connected and equivalent in an attempt to justify blanket discursive, if not military, responses. Jonathan Raban (2006) for example, writes, ' "The terrorists" used once to mean the dubious entity of al-Qa'ida. Now it's an umbrella term, spread ever wider to shelter an astonishing variety of administration-designated bad guys: Hamas, Hizbollah, Kashmiri separatists, the Taliban, Ba'athist insurgents, Sunni jihadists, the Mahdi Army, the governments of Iran, Syria, North Korea'.[8] Relatedly, John Rentoul (biographer of Tony Blair) identifies these discursive connections in the former British Prime Minister's rhetoric: 'He connects everything. He connects the domestic war against terrorism. He connects that with the situation in Lebanon, in Iraq, in Afghanistan and back to 9/11. He says it's all part of the same thing and is all part of this struggle between democracy or freedom, and radical extremist Islam'.[9] If, as we specified in our Introduction, a discourse refers not just to a set of statements but also to the rules and practices by which such statements are produced, then we see here how the War on Terror serves as a discourse in which statements that make such connections become intelligible. And as we saw in our analysis of CNN's coverage of Iraq in Chapter 4, news discourse can operate in a manner that can privilege one political discourse over another. We see that here in relation to the practices of television: its use of archives, templates and sequences serve to sustain the War on Terror discourse. This particular historicising of terrorism as part of an endless and boundless continuum of struggle against a common enemy is hugely advanced by the effortless capacity of television news to reflexively re-frame and renew its archived terror histories in covering new events.

Media reflexivity

Rather than mediating (and mediatising) a constant, even relationship with the past, television reflexively constructs the present in an uneven and often concentrated way, through a prism of archival representations (and vice versa). This process is vested with an accumulative acceleration as more of recent news history is first 'captured' and disseminated via television. This applies no more so than to the conflicting times of the opening of the twenty-first century. Notably, this period is marked by a massive growth in the capacity of new digital technologies to record, store, and manipulate the images, sounds, and graphics that combine to comprise the content of television news. Of course the value of the televisual archive rests on the uses it is put to in the present and in the future. As it is, the prolonged media-led dwelling upon 9/11, as one of the biggest news stories in US history at least, is one of the most discernible trends in this century's television history, yet the final (and historical) impact of which remains to be realised. As we have suggested, the recycling and reusing of recorded footage and photographs from catastrophic events may function as a process through which a (mass media-projected and presumed) community comes to terms with them. At the same time, television news in particular, through its instant archival access and compulsion to repeat, reopens wounds from months and years earlier, affording immediacy and freshness to these events as though they were hours, rather than years, old. This is in addition to the dramatisation, reconstruction, and part-fictionalisation of events that forge a symbiotic and even intersecting relationship with 'news' coverage (which we return to consider in Chapter 7).

The archive, as facilitated and accessed through the new 'technologies of memory', has been characterised as a matter both of societies' representations of the past to themselves and also as taking on a life of its own, thus a 'prosthetic memory'.[10] Television news, although not constitutive as an archive as such, nonetheless is entirely dependent on one – otherwise all coverage would be talking heads live to camera, as in the days of television's tentative beginnings. However, it is precisely through its self-aware historiography that the medium is empowered as the arbiter of new and unfolding events as it explicitly promotes its repertoire of those preceding and connected narratives, out of the combination of which the present is constructed. In its overwhelming focus upon its own activities, some critics argue that the media has become 'detached' from the 'reality' it seeks or claims to represent. This is not just a question of the promotional branding of different news organisations, networks, or programmes. Rather, there is a wholesale consumption and reconsumption of television news discourse (rules, roles, practices, content) that is part-constitutive of that which today passes as 'news'. For Niklas Luhmann, for example, the mass media constitute a self-referential system that can become detached from the outside world as such, reacting predominantly instead to its own operations. He argues:

> the mass media disseminate ignorance in the form of facts which must continually be renewed so that no one notices. We are used to daily news, but we should be aware nonetheless of the evolutionary improbability of such an assumption. If it is the idea of surprise, of something new, interesting and newsworthy which we associate with news, then it would seem much more sensible not to report it in the same format every day, but to wait for something to happen and then to publicize it.
>
> (2000: 25)

As we explored in Chapter 2, television news partly orients itself around and in the present, and in anticipation of the immediate future, no matter what, or rather what is not, transpiring (or potentially about to transpire). However, news today, as well as history, also appears to be shaped from television's accumulative authorial signification of its past, as TV news increasingly connects and serialises events that it reports on.

In fact, if we take the media event analogy, the War on Terror appears as one extended story within which 'new' occurrences (and on all sides) have a 'post-9/11' referentiality. Unlike traditional media events, however, the serialisation of attacks, atrocities, and warfare into the War on Terror schema is tied to a narrative seemingly without the prospects of closure, a conflict with little hope of even medium-term resolution. So, in addition to the real-time reflexive environment of the global media in which there are represented the unfolding verbal and military exchanges between various political, religious, (inter)national, and ethnic groups that comprise the news landscape, there is the less-commented-upon fact that these are interwoven with and sustained by the archival powerhouse of television. The diminishment of 9/11, and those events both seared and serialised with it in a global consciousness of the War on Terror, is not configurable with news agendas, as they themselves would be massively diminished without the War on Terror. The televisual past thus weighs heavily on the prospects of liberation from a pervasive conflict that is increasingly characterised as 'war without end'.

Mixing times: liveness and archives after the 7/7 bombings

Figure 5.2 illustrates the immediate capacity of television news to place unfolding events in a War on Terror schema through serialising templates in a narrative trajectory from 9/11 to the present – here, the July 2005 London bombings. This is achieved through a combination of multiple temporal and spatial layers that embed the still unfolding story of 7/7 into a powerful visual and oral narrative. The archival material – footage of the aftermath of terrorist attacks familiar (through its repetition) to Western news publics – is arranged chronologically. The audio commentary from the Sky reporter Tim Marshall, however, connects each attack template with Britain, as though they point inexorably to the London bombings, culminating in the 'striking similarity' between the Madrid train attacks and the bombing in the English capital. Following the extract shown in Figure 5.2, the final template in the sequence is used to develop a more detailed comparison. The centre of the television frame is split centrally to form two windows, one headed LONDON, the other MADRID. Footage and stills from each event are shown in a monotone blue under their respective heading, and

Template	Voice-over (Tim Marshall)	Televisuality	Video
1 New York	Ever since September the eleventh, 2001, the British authorities have feared an attack	Top left: *Sky News* logo and time. Template location given in each instance	Twin Towers, New York: billowing dust cloud from plane attack; crowd scattering; sounds of and shouts of alarm: 'Move! Get down!'
2 Bali	Britain's died at Bali in 2002 as the War on Terror and of Terror got into full swing	Top right: TERROR ATTACK (red button for more information)	Twisted wreckage of night-time shot of building silhouetted against flames' close-up of burning building; injured person being stretchered away from the scene
3 Istanbul	In Istanbul, in 2003, British interests and lives were directly targeted with explosions at the consulate and at the HSBC bank	Strapline: SKY NEWS FLASH: BREAKING NEWS: POLICE: AT LEAST 37 FATALITIES CONFIRMED AFTER BLASTS	Aerial footage of scene of debris; men digging through rubble with bare hands; cars on street with windows blown out; survivor with bloodied face against backdrop of wrecked building front, who says to camera: 'I'm English'
4 Madrid	Geographically, things got closer to home in Madrid, last year. That attack was carried out by an Islamic terror group. London bares a striking similarity	Bottom: Rolling text of messages from survivors and concerned relatives/friends interspersed with LONDON TERROR ATTACKS text	Train with bomb wreckage and emergency workers; covered body on stretcher being passed along line of emergency workers; another covered body on stretcher carried away from train

Figure 5.2   Extract from *Sky News* recorded report, 7 July 2005.

a large black box with white capitals appears and enlarges in the centre of the screen, reinforcing the commentary: TRANSPORT NETWORK TARGETTED; RUSH HOUR ATTACKS; MULTIPLE ATTACKS; COINCIDE WITH MAJOR EVENTS. This is accompanied with Marshall's voice-over:

> Both operations targeted the capital cities' transport network. Both took place during the morning rush hour. Madrid and London suffered multiple, closely-timed attacks. And on both occasions the attacks coincided with major events: in Spain the election, in Britain G8. The Madrid attacks indirectly led to a new Spanish government pulling its troop out of Iraq. Already a previously unknown Islamist group called al-Quaeda in Europe is saying it carried out the London bombings in revenge for the British presence there. There's no reason to believe the claim, but the motive is likely to be connected.
>
> (Tim Marshall, *Sky News*, 7 July 2005)

So, the audiovisual template series is used to begin to shape both an interpretation of the unfolding terror attacks on London and a speculative frame as to the likely motives of the attack. The series even implies potential political consequences in the United Kingdom through referencing the fall of the Spanish government and their withdrawal of troops from Iraq as a response to the Madrid bombing.

The archival footage both adds a series of atrocities to the mix (amplification) and also seeks an immediate explanatory and familiar narrative in which to place the shock of the news and the tremendous uncertainties as to the true nature and consequences of the attacks (containment). However, *the media event continues on-screen in real-time*. The liveness of the breaking news is maintained over the top of the pre-recorded report as conveyed through the text and graphics detailed in the Televisuality column in Figure 5.2. The quantification of the dead and the injured (a media obsession which we consider in Chapter 6) is updated via the bold text of the strapline across the bottom of the screen.

At the same time, the screen is employed as an emergency message board for those either reassuring friends and relatives of their safety or seeking news from their loved ones. This follows the trend developed by news networks and other channels on 9/11 when the mass medium of television functioned as an instantaneous and ubiquitous hub in a global network (see Chapter 2). In this way, television is situated in a new kind of media event that combines the properties of broadcasting (to a simultaneous mass audiences) with a potentially dialogic space (for communication between a small number of individuals relative both to the audience reach and to the actual numbers watching). Although, as noted in Chapter 2, we would caution as to Friedman's (2002) assessment of the medium offering significant 'participatory space' to viewers, the incorporation of an emergency on-screen message board does afford a more intimate and immediate televisual engagement with the unfolding event. The array of names and personal messages rolling continuously across the screen combine intimacy and spontaneity, yet also underscore the fears and the anxieties of the ordinary people who are in some way caught up in or proximate to the terrorist attacks. In this way, putting aside the communications from or for those limited number of individuals, television – and in this example without images – amplifies the human tragedy via communicating the randomness of the ordinary people in some way affected by the bombings. The incorporation of news publics through their inflection in breaking news via the ever-growing functionality of television and the growth in the use of so-called citizen journalism and amateur recordings contribute to the renewing of media, which we consider in Chapter 6.

Twenty-first-century Vietnam

It is notoriously difficult to make claims relating to the history of a period until sufficient information has accumulated. Such insight is usually only claimed to be possible with the benefit of epochal distance. But with the significant aid of the mass media, we appear to historicise our recent past like no other culture before us. We have so far suggested ways in which television news keeps past events alive and dynamic within current news agendas, and particularly those that have occurred in the period when digital recording and archiving technologies have been in the ascendancy and have proliferated beyond so-called traditional news organisations and news gatherers. At the same time, one can characterise the self-referentiality of the media (which includes a good deal of reliance upon their own archives) as an intensification of a highly selective past: In Luhmann's (2000) terms, the mass media operate as a 'recursive' system. This self-generating televisual past, we have suggested, is structured and ordered through schema and templates which shape incoming information as 'news', and also determine that which is defined and included as news and that which is discarded. A key issue here in terms of the relationship between television and terror is the disproportionate accumulation of terror events into an intense 'attractor' of yet more events that are deemed (by the media) to 'fit' the self-generating and dominant schema. Of course, there have always been trends and cycles in news reporting around events, conflicts, 'moral panics', and so on; yet we are now living through a period of an unusually intense 'extended past' in news reporting, to reconfigure Helga Nowotny's (1994) notion of an 'extended present'. We now explore these issues in extending the amplification component of our television and terror thesis.

One of the consequences of the proliferation of news providers and broadcasters is an insatiable demand for 'new' information to fill the space. As noted earlier, the vacuum of extended time is partly filled with the televisual discourses of the present and their endless speculations as to the course of future events. However, the scarcity of genuinely 'new' and newsworthy events requires the recycling and invoking of those past in order to help sustain coverage that meets a presumed relevancy threshold of audiences. This involves something of a paradox in television news texts, in that they strive for innovation in seeking out all that is 'new' in terms of content. Yet, as we have argued, although immediacy, temporality, and televisuality are the dominant modes of conveying and constructing the medium's apparent operation in and of the moment, this applies equally to 'old' content. Furthermore, television news' use of archival material, although sometimes highly signified as 'past', is often not. Either way, much of this content is still fed through the televisual apparatus of and in the present, simultaneously renewing and reshaping that from the past in framing and interpreting current events. We will now consider these issues in relation to one of the most enduring media templates of contemporary conflict, namely the Vietnam War.

From a Western news perspective, apart from during the lead-up to the holding of elections and the quantification of the accumulating casualties (which we examine in Chapter 6), most days in Iraq since the postwar period looked much the same. So, a key challenge for television and other news reporting of the aftermath of the Iraq war has been how to sustain viewer interest in an unchanging, ongoing, seemingly horizonless story. The template to which the US (and the UK) media turned to push the occupation of Iraq story to a critical and thus more newsworthy juncture was that which had been established as the dominant historical reference point in the reporting on most of the US overseas military ventures in the modern era – the Vietnam War. The resonances of the military and political failures in Vietnam in the US collective and journalistic psyche have been carried since by and through the same media deemed to have been partly responsible for this 'defeat'.[11] Contemporary politico-media-military discourses on Vietnam can be considered to be a form of 'postemotionalism' in Stjepan Meštrović's

(1995, 1996) definition, namely the manipulation and promotion of emotions from history 'that are selectively and synthetically attached to current events' (1996: 11). And to draw upon another of Meštrović's formulations of this idea: television can be said to effect a 'postemotional mixing of emotional memories with mythical historical events such that history and the present become rough equivalents' (1996: 22). In this way, the use of a Vietnam template not only adds an element of interest by way of a historical comparison with current events but is also employed as an immediate default cautionary frame through which US military ventures, particularly involving the loss of life of US troops, is assessed, and challenged. For example, G. Thomas Goodnight identifies two weeks of early April 2004 as a period featuring sustained political use of what he terms the Vietnam 'metaphor' and 'deliberative analogy'. He argues:

> When the '*lessons of history*' implied by a metaphor move from the status of *guidelines* to *rules*, then the over-heated and over-repeated metaphor generates an always ready discursive field of comparison. Such fields constitute, in popular nomenclature, a 'syndrome', a set of inhibitions, worries, and guilt ridden discourses characteristic of a need to avoid choices, no matter how remotely, that may implicate one in repeating a past mistake.[12]

In respect of the mass media, however, the term template is more appropriate in accounting for its recursive use as part of the archival memory of the media itself, and in the case of Vietnam, this is doubly so, given the US media's reflexive culpability.

As we have argued, the Vietnam template was employed by and through the US media in coverage of the 1991 Gulf War to purge the social memory of America's military and political failing *and* the myth of the media's (especially television news') culpability in this failing, and thus was more of a *retrospective* template (past-oriented). However, its use in the aftermath of the 2003 Iraq war was as a *speculative* template (future-oriented). The speculative template functions as a pre-emption or premediation of events; a means to provoke debate and action to respond to the prospects of the repetition of the past mistake. For example, shortly before the 2006 mid-term US elections, Thomas L. Friedman employed the Vietnam template in a *New York Times* op-ed: 'in time we'll come to see the events unfolding – or rather, unraveling – in Iraq today as the real October surprise, because what we're seeing there seems like the jihadist equivalent of the Tet offensive'.[13] Friedman acknowledges the generational shift since Vietnam and explains for the benefit of readers' 'too young to remember' how the Vietcong and North Vietnamese attacks in 1968–1969 – 'delivered, through the media' – undermined US support for the war and hence the possibility of victory'.[14] Friedman's comments immediately entered the reflexive swirling politico-media discourses on the ongoing aftermath of the Iraq War. On the day of its publication, the op-ed was cited in a question put in an interview to President Bush who acknowledged that Friedman 'could be right',[15] and the article and Bush's response then shaped questions and answers in the following day's White House press briefing by Tony Snow.[16] This in turn was reported widely via other media. Hence, through the journalistic use of ready and familiar speculative templates to frame questions to politicians and those connected with events reported as news, any response (and also any non-response) from the actors concerned enters reflexively into the same story trajectory.

Although both retrospective and speculative media templates are a powerful framing and shaping mechanism of news stories in the mass media, it is television news that is most integral to the interaction order in which they are produced and presented. This is owing to the medium's capacity to instantly draw upon its archives to create anew or illustrate and develop a template employed in other public or media discourses related to a story. This includes the imposing of a particular visual or audiovisual narrative with a template series (as in the reporting of the 7 July London bombings, shown in Figure 5.2). And, in respect of television's articulation of the past in the present, one can point to the visual image as pivotal in the media sensorium.[17] For instance, Frank P. Tomasulo states the importance of recognising the 'increased reliance on media imagery to define and verify daily news events and the historically real in the modern epoch' (1996: 71). For today, it is templates that structure this history in television news and that also render it alive and dynamic. But it is the medium of television that appears to have an authorial relationship to this past – and even to photographs and to film – in its presentation of images and events within its own real-time interaction order, rendered in its pervasive and persuasive 'now'.

We speculate that it is problematic for US television news to employ *visual* templates of the Vietnam War owing to their vividness and intrusiveness. This is not to say that verbal or written templates are less powerful, especially in relation to the employment of the testimony of those with personal experience and memories of the Vietnam War (Appy, 2006). Rather, the visual can carry an explicitness that is presumed (by news editors and producers) to be unnecessary or even crass for a US audience. This constraint does not apply to British television news journalists, for example, who are much more liberal in their application of templates that do not possess such a difficult social and cultural resonance for their audiences. For example, on 18 October 2006, the same day as Friedman's Vietnam-themed *New York Times* op-ed, BBC1's main evening news programme the *10'Clock News* ran the story. This news package by Matt Frei (shown in Figure 5.3) is recorded

Matt Frei verbal commentary	Footage
Of all the war memorials crowding the centre of Washington none is more poignant than the black granite wall remembering Vietnam.	Visitors pausing and reading the names on the Vietnam Veteran's Memorial wall.
This war produced haunting images that have become emblems of military misadventure. In terms of lives lost it wasn't America's costliest foreign conflict, but it was the most bruising to its self-esteem.	Close-up shot of wall with reflections of visitors walking alongside and half-screen sized panel of wall fading into black-and-white still of 'Vietnam Napalm' fading quickly into a black-and white still of 'The Execution'. Medium shot of Wall with visitors standing alongside.
So is Iraq becoming another Vietnam? This was the Tet Offensive in 1968. In military terms indecisive, in political terms the period in which the American public tipped against the war.	Colour footage of US soldiers running and shooting, Banner in top-left of screen: 'Picture from CBS'. Final footage of soldier sitting against sand bags with head and eye bandaged.
So could this week's violence in Iraq be the same? One leading commentator thought so. And guess who seemed to agree.	Cut to four men pushing stretcher along presumably Iraqi street and shot of vehicle ablaze and dense smoke and sounds of sirens.
	Stills of rows of coffins draped in Stars and Stripes and US soldiers standing over them.
Coffins back from Iraq, more than 70 so far this month. Vietnam produced ten times as many and most of them had not volunteered. Yes the American public quietly abhors this war. But this is the world after 9/11 and only a single protestor stands vigil outside the White House.

Compare that to four decades ago. | Still of medium close-up of US soldiers carrying flag-draped coffin. Woman holding white posterboard with hand-written: WARS ARE POOR CHISELS FOR CARVING OUT PEACEFUL TOMORROWS. WHAT A DISAPPOINTMENT WE ARE in front of railings with White House visible beyond. And close-up.
Aerial footage of mass crowds in the National Mall. |

Figure 5.3 The Vietnam template. Extract from the *10'Clock News*, recorded report, BBC1, 18 October 2006.

at the Vietnam Veteran's Memorial Wall in Washington. It reveals the multimodal capacity of television news to mix and to organise various verbal, visual, and aural aspects into a powerful media template as it also, simultaneously, reports on the story of the use of the template in the United States.

The report shown in Figure 5.3 demonstrates television news' capacity to mix multiple media (photographic stills, film, and television footage), the synchronic with the diachronic, and to construct and inhabit a multi-dimensional space with its layering of the 'real' and the 'virtual', altogether indicative of a trend towards a more adventurous televisuality. Two of the most iconic photographic images from the Vietnam War: 'Vietnam Napalm' by Nick Ut (1972) and 'The Execution' by Eddie Adams (1968) are virtually projected with the Vietnam Veteran's Memorial Wall employed as a spatially symbolic screen. The actuality of warfare, its human cost, and its commemoration are visually fused as the template narrative shifts back and forth. From the names of those killed in Vietnam carved on the Wall, the report shifts to the visual iconography of the civilian human cost; then the actuality footage of that which is inferred as the 1968 Tet Offensive is followed by a familiar scene of the aftermath of an attack in Iraq. The same report later shows the iconic flag-draped coffins of US servicemen and women, a controversial image from both the Vietnam and Iraq War eras. This leads into a template of the differential public mass and limited protests, respectively, with a solitary contemporary protestor shown outside the White House compared with film footage of mass numbers filling the National Mall, Washington, some four decades earlier. The archive images and footage used here are not labelled as such but convey their age in the quality of the film. Thus the televisual signification of the past is one already formed and instantly recognisable in the contrast of the blurry, sepia or black-and-white images from the 1960s and 1970s, against the sharpness and clarity of the news footage of the digital age. It is this scopic versatility of television news – its capacity to plunder its vast archives to instantly, visually, and aurally frame retrospective and speculative templates in developing news stories – that affords it a narrative power in shaping events that is unmatched by other media.

Frei also interviews visitors to the Wall in his report and two are included on camera remarking on the template. For example, one unidentified visitor comments: 'We did not accomplish the goals we really wanted in Vietnam. Lost a lot of, lot of young people. We've got the same situation in Iraq. Our goal has not been accomplished'. Such use of the commentary of those co-present to a place or an event (in the past or in the present) provides another authenticating layer to television's scopic mix. Moreover, televisual history is made credible through the insertion of public opinion, in this example the spoken accounts of those who testify to that history drawn from their own living or secondary memory, who are co-present to the place full of memory – the Memorial Wall. The 'aura' carried by the remote and blurry televisual, filmic, and photographic past is thus combined with the intimacy of present day 'witnesses' to forge a compelling narrative organised around the Vietnam template.

Conclusion

We have outlined some of the transformations in the televisual news environment that have enabled the medium to reflexively orient itself to and shape the events it reports on through its instant archival access and its multimodality. Given that television is increasingly authorial of that which accumulates daily in news archives, it is highly likely that the recursivity of the medium – its reliance on and its presentation of itself – is likely to intensify. Consequently, the schemas and templates that are generated and sustained within this system effect rigid discourses reliant upon simplistic (familiar) versions of conflict and warfare. In terms of mainstream media, as driven by the repetitious television news, there appears to be limited opportunity for counter-discourses to emerge and to become established. The endurance of the War on Terror schema, for example, is indicative of the ease with which the present *and* the past are connected and serialised into an all-encompassing meta-narrative that both simplifies and amplifies the threats posed (to the West) and conjoins and rationalises the rhetorical solutions (Bush's 'axis of evil', for example). Television history is crucial to the War on Terror as it keeps fresh the currency of the past, as it speculates as to the future, in a perpetual or 'extended' present. The medium serves the purpose of the advocates of terror and the War on Terror through endless juxtaposition and repetition, sustaining visual and oral linkages between temporally and geographically separate events. As such, television news is increasingly part of, and thus constitutive of, those events.

It is to one of the more problematic and contested elements of the media's presentational regime of these discursive and actual conflicts that we now turn to address, namely the inclusion and exclusion of the wounded and the dead.

6
The Distant Body

Introduction

A key contention in recent writing on the subject of media and war is that an unprecedented 'chaos' has arrived now that technology enables the production and dissemination of images anywhere, instantly, by journalists and non-journalists alike (McNair, 2006; Tumber and Webster, 2006). Images such as those from Abu Ghraib, or of the Iraqi twelve-year-old Ali Abbas who lost his arms in a bombing raid, are held to epitomise the unruly information battlefield, threatening the capacity of state governments to control news and undermining the stability of state legitimacy. At the centre of such debates is the human body, and in particular representations of the suffering, injured, or dead body. Television news retains a peculiar position with regard to these representations; despite the excesses of the medium elsewhere, television news is still held as a bastion of taste and decency. In the first part of this chapter, we deal with this 'body paradox'.

We explore the contrary and contested discourses over the 'distant' bodies felled in the aftermath of the 1991 and 2003 Iraq wars, subject both to television news' sanitising and modulating framings and to its historical, comparative shaping. Furthermore, we consider the extent to which representations of the injured, the captured, and the fallen have ultimately left television with its own lethal legacy as a weapon of war. We contend that representations of the body are a tool in the 'weaponising' of television, as various forces in the War on Terror use graphic representations for symbolic purposes, notably as trophies of war. While television channels attempt to contain these horrors, even sanitised footage can invite the viewer to imagine beyond what is shown and seen, potentially instilling even greater anxiety and fear in viewers.

This reinforces our argument in Chapter 4, in which our analysis of audiences' responses to footage of the Baghdad skyline during the 2003 Iraq war suggested viewers are left to 'do work' in constructing a version of the reality the media present so selectively. Whether or not this results in a universal, amorphous, 'liquid' terror (Bauman, 2006) that seeps over all audiences, there can be no doubt that television news has not been able to avoid a central role in the propagation of terrorism in recent years.

Below, we explore some of the paradoxes in a broadcast culture in which the form of programmes – as much as the time of screening – shapes what is deemed as viewable for and by UK audiences (in particular). We argue that the reporting on the continuing aftermath or civil war in Iraq is indicative of a 'moral crisis' in television news that operates on a number of levels. This includes the production of what we are calling a 'new ecology of images': the manner in which operational difficulties for journalists in conditions of continual near-civil war and an exhaustion of terror stories from Iraq conspired to effect a remote and thus critically disengaged news discourse over the long term. For instance, it is possible that the 'reality' of the post-war Iraq for Western audiences is conveyed more credibly through quantitative body counts than through any sustained in-depth analysis. Whether Iraq has entered a 'civil war' or been a 'success' appears a numerical matter. However, we conclude that although news reporting is constrained by limited access to the sites of conflict and by mostly self-imposed sanitising of footage, it is ultimately the frequent televisual representation of suffering, injury, and death that has illuminated a disjuncture between a rhetoric of 'success' and a reality of insecurity in Iraq.

Television and the body paradox

In the opening to this book, we identified the turn of the 1990s as significant in ushering in a period that featured a new mono-global tele-visioning of conflict. How Western TV news operated to contain excesses in that period is useful to contrast to the image avalanche of the post-9/11 era. In this latter period, the containment of censorship (or at the very least the sanitising of atrocity images) has become quite a different proposition. For example, one of the since iconic 'unseen' images of the 1991 Gulf War is Ken Jarecke's haunting photograph of an Iraqi soldier's body which sat charred in the front of a burnt out vehicle on 28 February 1991. This was part of a convoy returning to Iraq on the Basra Road named the 'Highway of Death' following the aerial obliteration of the retreating forces by the Coalition. In the closing days of the 1991 Gulf War, Jarecke could not find a US publisher for his photograph, and the Western news programmes, dominated by Coalition precision-weapon pool-footage, would not touch it.[1] The Jarecke photograph became an icon of the 'unseen' 1991 Gulf War (and also emblematic for anti-war protestors), even though by now the sanitised history had already become the received US collective myth. A thousand more atrocity photographs of the true and grotesque consequences of the Coalition 'smart' bombing of Iraq at the turn of the 1990s were not going to change this. In sum, the 1991 US television news industry mostly colluded in applying a sealant to the 'sanitised victory' over Saddam and effected the overdue purging of their collective guilt being long demonised for the 'losing' of the Vietnam War (in effect one myth was replaced by another[2]). Nobody, including Jarecke, was allowed to spoil the euphoria and relief.

Since the early 1990s, with the shattering of the mono-global picturing of conflict, one might expect the sheer availability of the images of conflict to transform television news into a conduit for visual challenges to the selective and politically motivated accounts of government. Yet, the sanitising of warfare remains a central part of the strategy (although with limited success) of that which Martin Shaw defines as 'the new Western way of fighting "risk-transfer war"' (2005: 71). Thus, part of the essential management of contemporary warfare is that 'suffering and death must be unseen; indirect, less visible and less quantifiable life-risks are more acceptable'. For example, the 2003 Iraq war was (like 1991) very effectively managed by the Pentagon. Most news organisations' critical capacities were effectively neutralised by their limited options for reporting, namely (i) to be 'embedded' with US or UK forces', (ii) to be 'housed' at the US 'information centre' Centcom at Dahar, or (iii) to risk deploying so-called independent personnel in the war zone. Of course, in times of war, there is a greater if mostly unwritten obligation on a country's media not to broadcast or publish material during the period of operations that would undermine military operations or morale. Yet, amid the swirling discourses of media renewal there is a new and growing tension between the highly accessible content of the Internet – and public knowledge of this content or at least its availability – and the content of mainstream news. The latter refers to what is produced, published, broadcast, regulated, and mostly consumed from those media outlets still (accurately or otherwise) viewed as 'mainstream' and which are most immediate and widely referenced in everyday public debates surrounding news events. Since the turn of the new century, the Internet can be described as weaponised (in respect of some of its content) and weaponising (in respect of its sourcing of other media), but no more so than television news.

Moreover, the renewal of media, that is the portability, simplicity, and connectivity of audiovisual recording devices as they feed global networks via the Internet and television, has ushered in an age of untrammelled terrorist opportunity. The business of news in Western democracies and elsewhere inevitably affords value to terror and insecurity, marketing a global theatre (with script and audiences) for the potentially unlimited penetration of terrorist propaganda. Television has become weaponised through its use as a key vehicle in the displaying of acts and the threatening of acts of terror to mass audiences. Yet terrorists are not required to phone news network programme controllers and editors to request a slot. They either record the act themselves and post the video on the Web or rely on news organisations and the bystanding public to do the recording for them. Ultimately, then, it is television that recognises, structures, and scripts terrorist atrocities (through their use of the footage of those atrocities) as part of news narratives, affording them the oxygen of publicity.

Yet in Western liberal democracies, suppression of information is not an option. Television news thus responds to its own amplification of fear and insecurity, as we have suggested, with various devices and even strategies of containment. But is the medium (and its audiences) ultimately a hostage to its own devices – as these are the modern modes of news production and presentation – so that immediacy, repetition, and saturation have accelerated the weaponising process? As Peter Preston (2004) asks, 'If the malignant message is itself a device, a weapon of mass hysteria, how do we defuse it?'[3] And beyond the responsibilities of broadcasters, are audiences themselves complicit in acts of terror through their responses or non-responses, and through their viewing or choosing not to view? In this chapter, we address these questions in the context of the renewal of media having compromised television news: The medium modulates between functioning as a weapon of terror – delivering and concentrating the propaganda of terrorists and feeding the insecurity of nations – and distancing and insulating audiences from both the inconvenient and the unwatchable.

These issues are significantly connected to the very nature of graphic and disturbing images and footage and what is, what is not, and what should be shown on mainstream television news, according to broadcasters, regulators, and audiences. Some critics argue that more of the 'reality' of warfare should be broadcast. Philip Seib, for example, clearly demarcates the obligations of news producers and publics in this respect: 'If the news media's job is to report war as it is, not sanitize it, then news organizations should deliver undiminished reality to their audiences...The public must decide for itself how to deal with reality' (2004: 40). However, what actually appears on screen is in large part dependent on programme editors and producers' presumptions as to the sensitivities of their audiences, and, in our age of media excess, TV journalism often shifts from a 'we could not see' to a 'we could not show' defence of its sanitising frames. The history of television is that of a medium charged as a bastion of 'standards of taste and decency' in a way in which other media – notably print and cinema – have not. Despite years of deregulation and the withering of taboos around the 'fictional' depiction of graphic acts and scenes of sex and violence, sensitivities to the actuality of mainstream television news seem peculiarly preserved. That is to say, the reporting and the representing of catastrophe and warfare – as noted earlier the main business of news – are the genre most restrictively 'produced' on television. To provide one example of the debates around the TV news broadcasting of images of violence and death, in 1999 the Sierra Leone freelance cameraman Sorious Samura won the Rory Peck Award[4] for his footage of rebel soldiers attacking the capital Freetown. This included shootings and deaths on the street and the involvement and treatment of child soldiers. Some of this footage including a child soldier being captured and beaten by the opposing army was shown on a *Channel Four News* programme. The programme anchor Jon Snow, the former BBC war correspondent Martin Bell, and others then debated the difficulties posed for broadcasters in using graphic and disturbing images in news programmes:

> Snow: I looked at your footage last night. I just could not bring myself to continue watching. The child that was beaten in that picture in many ways was even more horrific than the people that were shot dead. It was unimaginable. And if I can't watch it why should I ask other people to?

> Bell: There is a 9pm watershed which makes it possible to put more explicit footage on after that. But the programme editors don't like to do it. Not only are they not pushing at limits but they are aiming off on the side of caution in order not only not to upset people but not to endanger their own careers...I don't think anyone is arguing that you should show absolutely everything that you have

got... But you have to show enough to give some indication of the reality of what's going on and British news broadcasters have been so timid for so long.

In this way, there is a 'body paradox' in relation to the representation of injury, violence, and death on television news. Firstly, there is recognition (on the part of broadcasters, regulators, and audiences) that there is material that is unshowable and unwatchable, and thus much of the actuality of human injury and suffering (especially that inflicted by humanity) is filtered out of the daily content of TV news programmes. And, secondly and partly as a consequence, what is shown is mostly formulaic. Thus, the contemporary modes of news production (immediacy, repetition, and saturation) in terms of the threat to the Other (notably those not part of the intended or presumed audiences) are said to inure and diminish the potential for ethical response and responsibility. Susan D. Moeller (1999: 14), for example, claims that media 'distortions' result in 'compassion fatigue': 'Sensationalized treatment of crises makes us feel that only the most extreme situations merit attention (although the media still self-censors the worst of the stories and images from crises...)'. So, a 'low intensity' or at least consistent coverage of different crises and catastrophes appears to be the unsatisfactory norm. And when television news does provide coverage that genuinely shocks and disturbs audiences, one response is to ensure that this is protected against in the future, for instance via Grusin's (2004) 'premediation' strategy, introduced in Chapter 1.

One explanation for why the representation or the *pre*sentation of actual images of human suffering and death on television should be so provocative compared with other media is related to the debates we outlined in Chapter 2. The temporality of television – its continuous visual simultaneity of representation (actual or constructed) with that of the viewer – actually makes it more 'intrusive' than any other medium, in that it moves with and mimics the passage of clock time. For example, Scott Lash (2002: 71) argues:

The mass media and new media are... media of not representation but of *pre*sentation... They turn up in your house and present themselves. They work unconsciously and pre-consciously... The media come to you in 'time in'. And often they will not turn off, will not stop producing and delivering messages to your house, presenting messages in very close to real time.

We consider that this argument is most applicable to television, given that it is the medium's ontological presence, continuousness, and connectedness that both amplifies distant and diffuse threats and also reassures through the same devices. Again, this sensitivity has developed out of a public, government, and media discourse on television being subject to explicit standards of taste and decency often declared for the 'protection' of some group or community perceived as 'vulnerable' to images of terror (and most often children). However, this only partly explains the modulating capacity of television news to provoke and inure in its presentation of bodily suffering and death. For instance, David Campbell (2004) argues that there are three 'economies' of context intersecting which restrict the inclusion of images of death in contemporary media:

> In relationship to images, context involves three dimensions: the economy of indifference to others (especially others who are culturally, racially and spatially foreign), the economy of 'taste and decency' whereby the media itself regulates the representation of death and atrocity, and the economy of display, wherein the meaning of images is produced by the intertextual relationship of captions, titles, surrounding arguments and sites for presentation.
>
> (2004: 70)

In relation to the first economy, the persistent presence of wounded, dying, and dead Iraqi civilians on UK/US television screens since April 2003 suggests a strong context of indifference (if one can 'measure' indifference by noting a lack of effective collective outrage). This extended period of mostly 'low-intensity' coverage of the human casualties of the Iraqi 'insurgency' and sectarian conflict is examined later in this chapter. The second and third economies in respect of television often combine to employ cultural and political templates that package presentations of the body in ways acceptable to particular audiences. We turn to this next.

Displaying and hiding the body

Despite the operation of these economies of context, in the post-9/11 era, the injured, captive, and mutilated body has become a key instrument in the weaponising of television, and increasingly central to the waging of the War on Terror by all sides. This includes the Pentagon's strategy of publishing photographs of the often contorted faces or bodies of those terrorist 'kills' it most prized as 'evidence' of its progress in its pursuit of the post-9/11 'most wanted' lists of suspects. For example, four photographs of the bloodstained and contorted faces of the sons of Saddam, Uday and Qusay Hussein, were widely broadcast on their release by the Pentagon in July 2003. Similarly, the killing of Abu Musab al-Zarqawi, notable for his links to the bombings, assassinations, and beheadings of the insurgency in Iraq and for merging his organisation with al-Qaida, was followed with the Pentagon issuing a photograph of his bloody and swollen face which was published and broadcast globally.

The televised history of contemporary war is also marked by made-for-the-medium propaganda videos of the captive body. In August 1990, Iraqi TV footage (rebroadcast in the West) of Saddam Hussein tousling the hair and patting the arm of Stuart Lockwood, a British seven-year-old, and others who were his 'guest' human shields provoked government outrage in the United Kingdom and the United States. Over thirteen years later, Saddam is the captive paraded in US military video footage, remediated around the globe. However, the images of the former Iraqi President's capture – a seemingly old and defence-less man after emerging from living in a hole in the ground for some time – actually contradicted the Western politico-media discourse that had accumulated since the late 1980s of Saddam as an all-powerful tyrannical monster. Furthermore, the Coalition authorities released a video of Saddam's medical examination which took place soon after his capture and included the taking of mouth swabs for DNA testing. These images were intended to exert maximum humiliation on the enemy and to demonstrate to Iraqis that after decades of dictatorship this was no longer a man that they needed to fear. However, the release of the footage drew some criticism, for example, as Jonathan D. Moreno argues, 'Medical matters go to the heart of our common humanity, so distor-tions or manipulations of medical values imperil us all.... when medical procedures are exploited to make a political point it is not only that the rules have changed but that there may no longer be any rules at all'.[5]

These concerns were largely drowned out by the euphoria of the capture of the former Iraqi leader, but it is one of numerous examples in this period of deployment of the very blunt propaganda weapon of images of the captive, injured or dead body. And the global media 'vector' (Wark, 1994) into which these pictures are released does not mitigate the cultural, religious, and spatial sensitivities of the millions who come to view them within a matter of hours. However, it is the media vector that has amplified uses of the body as a trophy of war. These instances do not always have to be shown or seen in their horrific detail to significantly shape television as a weapon of warfare whose containment strategies (and particularly around an 'economy of taste and decency') are sometimes unable to 'defuse the message'.

As noted in Chapter 1, the greater availability and portability of audiovisual recording devices have allowed mainstream and non-mainstream journalists, photographers, and bystanders with recording facilities more frequent and faster proximity to events. Mistreatment and mutilations of the human body on all sides of twenty-first-century conflict are much more likely to be electronically witnessed and recorded in the era of media renewal. There may be some time, perhaps even a period of years, between the recording and the emergence of footage, as with the graphic images of the mistreatment of Iraqi prisoners by American forces in Abu Ghraib prison. Or, the mistreatment of the body may enter much more immediately and reflexively to shape public opinion and even government policy, as noted earlier in respect of debates around the 'CNN effect'. For example, the Clinton administration's decision to pull US troops out of Somalia was linked to the impact of scenes on US television news and around the world showing mobs dragging the bodies of American soldiers through the streets of Mogadishu in October 1993. The public display of the mistreatment or humiliation of the body is an effective weapon of terror and warfare. Mark Boden (2004), for example, argues:

> The mutilation and public display of bodies follows a distinct pattern. The victims are members of a despised Other, who are held in such contempt that they are considered less than human. Respectful treatment of the dead is the norm in all societies, and a tenet of all religions. Publicly flouting such basic dignities is a communal expression of hatred designed to insult and frighten. Display of the mutilated remains must be as public as possible...The crowd, no matter how enraged, welcomes the camera – Paul Watson, a white Canadian journalist, moved unharmed with his camera through the angry mobs in Mogadishu on Oct. 4, 1993. The idea is to spread the image. Cameras guarantee the insult will be heard, seen and felt. The insult and fear are spread across continents.[6]

Under the saturating and extensively connected conditions of contemporary mass media, there is a more substantial guarantee of reaching the intended audiences, even with the varying economies of context mitigating against the dissemination of images of the dead, as argued by Campbell, above. For example, on 31 March 2004, four

American contractors were shot by what was reported to be insurgents, and their bodies burnt and dismembered by a cheering civilian crowd in the Iraqi city of Fallujah. Two of the remains of the corpses were tied to vehicles and dragged through the streets, while two others were hung from a bridge over the Euphrates River. Although most of the graphic scenes were edited out of reports broadcast on US television news programmes, the showing of parts of the video (accompanied by the reporter's verbal description) is sufficient for audiences to *visualise* in their own minds the images on which this story was based. In the United Kingdom, *Channel 4 News*,[7] reporting on the same story, showed an extract from the video of a corpse being dragged along a street in Fallujah, but with the body being blurred from the footage. In this example, UK television news imposed its own standards of taste and decency, presumably in accordance with its obligations under Section 1 of the Programme Code set out by the British regulator Ofcom (Office of Communications). This is headed 'Family Viewing Policy, Offence to Good Taste and Decency, Portrayal of Violence and Respect for Human Dignity'.[8] But television, acting as a buffer and as a container of terror, may conversely accentuate the impact of the pixellated or removed images. By protecting the viewer from the 'unshowable' and the 'unimaginable', the reported yet unseen images or events can be further mystified and amplified to a potentially greater effect than if they had been broadcast. Of course graphic or explicit images do not necessarily equate with moved, disturbed, or shocked viewers. Terror can be very effectively communicated in the depiction of the horror expressed in the eyes of a witness, the absence of victims, the marking of a mass grave, and so on. Moreover, and under the conditions of media renewal, we ask, are the various local or regional 'economies of context' in news presentations of acts of terror massively out-of-synch with the fears already inscribed upon the populace in the very act of reporting?

One position in response to this question is that media renewal contributes to a rather unchecked 'negative globalisation', notably articulated by Zygmunt Bauman. He argues, 'In the liquid modern world, the dangers and fears are also liquid-like – or are they rather gaseous? They flow, seep, leak, ooze...No walls have been invented yet to stop them, though many try to build them' (2006: 97). Global terrorism thrives in precisely this environment in which we are intimately and inextricably connected to the instantly disseminated currents of threat and fear. Maximum exposure of terror acts is guaranteed through use of minimum media. For example, the impact of the kidnapping and execution in Iraq of the civilian Americans Jack Hensley and Eugene

Armstrong and the Briton Ken Bigley was amplified by the circulation of video recordings of their captivity and their decapitation in September and October 2004.[9] Terrorists have achieved the weaponisation of television through the delivery of audio and videotapes to TV stations and via the Internet. Equally, families of hostages have used the same media to lobby directly to the terrorists, their sympathisers, and those that may have influence over them. Bigley's family, for example, used Arab TV to make impassioned pleas for his release. Furthermore, the kidnappers led by Abu Musab al-Zarqawi (the al-Qaida leader in Iraq) followed the actions of other hostage-takers in Iraq in dressing Bigley in an orange jumpsuit. This was intended to re-sign the dressing of al-Qaida suspects in the same uniforms detained in the US prison camp in Guantanamo Bay, Cuba, in the months and years following 9/11. Hence, a communicative chain or network is constructed that for periods can prosper on the agenda of mainstream news. One might infer this acts to sustain the presence of terror and terrorism in audiences' consciousnesses.

Terrorist threats and actions are thus reflexively communicated to us, their intended targets, with 'the whole-hearted cooperation of the mass media' (Bauman, 2006: 108). Reflexively is a key term here: journalists may be *knowingly* used by participants in contemporary conflicts but continue regardless because this yields access to high-value news stories, such as interviews with statesmen or terrorist leaders. Hence, television news is one of the principal vehicles of the propagation of terrorism, and yet, as noted above, media suppression or greater regulation in Western liberal democracies is not an option. The partial or heavily edited broadcast of terrorist videos by Western television news programmes does not necessarily diminish their intended impact to disturb and to terrorise. McNair, for example, makes this point: 'the knowledge that they [decapitation videos] were available to be seen on the web – that they existed, out there in cyberspace – had a profoundly disturbing emotional impact. They brought geographically distant atrocity into the living room, from where it entered the collective imagination as the stuff of nightmares' (McNair, 2006: 8). And for those with the curiosity to see the macabre video in full, the Internet provided uninhibited access. For example, as noted in our opening chapter, one project ethnographer discovered that a group of British teenage schoolchildren had downloaded the video of the execution of Ken Bigley onto their mobile phones. When asked their motives, they explained they were curious as to 'what a beheading looked like', having never seen one before. They certainly were not alone in the accessing and viewing of the terror video online with reports of over a million downloads from one particular site within a few days of it being posted.[10]

However, for audiences curious or otherwise, television news showed 'enough' of the Bigley video to highlight how minimal technological resources can translate into the effective global propaganda of terror. Hence even by providing fleeting glimpses of acts of terror, television struggles between amplification and containment and is ultimately implicated in a crisis of news discourse.

Another example of the media's difficulty in dealing with images they deem too graphic for public consumption (especially in the United Kingdom and the United States) followed the Madrid train bombings in which 191 people died and over 1400 were injured in coordinated blasts in the morning rush hour on 11 March 2004. The following day, most British national newspapers published a key photograph (some on their front pages) showing rescuers attending to the injured, who were strewn sitting or lying amongst the ballast on tracks next to a wrecked commuter train. In the original photograph, there appears to be a bloodied limb in the foreground. However, a number of newspapers (*The Times*, *Daily Telegraph*, and the *Sun*, for example) 'airbrushed' the body part from the image, whereas the *Guardian* reproduced the photograph in black and white turning the body part grey and thus rendering it virtually indistinguishable.[11] This is not to suggest that the original photograph is more or less shocking or disturbing, but that this kind of immediate doctoring of an image is indicative of a particular perceived British sensitivity that feeds (however naively) into the media's containment of terror events.

Some terrorist atrocities, in which the nature of the images immediately renders the event explicit in particular ways, are more amenable to the containing mechanisms of television, notably repetition and saturation. 9/11 is the defining example of media-delivered terrorism that has since been minutely ground through more or less every representational or presentational device that television and other media have to offer. It has been documented and rendered familiar in an apparent determination to historicise the event – as though this may diminish its impact. To return to Silverstone's argument (explored in Chapter 2): 'the endless repetition of image and the reiteration and reinforcement of narrative cements a version of the world which moves imperceptibly but entirely into the familiar and unexceptional' (2002: 10). The unimaginable becomes imaginable – brought into our everyday discursive realities (see Chapter 8), visibility assuaging the fear of the unknown. However, in editing and sanitising other images of terror as a means to protect the viewer in the name of 'taste and decency' – through opening up the potential for the imagination of horror rather than closing it down – is the medium doing the terrorists' bidding? If television structures, concentrates, and delivers the terror message to mass audiences, then is it inextricably a weapon of terror?

The moral crisis

If we look at the presenting/sanitising debate through a different dimensional context, to continue with Campbell's (2004) model, above, namely 'the economy of indifference to others (especially others who are culturally, racially, and spatially foreign)' (ibid.), then we come closer to illuminating this aspect of the crisis of television news discourse. That is to say, if there can be some justification for attempting to delimit the terrorist strike on *our* military or civilians by restricting dissemination of the images of their injury, then the imperatives are very different for the broadcast of the suffering of others either inflicted by *our* governments or in our name, or as a consequence of our (and our government's) inaction. In fact the very motivation often given for the depiction of human suffering of the other is to provoke (news publics, home or foreign governments') military intervention, or at least humanitarian aid. Under the conditions of media renewal, however, there is the potential for an unrestrained connection to the distress of others. Audiences are subject to an array of catastrophes, conflict, and warfare, producing a glut of images of the distant suffering body. As we have suggested, this is mitigated to some extent as niche news channels and programmes disperse the terror of the world according to broadcasters' assumptions as to the political, cultural, and moral sensitivities of those presumed to be watching. However, knowledge of the potential horrors and fears of that which has not been fully exposed being just over the horizon or available in the ether in our living rooms does constitute an everyday presence, no matter how 'virtual'. Television news connects us with these daily terrors even and perhaps especially when it does not fully reveal them to us, i.e. in attempts at containment.

This explains the seeming contradiction in assessments of the impact of the media on a mythical moral collective, for example, as set out and critiqued by Susan Sontag (1979/1977, 2002, 2003). Sontag writes, 'The first idea is that public attention is steered by the attentions of the media – which means images', whereas 'the second idea ... is that in a world saturated, even hypersaturated, with images, those which should matter to us have a diminishing effect: we become callous. In the end, such images make us a little less able to feel, to have our conscience pricked'.[12] However, as we have argued, television news modulates between bringing the world's wars and catastrophes onto the West's horizon of responsibility and in blocking them from view. For example, the reporting on the continuing 'aftermath' of the Iraq war is indicative of a moral crisis in television news that operates, as we examine below, on a number of levels. There, the reporting of events as news always requires some degree of novelty, exception, or shift in relation to an ongoing story. Through 2004 and 2005, with little sign of a significant shift in US/UK military or political strategy in Iraq, the threshold for reporting on the continuing carnage beyond a mere daily tally of the dead increased. Moreover, the moral crisis in news discourse stems from an utter equivalency of reporting deaths from and at a distance. Philip Gourevitch, for example, states, 'The piled-up dead of political violence are a generic staple of our information diet these days, and according to the generic report all massacres are created equal: the dead are innocent, the killers monstrous, the surrounding politics insane or nonexistent'.[13] Although writing of the reporting of the atrocities in Rwanda in 1994, Gourevitch's words are eerily applicable to the Iraqi civilian death toll accumulating distractedly on our television screens today. Thus, a key challenge for the sustaining of news of mostly non-Western casualties from Iraq (or elsewhere in the world) over a long period in the UK, for example, is how to differentiate one day's scenes of aftermath from the hundreds of days before. Stasis, even of the most terrible of circumstances, does not sustain news interest for very long.

Although a great deal of the work that has addressed the moral aspects of the representations of and responses to images of distant atrocity in the media has focused upon the photograph (including the considerable contribution of Sontag), it is television that is the medium most indicted for saturation and the harbinger of compassion fatigue. A defining television story in this respect was Mohammed Amin and Michael Buerk's harrowing BBC news film of dead and dying emaciated Ethiopians in Koram – and especially children – at the height of the 1984 famine.[14] These images quickly reached a global audiences and are widely credited with the Live Aid phenomenon and an outpouring of vast institutional and public sums in aid, including an immediate £1.8 million emergency donation from the EEC reported just two days after the Amin/Buerk report was first broadcast. In this respect, as we note in Chapter 3, actors (in this case media, news publics and policymakers) can adopt an immediate framing of an event, resulting in a significant response (if not significant shifts in Western policy on debt relief and aid to developing countries). However, the interesting analytical question is why? Why did this particular set of images appear to stir the West into some kind of collective action, given that other pictures of the consequences of famine had been broadcast and published before? Explanations include the fact that these images were unusually graphic for inclusion in television news (then and since) and the 'photographic' quality of the footage, in that the camera tended to run for longer, lingering on the suffering, rather than the more rapid style of film shots associated with TV news. For example, William Lord, an ABC executive news producer of the time is widely quoted in this respect: 'It was as if each clip was an award-winning photo'.[15]

Despite the acclaimed impact of the Amin/Buerk footage, there soon emerged acknowledgement from within the media of the potential 'limits' of the repetition of their images in the context of news programmes. For example, Lane Venardos (a CBS executive news producer) was quoted in November 1984: 'The residual impact of putting those pictures on the air night after night can have a negative impact... It is possible to overdo pictures of helpless children with bloated bellies'.[16] In our picture-saturated media environment, there seems to be little alternative to the cycle of diminishing interest from increasing exposure: The image or footage deemed 'exceptional' is repeated until it enters the domain of the familiar, and sometimes the iconic, by which time it signifies its history as a media image and is no longer exceptional. And if one of the functions of the recording and the dissemination of shocking images should be to engender political change, as Sontag demands, then television news does appear to be caught in a moral crisis between sanitisation and saturation.

However, John Taylor questions the use of the notions of 'surfeit, voyeurism, and compassion fatigue' in combining as an effective critique of press photography. He argues that use of the latter phrase 'claims the moral high ground': 'It hints at an earlier stage when compassion was intense but which has simply become spoiled by the abundance and voyeurism of media coverage' (1998: 19). Taylor defends photography from charges of failing to awaken the conscience of viewers arguing instead that indifference towards the suffering of others in part emerges from what he calls 'the ecology of images' (1998: 20). Thus, 'the way [images] are stored, marketed and sold, converges with the way that press (and broadcasting) managers restrain horror on behalf of 'citizens' who they assume would prefer not be disturbed' (ibid.) In this way, the irresolution of the sanitising and saturating modulating modes in the media coverage of injury, violence, and death is partly institutionalised in the operations of news gathering and distribution. This moral crisis is made more explicit in the circumstances when even those who are involved in the production and presentation of news appear to lose faith in their capacity for reporting the main story of the day. In modern times and under the conditions of media renewal, this crisis has become entrenched with what we are calling a new ecology of images, notably established in the television news reporting of the aftermath of the war in Iraq. And it is to this defining period of moral crisis in the media that we now turn to address.

The accumulating aftermath

This moral crisis of news discourse is very evident in UK and US television news coverage of the aftermath of the 2003 Iraq war, with a growing frustration on the part of some broadcasters (and notably *Channel 4 News*) with a credibility gap opening up between broadcastable material and the 'reality on the ground' in Iraq. This point is graphically and perhaps ironically illustrated by members of the *Channel 4 News* team in a documentary – 'Iraq: The Hidden Story' – broadcast on Channel 4, in which direct comparison is made between what was shown and that deemed unshowable. In relation to such persistent horrors as the daily carnage in Iraq since 2003, questions are raised as to whether the news agendas and programming that have sustained this coverage are anywhere close to being 'proportionate'. Such is the daily regularity of instances of injury and death – to Iraqi civilians, police, government officials, militia, and Western military personnel – that the news value of these reports appears to diminish. The threshold for their inclusion and positioning in news programmes, usually discussed in terms of body count, has increased as the conflict continued.

At the declared 'end' of the war in May 2003, most Western media organisations pulled out of the conflict zone. Committing personnel and equipment in the build-up to and for the duration of the war stretched the resources of many news providers. After the Saddam regime had fallen, there was not considered a need for a mass journalistic presence as the 'media event' of the 2003 Iraq war was over. This proved to be one of the greatest ironies in the media coverage of conflict of the new century, in that the defining news story – the 'aftermath' of the war – was just beginning as the news organisations pulled out. This comparison is indicative of the disproportionate nature of the media event explored in Chapter 2. We suggested that when television news is most engaged with an event in terms of time and resources, it does not necessarily equate to greater insight into that event. Rather, such coverage tends to be subject to greater management and scrutiny (by editors, regulators, government, and news publics) and is more timid as a consequence. Coverage of post-war Iraq, however, also held very significant challenges for journalists, and as with the war, access – although restricted by different factors – was again a key issue.

Over this time the 'insurgency' that was replaced by even more lethal sectarian attacks moved sporadically around news agendas. Despite frequent speculation (in and by the media) as to a 'tipping point' in terms of the imminence of full-blown 'civil war' that might signify a final failure of the Western occupation of Iraq, the intermittent television news coverage of the injured and the dead (either in visual or in numerical discourses) did not seem to have a significant impact on the strategy – or even the rhetoric – emanating out of Washington and London.

One mechanism often employed by editors and reporters to push Iraq up the news agenda is through aggregating the total human (and other) 'costs' of the post-war military engagements. This is often undertaken on anniversaries (for instance, of 'the end of hostilities') and when the numbers of Western military personnel killed have reached a round number, such as 100 UK or 2,000 American servicemen and women fallen in Iraq. This process is external to television's economy of time that drives news (identified in Chapter 2) but nonetheless shapes its modulating flow. In one respect, these numbers are significant markers for the framing of an evaluation of an ongoing conflict, in that they have a certain recognisable resonance in political discourses in figuring a human 'cost' of a particular event or military campaign. This is particularly so in their comparability with other events or conflicts which are familiar in the social and media memory of news publics (see, for example, our consideration of the enduring Vietnam template in Chapter 5). However, this kind of quantification as a determinant of newsworthiness is also quite random in its timing and thus in the way it intersects with other aspects of the story or with news cycles. There is no doubt, though, that on these occasions a range of news media employ more lengthy, retrospective, and comparative analyses and, in so doing, potentially engage greater political and public debates.

For instance, on 1 February 2006, many British national newspapers devoted front-page headlines, inside pages, and leader columns part reporting, part commemorating the death of the hundredth British member of the military to die in Iraq. For example, *The Daily Telegraph* ran the headline SACRIFICE: THE 100TH BRITISH SERVICEMAN DIES IN IRAQ, above a photograph of Cpl Gordon Pritchard who was killed by a roadside bomb in southern Iraq. On the same day, *The Independent*, often devoting prominent space to images, headlines, and text critical of the Iraq war and its aftermath, filled its front page with the names of the 100 British dead and their affiliation and the date of each of their deaths. This list was printed in an uppercase style on a black background, perhaps a style evocative of the names of the dead engraved on the Vietnam Veteran's Memorial wall in Washington – a kind of reverse template. On the following page, the newspaper printed all the available photographs of the soldiers who had been killed. Television news also widely marked this 'grim milestone' the day before with coverage of anti-war protestors placing 100 crosses in Parliament Square and interviews with members of bereaved families.

However, whereas the numbers of Western military personnel injured and killed are regularly quantified (and cumulatively so) in UK and US news, the number of Iraqi civilian casualties became more central to a politico-media discourse on the extent the whole Iraqi campaign was a 'success' or 'disaster', as UK/US military engagement in the country appeared to be entering its final stages. In the sprawling and violent mess of post-war Iraq, although it is footage of non-Western bodies (and more often bloodied survivors) that are shown with most regularity in Western news programmes, it is their quantification that has become most contested. This is not just an issue of the difficulties in collecting and accurately classifying and verifying reports of Iraqi 'noncombatants' in a country close to civil war. Rather, as Shaw (2005: 119) writes, 'Body-counting is *an intervention in the risk-economy of war*, to make the risk-experience of civilians (and, for a few, enemy combatants too) as "valuable" as the exposure of Western soldiers, and to make it significant for politicians, so that they in turn won't risk more wars of this kind' (original italics). Thus, the Iraqi civilian body count has become a key component of the mediated discursive struggle over the 'success' or otherwise of the Western military strategy. Quantification of death is seemingly entwined with the legacy of the key players – and not least Bush and Blair.

However, whereas the media and especially rolling news formats are heavily reliant upon the uses of experts and expert sources in their interpretation of events and public, political, and military discourses, these were significantly undermined in relation to the accounting of the civilian death toll as a consequence of the Iraq war and its aftermath. The huge variance in reported estimates of the numbers of Iraqi civilians killed since the launch of the invasion diminished the capacity of those opposed to the war to forge a consistent or coherent critique around the accumulative human cost to ordinary Iraqis. For example, in December 2005, the US President finally put a figure on the (total) number of people killed in Iraq at that time at '30,000, more or less'.[17] Less than a year later, one study published in *The Lancet* found that an equivalent of 2.5 per cent of Iraq's population – 655,000 – had been killed since hostilities began, and the authors conclude, 'Although such death rates might be common in times of war, the combination of a long duration and tens of millions of people affected has made this the deadliest international conflict of the 21st century, and should be a grave concern to everyone'.[18]. And in the same month as the publication of *The Lancet* article, the widely cited online 'Iraq Body Count Project' was reporting between a total of between 45,000 and 50,000 civilian deaths as a consequence of the 2003 invasion.[19]

The lack of verifiable and precise figures reflected in the absence of a media-critical consensus on the cumulative and long-term extent of the civilian costs of the war and post-war is also related to the event-driven nature of the coverage from Iraq. Despite and because of the continuity of the daily casualties, its prioritisation in news agendas rested with the reaching of a moving body count threshold from a particular incident or aggregated over a particular day. Yet, even aggregated thresholds of body counts have ultimately diminishing news value unless (and only temporarily) a round number deemed in some way significant is passed, or unless a day or month is exceedingly more bloody than those which preceded it. Quantification, as a standard criterion of news, contributes to a moral crisis of the media's engagement with the post-invasion accumulating casualties in Iraq. Luhmann (2000: 27), for example, argues that the use of quantities in news is one 'principle of selection' of the 'function system of the mass media'. He suggests that 'quantification can generate sudden moments of insight without any substance' (2000: 28). And it can also be considered one of the many 'signs' of the injuring and violence of warfare that displace their consequences from view.

From this perspective, the prospects for television news delivering much more than a sanitised, banal, and self-constrained version of the suffering in Iraq and elsewhere are bleak indeed. However, the new ecology of images that defines this period is also a product of the specific operational difficulties of Western news gathering under conditions of continual near-civil war. Most journalists in much of the post-war period have had to remain confined in the heavily fortified and isolated diplomatic or government Green Zone in Baghdad where the US occupation and other authorities are housed. Consequently, local video journalists record footage of daily life and death in Iraq, and these images are interpreted by correspondents housed in the Green Zone, or in the country of broadcast. However, according to Jon Snow, the news coverage is diminished: 'Without the human dimension of the reporter, the pictures become so much wallpaper – more blood, more bodies, more mayhem – but no enquiry into what actually happened and no talking to those who were present. The pictures simply lose their impact'.[20] The new ecology of images is thus founded upon a disjuncture in the very phenomena that is the driving force of television journalism (examined in Chapter 2), namely immediacy and intimacy, derived from access and proximity. As a consequence, the viewer is 'twice-removed' as a witness to the daily atrocities in Iraq. The greater the distancing modes of presentation (structural and arbitrary) the further there is a shift to containment. And, as a corollary of this, to draw on the work of Luc Boltanski (1999: 23), the potential for a politics of compassion is diminished in response as viewers are made more remote.

Conclusion

In sum, whereas the casualties of conflict were largely absent from UK/US television news screens during the 'event time' of the 1991 and 2003 wars, the images of injured and dead Iraqis – even in a highly sanitised form – became the dominant signifiers of the aftermath of the 2003 invasion. The Vietnam template used by the media and even by President Bush to frame this period, although in different ways and for different ends, nonetheless evoked the idea (however accurate) of the daily drip drip of bad news having a cumulative impact. So, despite the political rhetoric of elections, democracy, and freedom, the credibility of the public politico-military discourse of a likely 'successful' end point to the occupation of Iraq was rendered incomprehensible by the civil war consistently unfolding on television screens around the world. Despite the mostly self-imposed restrictions of what could be broadcast of the actual terror of life in much of Iraq, what was reported and shown illuminated a disjuncture with the political spin of any kind of progress and the feasibility of any of the numerous announcements as to the planned withdrawal of Western military forces.

However, this disjuncture was mirrored by a new ecology of images and a moral crisis in the media itself. The controversy over what should or should not be broadcast and the enduring body paradox and the difficulty of gaining access to the 'reality on the ground' combine to stretch the capacity of Western television journalism to investigate the 'real' Iraq.

We now turn to address television's presentation of war and terror by assessing the role of drama and documentary in rendering these realities. If news reporting is in crisis, do other formats offer more credible or reliable representations?

7
Drama and Documentary: The Power of Nightmares

Introduction

In examining the television interaction order and the relationship between on-screen interactions and the off-screen perceptions of security of audiences and policymakers, the role of drama and documentary is particularly interesting. Woven into the schedules alongside news, these formats present renderings of many of the security salient events constituting news in recent years. Entertainment, as a cultural genre, is not antithetical to politics,[1] despite Postman's (1986) concern that we are *Amusing Ourselves to Death* (or to political stupidity). Elizabeth van Zoonen (2005) argues that entertainment can provide a context for viewers to contemplate their role as citizens and their political engagement; that entertainment can thereby make citizenship pleasurable (cf. Livingstone, 2005). Our audience analysis reveals the manner in which television viewers understand 'actual' events through analogy to television fictions. Some interviewees suggested they enjoyed being provoked to think 'deeper' about events by documentaries such as *Panorama* and the films of Michael Moore. If, as we argue in Chapter 8, citizens' perspectives emerge from the interaction of their political, media, and experiential discursive realities, then drama and documentary are a part of anyone's media discursive reality. This chapter features a comparative analysis, examining how drama and documentary remediate (critically or uncritically) actual security events present in news.

24 and *Spooks* offer alternative renderings of state-led domestic counter-terrorism efforts before and after 9/11, including policy matters such as 'jihadi' terrorists, rogue states, uncertain politicians, and frightened citizens. Each deals with political controversies such as the

security–liberty balance and torture. Though each has a distinct televisual style, representing in different ways a situated network of characters interacting at speed, both dramas use split screen, captions, maps,
and other devices we see in television news to present local, national,
and global insecurities, as well as remediating 'real' television footage
from parallel events. The inescapably national renderings of security
issues – *24's* America versus *Spooks'* Britain – offer alternative perspectives akin to their parent companies' news channels, Fox versus BBC. But
our focus in this chapter is primarily on how each render a 'picture' of
security issues and catastrophic events within a time/space network or
interaction order. Our particular interest is in how these entertainments
might create insecurity for audiences. The methods by which anxiety
and fear are created in or dissipated by drama may tell us something
about the relationship between television news and cultural levels of
fear and anxiety.

We argue that dramas such as *24* and *Spooks* prioritise immediacy
and excitement over comprehension or reflection, and may serve to
reinforce certain assumptions about terrorist threats. By contrast, we
also study two controversial documentaries aired on British television
since the 2003 Iraq war. *The Power of Nightmares*, a series of three
documentaries aired on BBC2 in 2004 and repeated in 2005, represented an unusually high-profile challenge to the assumptions of the
politico-media discourses of the War on Terror. In fact the series drew
together various academic arguments (e.g. Kepel, 2004) to present a
perspective that seemed to contradict prevailing media and government
discourses to such an extent that the broadcast of its promotional trailers
were suspended owing to the killing of the British hostage Kenneth
Bigley (Beckett, 2004). By contesting the 'reality' of threats faced from
terrorism, the documentary stood in lonely opposition to the inflation and amplification of threat by officials and media in the post-9/11
period. We finally turn to a *Dispatches* documentary, 'Iraq: The Hidden
Story', another televised essay that argues that life in Iraq is simply
impossible to report because it is too dangerous for journalists to operate.
This again challenges and perhaps undermines television news coverage
and official pronouncements on conditions in Iraq.

Drama: *24* and *Spooks*

It is noteworthy that as political and military situations change, so do
the concepts and metaphors used to describe them. The transition from
a Cold War state-dominated world order to a more globalised era of

multi-level governance by state and non-state actors has coincided with a transition to new concepts and metaphors such as scapes (Appadurai, 1996), flows, and networks (Castells, 1996, 1997a,b; Urry, 2000, 2003). Even an establishment figure such as General Sir Rupert Smith, NATO's Deputy Supreme Allied Commander Europe until 2001, has adopted the rhizome metaphor prominent in the work of radical social theorists Deleuze and Guattari: war has been transformed, he writes (2005), because the enemy, terrorism, is 'rhizomatic' – propagating like underground roots, from nodes, horizontally.

If policy practitioners and academics use such metaphors to help themselves understand the 'real' interaction order, perhaps we can do the same when examining contemporary fictional representations. For instance, in the work of Urry, and Deleuze and Guattari, 'the social' is ontologised as fluid, as composed of flows of materials and people, with rhythms, intensities, and tempos. These flows have intentional, vectoral directions, located relationally rather than through any transcendent or structuralist coordinates (see literature review by Albertsen and Diken, 2001). Does this not characterise the movement of agents and villains in the crime and thriller genre – assembling then vanishing, reliant on a mix of technology and human intuition, located in relation to moving targets rather than fixed points?

But this seems unrealistic, for are not our societies composed of institutional sites rather than sloppy flows? One may suggest an institution such as 'the White House' is simply an enduring 'intensity', but not many people will understand it as such. Helpfully, Deleuze and Guattari offer some solution through their ontology of *lines* that cross 'the social'. First, *molar* lines mark segments of the social – institutions that territorialise and bound human activity. Second, they identify *molecular* lines – rhizomatic movements (above) that are not necessarily bounded – that seek de-territorialisation. Thus, 'the social' is conceived of the twin pressures of de- and re-territorialisation (there is a third line we shall come to later). Hence, Deleuze and Guattari title their work *Capitalism and Schizophrenia*; capitalism is a constant process of creative destruction, in which things are continually broken down but reassembled afresh. Existing institutions are not permanent, but in the course of human activity (competition, work, demand), new ones emerge. This overlaps with our interest in processes of control and chaos – processes also important to narrative in television drama. How does television render the twin processes of chaos and control as they unfold across networks or flows of social relations? *Is television schizophrenic?*

Relational networks and connectivity

Virilio has written that of the dimensions time, space, and speed, it is speed that is now the defining standard of social life – the 'cosmological constant' (Virilio, 1997: 37). He argues that comprehensive connectivity through communications technologies means the demise of the journey, of trajectories with beginnings and endings. We can get where we want to go instantly. Trajectory has been replaced by 'trajectivity', he suggests (p. 24). But we see in the worlds of *24* and *Spooks* that 'the social' is still composed of multiple interlocking trajectories, criss-crossing pathways. It is more complex than Virilio will allow (cf. Thrift, 2005).

In *24* and *Spooks*, characters are constantly connected through mobile phones. Most plot developments occur through mobile phone calls. In *24*, Bauer is told something: he drives off to act. In series 1, the villainous Serbs call him to reveal where they are keeping his kidnapped wife and daughter: he gets angry and drives after them. His wife steals a phone and calls him to tell him it's a trap, so he does something else. And so on. The main effect of phone connectivity is to highlight the synchronicity of one event to others. This is depicted chiefly through split screens (constructing the simultaneity we discussed in Chapter 2). When two people talk, the screen splits in two. For a moment, the audience gains power – they can see whether either party is hiding something. For instance, Bauer phones his daughter and tells her he loves her just as he is tracking a bad guy. But these split screens can split into four, to show each character from two different angles. Of those four splits, two will be on hand-held cameras, two still cameras, so we become unsettled. Any power the audiences had is taken away. And then if a third party (back at headquarters) is listening to the phone call, we get three characters – that is six simultaneous images. Suddenly your eyes cannot keep up with everything. The audiences must learn to watch through glimpses. Like the guards in Bentham's (1995) panopticon, we can see all the characters/prisoners in their (screen) boxes, but this is an overburdened perspective. Watching this 'live' footage, we are always on the verge of missing something.

Furthermore, as we see all the characters in different places at once, driving around, connected by their phones, we see how they never reached a settled place. Nowhere is safe. Place equals danger. Each time the wife and daughter get freed from the Serb kidnappers and taken to a safe house, the safe house gets ransacked and they get kidnapped again. Trajectories get entangled, bringing frustration and delaying any resolution. Each time Bauer unearths a traitor in his CTU offices who is transferring information to the baddies, the traitor is kicked out or killed, but then the camera zooms in on another character making a secret phone call to the baddies. There is *always* a danger inside. This also means all flows of information are provisional and suspicious. Bauer gets sent instructions, but can he rely on them? But when a character has their phone turned off or loses reception, time and time again something terrible happens to them because they missed a piece of information. In *Spooks*, Tom's bitter ex-girlfriend posts his mobile phone number on sex calling cards in nightclubs with a photo of Tom in James Bond-style tuxedo and tagline 'On her majesty's sexy service'. To own a phone is to be vulnerable, but only through our phones can we move towards safety.

The final depiction of these uncertain spaces and accelerating events that could induce anxiety among audiences occurs when the four-way split screen goes silent in *24*. We are watching four things happening on the screen, and we can only watch. We cannot hear. The already ostensibly powerless audiences are put at a further remove from the action.[2] And then the clock comes on screen, and we see the faces in agony but only hear the clock ticking.

Agents' time and citizens' time

24 is supposed to be set in 'real time', that is, we see the events as they happen. More accurately, the show is set in 'clock time' (Adams, 1995). A digital clock graphic is imposed on the action every eight to ten minutes to remind us that time is running out for Bauer. Clock time is a highly constructed form of time, which is perhaps easier to manipulate than 'real time'. Indeed, *24's* clock time plays two tricks on the audiences. First, you do not see an hour of real-time action per episode, you see forty-three minutes, because it was shot with US television commercials in mind. Indeed, the clock graphic appears on screen to mark a commercial break, and it skips forward five minutes in the story. So the entire premise may be that we are seeing an hour, but we see forty-three minutes. Time is condensed. Second, this 'real time' is also stretched. Bauer reminds us at the start of episodes, 'this will be the longest day of my life'. There is just too much for one day! And yet, it's less than a day. So our 'sense' of time is suspended. At first glance there are echoes of Samuel Beckett's *Waiting for Godot* in series 2 when Bauer says, 'we're running out of time. We're all running out of time'. In Beckett's play, the characters kill time with jokes and laments as they wait painfully for the mysterious Godot (death, God ...) who never arrives (and may never). But while *24* does play with our sense of time, it does not take place in an entirely a-temporal vacuum. A resolution will come; Bauer will save America.

What dictates how long it takes to move from suspended state to resolution, or indeed how long anything will take to happen, is the length of time it takes Bauer and his CTU team to process information. One commentator notes:

> Plot events are conditioned by the character's ability or inability to process information in real time. There is no shortage of information; what is lacking is processing power... At the same time, the rule is that all data will be processed, given sufficient time.
>
> (Baldwin, 2003: 5)

So real time is in fact processing time: 'a day corresponds to the time taken to process and act on all available intel[ligence]' (Baldwin, ibid). Viewers aware of miniseries' conventions will expect that a resolution must be found in twenty-four hours, and within each hour. But each resolution depends on processing information – on decoding a file on a suspect, on transferring a name or a photo to Bauer's onboard car computer so he can save or kill the target. So each 'day' becomes that time period within which information is processed and acted upon to bring about resolution. While processing time plays a role in dictating action in *Spooks*, a single episode can be set over weeks or months. The world is not threatened and saved in a day. This implies long periods of waiting and inaction. We see more of characters in the pub, having a glass of wine at home, or debating their purposes at work. We have seen in previous chapters how rolling news fills gaps between new news with speculation, and perhaps it is no coincidence that the characters in *Spooks* are more reflective than those in *24*. They have time to think. The plot is moved forward through talk whereas *24*'s plot is driven by visuals and simultaneity. We shall return to this below.

The computations and processing 'real time' of these miniseries are not dissimilar from the 'real time' of news on CNN or BBC News 24. Recall our analysis of the opening phase of the 2003 Iraq war in Chapter 4; the pace of news oscillated as journalists computed the data to hand in order to present something concrete to viewers. Reporters tried to piece together fragments of information about the possible launch of a pre-emptive decapitation strike targeting Saddam Hussein and waited for confirmation from the White House. Upon confirmation, the news speeded up as anchors and interviewees rushed to interpret this event and its implications for what happens next. This uneven rhythm contributes in both *24* and twenty-four-hour news to oscillating levels of anxiety; that is, to the modulation of terror.

The urgent temporality of counter-terror agents in *24* is contrasted with a slower pace of ordinary life for ordinary citizens (and again invokes a discussion in Chapter 2, on the 'flow' of citizens' everyday lives). Series 2 begins with Jack Bauer and his daughter Kim mourning after their wife/mother died at the end of the first series. Their mourning is very slow. We see shots of Jack thinking, and awkward conversations between the two. Their slowness is made clear when the President suddenly calls Bauer to return to CTU and prevent the latest crisis. The call interrupts the natural flow of time and natural period of mourning. But Bauer declines the offer and the episode continues to plod, with Bauer's mourning an obstacle to the show 'picking up pace'. Finally, we see Bauer enter the CTU headquarters, take off his lumberjack coat, to be an agent again. Suddenly the episode picks up pace. Bauer makes connections and orders suspects to be brought in. He begins to order the network. He has stepped out of normality into the exciting world of counter-terrorism.

In fact the agents in *24* and *Spooks* are for the most part disembedded from the society they seek to protect. This disembeddedness is both temporal and spatial. The boundary of ordinariness and agency work is represented through the threshold of headquarters. The very first episode of *Spooks* features an MI5 press officer giving a guided tour of the outer MI5 buildings, but this cuts to the lead trio of agents, Tom, Zoe, and Danny, entering the secured inner core. A split-screen CCTV shot of Danny entering adds to the sense of pace surrounding these heroes. In both shows, the public are rarely involved, except as unwitting obstacles to the agents' progress. In series 2 episode 1, Zoe is recognised on a bus by an old school friend, Sarah, who is overweight, slow, and ignorant of the clearly more urgent narrative of the security crisis Zoe is preventing. Zoe has to avoid Sarah to stop being slowed down. In episode 3 of that series, Zoe finds herself enjoying working under cover as a schoolteacher. Her boss at MI5, Harry, mocks her:

> Quite beguiling, isn't it? The simplicity of the outside world. Dinner bells. Detention. Names on chipped coffee mugs. I know, you enjoy being part of something ordinary.

The agents of *Spooks* and *24* live and work in the extraordinary inside world. Society must be protected, and the agents of both shows are presented as having considerable discretionary powers here. In series 4 of *24*, the agents discuss the likelihood of terrorist attacks across the US sparking civil unrest and mass panic. They consider imposing marshal law. Earlier in the series, the possibility of closing down the Internet for security purposes (the entire Internet) was raised. The theme of absolute power in an emergency situation is also present in *Spooks*. In what is ultimately a simulated test of MI5's practices, the agents are told that the Prime Minister, Cabinet, and Royal Family are probably dead. Invoking Hobbes' *Leviathan*, an agent responds, 'The country's like a body with no head'. Tom, the main agent, wants to take control of the country and declares a state of emergency. He is told, 'On your head be it', and, when he is struggling, 'On the head of the king, let all the sorrows lie'. In representing society through Hobbes' metaphor of the ruling head and the social body, the drama again depicts the public as passive, ordered from above, and in need of protection. Are viewers to accept this positioning and feel grateful for the protection of the real MI5? Or, as we explore later, is this offset by the depiction of *Spooks*' agents as fallible?

The 'CNN effect' in drama

The 'CNN effect' model, as we explored in Chapter 3, referred to the manner in which the pace, speed, and extent of twenty-four-hour television coverage actually shapes events themselves, feeding back in a reflexive loop. That is, the policymakers involved in the event watch TV coverage of the event and modify their actions accordingly, such that it is possible that news media can determine policymakers' actions – journalists *forcing* intervention during a humanitarian crisis, for example. So in *24* and *Spooks*, to what extent are agents and policymakers portrayed as reacting to news, or do they actually control what appears in the news?

In *24*, the news media is portrayed as able to shape events. In series 2, a journalist, Wieland, gets information that a fictional president (Palmer) is aware of an imminent threat to the United States. Wieland does not know what the threat is, but nevertheless threatens Palmer that he will make a television report anyway. Palmer warns such a report would be against the public interest, as it would provoke mass hysteria, but Wieland invokes his professional right to break a story. Ultimately, Palmer orders secret service to take Wieland away and 'deal with this'. As the scene ends, the camera closes on Palmer, looking wrought and weighed down. Though we later discover Wieland was not killed, at this stage in the series, the audiences are given the impression that the White House will resort to coercion to control news media and prevent unhelpful 'breaking rumours'. This implies that an un-coerced media would be able to shape and possibly alter the direction of events.

The news media is less of an independent, powerful force in *Spooks*. In series 1, Tom orders a newspaper story that makes the front page of the next edition and expects journalists to hand over any information. In another episode, Kurdish nationalists hijack the Turkish embassy in London and take hostages to draw attention to their cause. The leader justifies the actions to agent Zoe:

> Zoe: This isn't going to help your cause.
> Leader: What are you talking about? The world's media is our there right now discussing our cause! Your people are listening. We have already won a great victory.

The Kurdish leader assumes a CNN effect model in which the group use the publicity provided by news media to create a newly informed public who will pressure their elected representatives to alter policy. However, Tom defeats them by using the media too. He orders the production of a news clip showing the Turkish embassy with hostages being released. MI5 funnel the clip onto a 'Channel 1' showing in the embassy. The Kurds are fooled into thinking the news on 'Channel 1' is not showing their actions. Their effort to use the CNN effect model is thwarted.

Given the susceptibility of journalists and malleability of news stories, it is perhaps contradictory that agents in both series learn about events by watching television in their headquarters or at home. Such news is taken as 'truth'. *Spooks* actually begins episodes with simulated TV news to introduce the storyline; the news tells the characters and us, the viewers, 'what is happening'. Hence we are presented with an ambivalent portrayal of the news media: news may be rumour, it may feature planted stories and news clips inserted by special agents, yet it is also reliable enough for agents to watch themselves.

Representing politics and terror

In *24*, fear and anxiety replace contemplation (Broe, 2004). The show depicts many 'realities' of the War on Terror and invites us to see them as part of a bewildering, exciting world defined by speed and threat. In series 1, produced *before* 9/11, integral parts of the show include torture, terror cells, and a detention centre that officially does not exist. The producer of the show Robert Cochran told the *Atlanta Journal Constitution* that the aim of the show was not political per se; rather, he said, 'we have a legitimate interest in telling stories that are grounded in reality, at least to a considerable extent grounded in reality' (in Watson, 2005). Perhaps it is not surprising that when our audiences talk about news and actual events in the War on Terror, they lapse into dialogue about movies and TV drama.

Even if the producer had no overt political agenda, by elevating fear and anxiety over contemplation in the treatment of real events, the producer positions audiences to relate to the signified real events not with a critical mindset but purely for their *immediacy*. Just as in much news coverage of the War on Terror, context disappears, as we see only the event in isolation. 'Suicide bomber kills 46' – yes but who are they, why did they act, as part of what campaign, in response to what? Series 1 of *24* is particularly culpable. The series relates to the 1990s' Balkans conflict and the role of the United States, in particular the role of a US Special Forces team led by Jack Bauer, in assassinating people in the conflict. The entire series is about Serbs seeking revenge for a secret attack by Bauer, yet nowhere in *24* is there any consideration of why US agents were secretly killing people in the Balkans.

Series 2 and 4 offer a more complex political reading, through an ambiguous treatment of Islam and terrorism. Series 2 contains a study of 'white fear'. An affluent Muslim man, Reza, is about to marry into a similarly well off white family. The sister of the bride, Kate, is repeatedly suspicious of Reza. Though the nature of her suspicion is unspecified, we find out she has hired a private detective to investigate him. The detective tells Kate that there is a link between Reza and a suspected terrorist. The camera lingers on Kate, drawing attention to her fears and her quandary: should she tell her sister – and this is the day of the wedding? Later, that morning, Reza, who suspects nothing, takes Kate for a drive and says the destination is a surprise. Kate is unable to act normally and actually gets out of the car, until Reza says he was taking her to see the house he had bought for her sister Marie, the bride. Kate's fear was unfounded. The 'white fear': has she misjudged him? When they return to the family home, CTU come to talk to Reza. Again, the camera stays on Kate through the whole scene, as if the story was not about Reza being interrogated but about *her* – about white people struggling with their racial prejudices. Marie is upset for Reza and herself and blames Kate for sabotaging the wedding. But under CTU questioning, Reza concedes he has been covering for Kate and

Marie's father, who are funding terrorists! CTU call the father, Kate looks shocked. She is now alone, and the camera closes on her bottom lip.

The issue of whether the United States can be 'home' to Muslims is repeatedly presented. Already in series 2, we see a terrorist decide not to detonate a bomb because he was touched by the generosity of a white American friend. Getting a puncture while driving to set off the bomb, the friend fixes his tyre and this act changes his mind. In series 4, Bauer is being pursued by armed guards and takes refuge in a gun store, which happens to be owned by a couple of Muslim men. The men reveal their father built the store up and they will not flee because they want to show America is their home. They stand with Bauer and fight, and cry with happiness when the gunfight is won. Against this, also in series 4, a Muslim man, Navi Azaz, who is part of a group planning terrorist attacks sits in a shop in which a television shows a hostage video he has played some part in. A customer walks in:

Customer: Have you been following this Mr Azaz?
Navi: <forced> Yes, it's horrible.
Customer: It makes it so difficult for the rest of us when people from home do these unspeakable things.

The customer, a 'moderate Muslim', is against terrorism but still refers to another country as home. But *24* rarely depicts matters as more complex than this, nor provides much geopolitical context. *Spooks* attempts to do both. The first episode to confront the issue of 'homegrown terrorists' came in series 2. In orientalist fashion, the episode opens in a Mosque bathed in darkness offset by greenish lighting, as creepy music plays. An imam pretends to upbraid a boy for poor study (infer: Muslims are deceptive and value scholarship), then tortures him, and dumps his body. Introducing the case at MI5 headquarters, Tom begins with the geopolitical context. With his boss Harry he discusses the imam:

Tom: He came from Afghanistan. I always saw that as a friendly place wrecked by Soviet Russia.
Harry: <wryly> How one forgets.

Harry implies that Afghanistan was an unfriendly place – and by implication, Afghanis were unfriendly people – *before* the 1980s Soviet invasion. The episode proceeds by telling a story of a battle within

Muslim communities in Britain between 'Islamic extremism' and moderates. In the 'Controversy' extra feature of the DVD, the writers speak of wanting to show 'two sides'. They note, 'All religions have their bad priests'. This simple good/bad dichotomy is clearly present in the 'bad' imam. He tries to recruit a Muslim boy to suicide bombing:

> Imam: Shall I tell you a secret? One day, England will become the house of Islam. No hamburgers. No tins of lager. All the people of this island will follow God and honour the prophet, peace be upon him.
> Boy: But how could that happen?
> Imam: By the blood of martyrs, my son.

The binary is muddied, however, when a moderate Muslim who helps MI5, called Halloun, makes the 'un-British' comment that the imam should be killed. Noting the embarrassment on Tom's face, Halloun apologises: 'I see. Do we have a clash of cultures here?' At the episode's climax, Halloun tries to dissuade the boy from blowing himself up by talking about football, playing on the complexity of the boy's identifications. It is perhaps regrettable that the difficulty faced by young people of negotiating cultural and political identifications is not presented until the very end of the episode, but it does raise the issue forcefully.

The representation of the national self-image in *Spooks* is an important counterpoint to that of *24*. In *24*, President Palmer represents the United States across series. In both his actions and speeches, he projects strength, dutifulness, and innocence (not in the sense of naivety, but guiltlessness), an ideal president, akin to the ideal White House depicted by *West Wing*. Facing a row with China in series 4, Palmer's reaction exemplifies this: 'We didn't bring this crisis on ourselves, but we're going to be the ones to settle it. This is a dirty business and we're going to have to get our hands dirty to clean it up'. Ends justify means, and the United States will be the decisive force. *Spooks* represents both the United States and the United Kingdom very differently. The tone is set early as the first baddie in the very first episode is American (an anti-abortionist terrorist), and when the real-life President Bush appears on a TV screen, he is in blue monochrome – the same CCTV tint used to depict suspects and criminals. The special relationship is evoked as Tom has an affair with CIA agent Christine, an affair of some tenderness but also mutual deception. Ultimately, she betrays him. Is this what British audiences should expect of the United States?

24's America is an innocent dragged into conflicts it must and will resolve, offering regular redemption. *Spooks'* Britain is a mistrustful place where pragmatism determines actions, motives are mixed, and a benign conclusion is unthinkable. In *Spooks*, Harry laments 'Suicide bombers in the heart of England', and invokes Peter Pan, a 'story about being safe in an eternal garden where you play in tree houses all day long'. England is a country that needs to grow up and face its threats, he suggests. But *Spooks* offers less hope than *24* that threats can be averted. While there are intra-government disputes between agencies in *24*, often based on 'bad' characters obstructing 'good' CTU agents, in *Spooks* there is residual conflict between arms of government and nobody is consistently good or bad. MI5 encounters hostility from the Home Office, Treasury, nurses, policemen, and most foreign governments. MI5 assassinates people that other branches of government have instructed to be left alone. Each institution has internal conflicts too – in one instance a leading army officer instigates a mutiny. But it is MI5's duplicity that is most interesting for the purposes of this book. Episode 5 of series 2 centres upon the level of terrorist threats Britain faces. It features a drill in which MI5 agents are told the Prime Minister, Cabinet, and Royal Family have been killed. In the first twenty-five minutes, agents discuss the number of threats they have identified that week, the number of dirty bombs being constructed in London at that moment, and even explain how different bombs work – educating the viewer on the nature of threat apparently faced. But twenty-six minutes in, an agent says of one suspected group, 'It was in the loony file. We mentioned it in the weekly report just to keep the numbers up'. MI5 is depicted as inflating threat levels. The episode suggests to the viewer that while there is a range of imminent threats out there, even MI5, our heroes in this series, cannot be trusted. *24* puts viewers in a passive position but with heroes to trust in. *Spooks* presents the same threats but only fallible heroes.

Crossing the line: heroes as war machines

We wrote earlier of Deleuze and Guattari's understanding of society as an ongoing process of de- and re-territorialisation, or forces of disorder and order. But they write of a third 'line' or tendency, a line of flight, which demonstrates the limits of this modulation between order and chaos. *24's* Bauer and *Spooks'* Tom each escapes the control or recapture by their institutions. It is important for understanding the representation of counter-terror in television miniseries that the heroes sometimes have to step beyond the rules and norms of their institutions to protect their societies.

Deleuze and Guattari (1987: 357–358) argue that nomadic cultures have often gone to war, become 'war machines', not against particular invading or controlling sovereign regimes per se but against the process of sovereign state-formation itself.[3] Hence, as Reid (2003: 65) points out, for Deleuze and Guattari, 'war is irreducible to sovereignty and prior to its law'. Sovereign powers can attempt to capture and direct this desiring war machine, but there is, to a certain extent, a desire 'in and of itself' that *can* exceed state control (Deleuze and Guattari, 2000: 27). Reid contrasts this with the writings of Foucault, for whom desire is never outside state power systems but created by them. Reid notes the connection between these competing conceptions of power and desire and competing conceptions of war. Foucault (1978: 92–102) had inverted Clausewitz's dictum that 'war is the continuation of politics by other means'; for Foucault state politics was a form of war. However, Deleuze argues, *contra* Foucault, that despite the attempts of power to codify the relationship between war and politics, there is an 'essence' to war that escapes these attempts at codification and that 'has as its object not war but the drawing of a creative line of flight' (Deleuze and Guattari, 1987: 422). This is in stark contrast to Foucault's bleak assessment of the 'omnipresence' that power achieves through its subsumption of laws deriving directly from war' (Reid, 2003: 61). War can therefore be considered as something 'both inside and outside the domains of state sovereignty', Reid notes (p. 61). This directs our attention to how states manage this irrepressible 'war machine', or bring under control this warrior tendency. This tension becomes visible in *24* and *Spooks*, where the hero agents regularly transgress the boundaries of law (and certain ethical norms regarding torture) because of an intense and slightly wild sense of injustice and duty. These moments throw into relief the presence and nature of the boundaries transgressed.

Hence when Bauer and Tom cross the boundaries, they become nomadic, for a time. They go off on their own, out of anyone's control. Their superiors deem them 'unreasonable'. But returning to Reid's definition of 'line of flight': 'A line of flight is the operation of deterritorialisation by which the dialectical stratification of relations between reason and desire are no longer defined in relation to reason, but take on aims of their own' (Reid, 2003: 81). That is, Bauer and Tom find themselves following aims other than, or in opposition to, those of the state. They find themselves in an intolerable situation and break free. In series 4 of *24*, Bauer defies a presidential order forbidding the torture of a suspect. A colleague tells Bauer, 'You can't expect to keep working *outside the line* and not expect consequences' (emphasis added). But it is worth asking whether working outside the line can alter the consequences; whether warriors like Bauer alter the conditions within which they act. Has not Bauer's habit of torture contributed to the normalisation of torture in popular culture and, indirectly perhaps, public policy?

Towards the end of series 2 of *Spooks*, Tom feels a double anger towards his job. His boss tells him to finish his relationship with the CIA's Christine, and this feeds a wider resentment towards bureaucratic impersonality – Max Weber's 'iron cage' of rationality. Tom's anger erupted when MI5 quashed the mutiny led by an army officer who complained about a lack of resources. The officer was killed, and Tom had been sympathetic to his complaint. He shouts at his boss Harry, 'Fuck you. If the new world order means ... destroying anyone who questions the political agenda, then I'm in the wrong job!' Tom identifies a homogenous authority complex that he labels the 'new world order', and we know he will not be bound by it. In the next episode Tom, in a driven state, outperforms the rest of MI5 to the extent that he humiliates Harry. But again, in the course of working towards objectives set by Harry, someone Tom cared for is killed and actually dies in his arms. By now, the miniseries is filmed in a cinematic mode, with operatic music and long still shots. The next and final episode of the series nods to Orson Wells' *The Third Man* (it is even playing in one scene) as Tom chases a mysterious agent through underground vaults beneath London (of course, this is the twenty-first century and the agents use GPS devices). The episode ends with Tom vanishing, apparently drowning himself in the sea, but with the possibility that he escaped with Christine – a 'line of flight' out of Britain. We see, then, how our heroes are sometimes called by a duty other or higher than the state, such as family, love, or beliefs. Or, they independently adopt alternative methods to better achieve the state's goals of public security, methods such as assassination and torture. Given our assumed sympathy for the heroes, do we then accept their redefinition of necessary methods?

Summary

24 and *Spooks* present an interconnected, perpetually insecure interaction order (or disorder). The order is constituted by slow, passive publics protected by fast agents operating in networks disembedded from the societies they protect. The dramas depict familiar political themes such as multiculturalism, national identity, and the role of the media, but in *24's* case, the immediacy and pace of the action prohibit consideration of these issues. And as dramas, they present us with an interaction order featuring heroes and villains, the heroes driven by their particular calling and altering the order where they need to. The greater nuance and moral ambiguity of *Spooks* may undermine certain simplicities in political and media discourse and lead audiences towards more critical engagement with the themes represented, but *Spooks'* world is still relentlessly insecure and full of threats.

Documentary: *Dispatches* and *The Power of Nightmares*

11 September 2001 acted as a catalyst for a public hunger in North America and Europe for information about Islam and terrorism. There was a marked increase in sales of the Koran to non-Muslim readers, and non-fiction titles such as *The 9/11 Commission Report* became bestsellers (that title was even re-published as a graphic novel). Novelists have also addressed these issues, for instance, John Updike's *Terrorist* (2006) and Jonathan Safran Foer's *Extremely Loud and Incredibly Close* (2005). Yet in documentary there was a pause, an apparent moment of cultural hesitancy in the 'shadow' cast by 9/11, before the release of any rigorous examination of the 9/11 attacks or its connection to the ensuing War on Terror. It was not until September 2006 that the BBC released Peter Taylor's documentary *Al-Qaeda: Time to Talk?* Taylor explored the notion that counter-terrorism campaigns prior to the War on Terror have ultimately resorted to political negotiation rather than purely military operations; by implication, should not US and UK leaders admit they must negotiate with Al-Qaeda leaders? (though given that the BBC gave him the time and money to explore his thesis clearly such questions were being considered in 2005). In the same week as Taylor's documentary aired, however, documentary or reconstruction films such as the BBC's *The Fall of the World Trade Centre* and Channel 4's *9/11: The Miracle of Stairway B* continued to de-politicise the events by concentrating on the individualised stories of victims or survivors of the structures of the Twin Towers.

We wish to examine two documentaries which challenged mainstream cultural discourses. The first is Adam Curtis' *The Power of Nightmares*, broadcast by the BBC in October 2004 and later remade as a film. Curtis argued that many assumptions about the War on Terror, such as the existence of Al-Qaeda, the threats faced by Western publics, and the motives of Western leaders, had been misunderstood or simply not questioned at all since 9/11. His provocative thesis was that in a post-ideological age, Western leaders struggling to offer any vision of a better society have resorted to depicting 'nightmares' such as terror threats in a bid to justify their authority. The second documentary we examine is Channels 4's *Dispatches* documentary, 'Iraq: The Hidden Story', broadcast in May 2006, in which presenter Jon Snow argues that the difficulty of reporting in Iraq makes it impossible for news media to present audiences with what is actually happening. Both documentaries challenge the 'reality' presented by news media and politicians. In so doing, they identify elements of the crisis of news discourse.

Both documentaries are essays. Alongside his controversial argument, it was this format, for Curtis, that led US television networks to reject showing *The Power of Nightmares*: 'What happens on US TV now is that you have a theatre of confrontation so that people avoid having to seriously analyse what the modern world is like – perhaps because of the emotional shock of September 11' (cited in Jeffries, 2005). As a three-part documentary, audiences were expected to follow a complex historical argument over a number of weeks. Curtis' motive was to provide a 'historical explanation for September 11'. He comments, 'up to this point nobody had done a proper history of the ideas and groups that have created our modern world. It's weird that nobody had done this before me' (ibid).

Curtis makes the case that a group of radical Islamists and American neoconservatives enjoyed a parallel historical development from the 1970s onwards, and that the ideas of each now propel violence in the War on Terror. Both sides revolted against liberalism, with Egyptian Sayyid Qutb providing the ideological critique from an Islamic perspective and Leo Strauss and his followers offering a parallel critique from within the United States. Both sides relied on 'necessary myths' – each claimed victory over the Soviet Union in the Afghanistan war and each argued liberalism offers a moral vacuum that weakens human beings. Both movements are led by intellectual vanguards who seek to (re)create strongly religious societies – neoconservatives uniting with Christian masses and intellectual descendents of Qutb such as bin Laden and al-Zawahiri seeking to overturn secularism in the Middle East. In this way, both movements have a mutual interest in defining world events as a battle between Islam and Western democracy, inflating the threat presented by the other and by liberal 'softness' in order to mobilise their putative constituencies behind their respective projects.

The thesis is not without problems. The leadership of the United States and the United Kingdom may feature some neoconservatives, but Rumsfeld, Rice, and Cheney and Blair, Straw, and Beckett are not neoconservatives. If they are not influenced by Leo Strauss or other neoconservative thinkers, yet they have been in the key positions during the War on Terror, then of what explanatory value is neoconservatism? Conversely, Curtis tends to underplay the role of Al-Qaeda, arguing it is not an organisation and was not called Al-Qaeda until 2001. There is much evidence to the contrary (Burke, 2003; Bergen, 2005), and the counterfactual always exists: 9/11 would not have occurred without the organised resources of Al-Qaeda. Curtis has since clarified his position: the Al-Qaeda threat is as an *idea*, one 'that inspires young, angry Muslim males in our own society' and others (Curtis, 2005). He claims the 7/7 London attacks vindicate his argument because the bombers were not part of an organised network but connected only to an idea. In creating an object of nightmares, a 'fantasy' or 'phantom' network that can be identified and eliminated, Curtis argues policymakers have confused the few followers of Qutb's ideas with Islam generally and have only alienated young Muslims further.

The Power of Nightmares set an important marker in debates about the 'reality' of terrorist threats, and we shall explore in Chapter 8 how audiences and citizens comprehend and negotiate such threats in their everyday routines. There is certainly evidence that policymakers have inflated the threat of terror. In Britain, in 2004, Leader of the House Peter Hain connected his government's anti-terror legislative agenda to Labour's strategy for winning the 2005 General Election: 'We are crowding out any space for [the Conservative Party] on the security agenda and that will make for an interesting political year' (cited in Phythian, 2005: 667). There is also the infamous 'dodgy dossier' in which the British government claimed Saddam could attack British citizens with WMD in '45 minutes'. In the United States too, works such as *The 9/11 Commission Report* and Ron Suskind's (2006) *The One Percent Doctrine* document the inflation of threat by elected politicians and the politicisation of intelligence. Curtis argues news media have failed to examine what Al-Qaeda is, due to their reliance on officials who have an interest in inflating threat levels. Unverifiable claims from security services or politicians make headline news, and few such stories are retracted when found to be false (Beckett, 2004). Where officials inflate, media amplify.

The Power of Nightmares attempts to de-mythologise Al-Qaeda and terrorism. This is achieved through tracing the historical trajectories that led to 9/11 and attacks since. The documentary format helps. Curtis mixes movie clips with footage of Qutb and al-Zawahiri and overlays serious material with occasionally humorous soundtrack choices. Curtis comments:

I use wit since one of the things I'm trying to illustrate is that we're living in a cartoon-like version of reality. Humour undercuts the mix of fact and fiction used by the politics of fear-mongering...and it's designed to undercut this completely unreasoned fear of Islamism.

(cited in Koehler, 2005)

Dramas such as *24* and *Spooks* are not factual but mythologise the reality they aspire to dramatise through features intrinsic to narratives such as heroes, villains, crises, and denouements. The factual basis of documentaries such as *The Power of Nightmares* can undermine the often simplistic or erroneous assumptions and characterisations that support the narratives of some dramatic miniseries and movies.

In the *Dispatches* documentary, 'Iraq: The Hidden Story', presenter Jon Snow argues that the 2003 Iraq war and its aftermath 'remains one of the least well covered conflicts of the television age'. The result is that 'we are profoundly disconnected from the real Iraq'. The unreal Iraq is the Green Zone in Baghdad, where coalition officials and their guests, including journalists, live behind a secured wall. Outside the perimeter lies the Red Zone, the 'real Iraq', where Iraqis live and where military convoys venture carefully, sometimes allowing journalists to travel with them. But this makes independent journalism impossible. Due to the risk of kidnapping and murder, it is too dangerous for Western journalists to leave the Green Zone, but if they travel with Coalition military, then they lose independence and are unable to talk to ordinary Iraqis. Western news organisations are forced to rely on Iraqi journalists. But for Snow, and other Western journalists interviewed, this is inadequate. Lindsay Hilsum of Channel 4 complains Iraqi journalists do '*their* journalism...They ask different questions' to those she would ask. Western newsrooms can add commentary and context, but they cannot be sure it is correct or complete. Snow examines the role of Iraqi citizens using the Internet and camcorders to produce their own reports of life outside the Green Zone, but argues that the 'Iraqi perspective' is not what Western audiences will connect to. They expect 'the human dimension', i.e. a (familiar) Western reporter asking questions of relevance to international audiences.[4]

Moreover, Iraqi journalists are constrained too. The documentary actually shows al-Arabiya journalist Mazen al-Toumeizi being killed by a US military helicopter as it fired into a crowd of civilians. Iraqi journalists dressed in civilian attire are at risk from US military, but if they wear armour they are mistaken for US journalists and at risk from Iraqis. In addition, as Iraq divides on sectarian lines, it seems journalists telling the news of one 'side' are protected while those seeking to be neutral or objective are at risk from all sides. Hence Snow's conclusion:

> Is there already a civil war? The answer is: we don't know. We've got no way of getting to the grassroots to find out how people really feel about each other, or whether this [potential civil war] is simply a manipulated thing from the top.

Why, then, does Snow's flagship *Channel 4 News* programme perpetuate the pretence that events in Iraq can be covered? As Joseph (2006) argues, why does it rely on second-hand camerawork from Iraqi journalists if Snow thinks it is unreliable and partial? As long as television news presents coverage of Iraq with the same professional gloss as coverage of any other story, why should viewers suspect the news is suspect? Would it not be a more radical step, with the potential for impacting on other news outlets, if *Channel 4 News* simply announced 'things probably happened in Iraq today but reliable reports are impossible to achieve so we won't lie to you, viewers, like the other channels'. Such a risky step might draw attention not only to the inadequacy of news that so frustrates Snow but also to the seemingly anarchy of post-invasion Iraq. For underlying Snow's argument about journalism is also a critique of the Coalition invasion. He uses the terms of the anti-war protests of 2003 by asking, 'if [viewers] had a full account, would they support what was being done in their name?' This also echoes a passage from his autobiography in which he recounts the 1980s Iran–Iraq war and the role of the United States in perpetuating it:

> as the marshy wastes and desert sands soak up the blood, there were decreasing numbers of personnel on hand to witness what was being done in Lincoln's name. It was so dangerous, so unreportedly big, and so unchangingly active a war, that newsdesks stopped sending. Thus there was simply no pressure upon anyone to end it.
>
> (Snow, 2004: 158)

The CNN effect returns. Snow implies that media coverage of bloodshed would have pressured policymakers into acting to end the Iran–Iraq war, just as more reliable and comprehensive media coverage of Iraq in 2006 may have altered public opinion and pressured policymakers to alter what was being done in the viewer's name.

But how can we be sure whether more 'realistic', graphic scenes from Iraq would alter audiences' opinions, let alone alter them in a particular and consistent direction? The documentary shows two unedited clips, one of a single suicide bomb and another of a US marine shooting an injured Iraqi in the head. We then see the edited versions shown by different news channels. Each channel edits differently – different proportions of blood edited out, different moments blacked out, and different sounds edited out. Prominent journalists discuss the merits of such editing. On the one hand, *The Independent*'s Robert Fisk argued:

> I've believed for many years now that journalism – in particular television journalism – by its failure to show the real horror of war, has become a lethal weapon, supporting governments that want to go to war.

On the other hand, Channel 4's Lindsay Hilsum invoked a less simplistic causal relation between images of horror and the meaning of an event:

> Like most journalists who work out there, I want to show more. If I've seen something, I want people to see it. But I've also learnt that it's not always the most gruesome pictures that really convey the story.

As we have discussed in previous chapters, it is possible that viewers forced to imagine a scene, blacked out in their news channel, may experience a greater horror than viewers confronted with gruesome pictures. And gruesome pictures may trigger an instant turning away from the screen, whereas the triggering of the imagination induces a moment of reflection and active mental construction of images.

Like *The Power of Nightmares*, 'Iraq: The Hidden Story' raised questions about the 'reality' presented to television audiences. Snow's thesis is that current reporting offers no coverage of the 'real' Iraq. As such, as one journalist pundit in the documentary, the BBC's Rageh Omaar, commented, 'Iraq has represented a fairly fundamental crisis for journalists'. And given the lack of solutions offered by Snow, this crisis is not over.

Conclusion

We have used this chapter to examine how drama and documentary have represented security-salient events in the post-9/11 period.

24 and *Spooks* offer a world of unremitting insecurity, with potentially catastrophic threats, fragile social and political infrastructures, and slow, passive publics thankfully protected by fast agents who act within networks that are somehow disembedded from our societies. A televisual style of relentless immediacy prohibits reflection on the themes represented, in the process reinforcing assumptions and mythologising institutions (the presidency, counter-terror agents, terror networks) already familiar to news and political discourses surrounding the War on Terror. But the two documentaries we have examined each serve to undercut these assumptions and challenge these discourses. *The Power of Nightmares* offers a historiography of the intellectual movements that became the politico-religious projects we know today as neoconservatism and Al-Qaeda, in the hope of making the latter appear less frightening. The producer, Adam Curtis, hoped this might undermine attempts by politicians to inflate threat levels and indeed by media to amplify and perpetuate these threats even further. Finally, where Curtis attempted to offer a reality so far untold on public television, Jon Snow's 'Iraq: The Hidden Story' attempted to expose the lack of reality offered by news coverage of Iraq. He pointed to various elements in the crisis of contemporary war reporting, to the extent that we might ask: why bother watching any of the apparently incomplete or false news we are offered (by his station included)?

In the next chapter, we further enquire into the relation between televisual representations of reality and audiences' perceptions of security by drawing on audience research. This allows us to assess claims made so far about the modulation of terror threats by news, drama, and documentary by joining up television content with the consumption of that content.

8
Security and Publics: Democratic Times?

Introduction: on the reality of terror threats

At stake in many public debates surrounding security before and particularly after 11 September 2001 has been the veracity of definitions of terror threats. Why are there always such differing viewpoints about the 'reality' of threats? Why, in August 2006, did British Home Secretary John Reid (2006) feel the need to bluntly say that critics of anti-terror legislation 'just don't get it' as to the threats facing Britain and elsewhere? Why do some people hold the view that the attacks of 9/11 or 7/7 were hoaxes or government conspiracies? Definitions of terror threats are vital to contemporary security debates because from those definitions all else follows: the attribution of hostile intent to certain groups posing the 'threat', the warranting of particular government policy responses to that 'threat', and citizens' feelings of (in)security and whether they carry on living 'normal' lives. Definitions of terror threat are integral to the legitimacy of security measures and whether citizens grant consent to those policies.

We have seen in previous chapters how television plays a role in modulating the representation of threat and terror. This chapter locates these representations within an interaction order that extends beyond the screen, into the lives of audiences and citizens, and that includes government policies and political addresses. We examine the relation between media representations of terror and audiences' perceptions of terror. The purpose of the chapter is to offer a tentative explanation of the differing perceptions of terror that lie at the root of so much security policy debates and practices.[1]

The variation or inconsistency of media representations of terror and threat is exemplified by a single edition of *The Independent* from Saturday

12 August 2006, with 'The enemy within?' as its front-page headline.[2] This was related to the ongoing story of the terror plot to blow up nine aeroplanes flying between the United Kingdom and the United States and recent police arrests of suspects. The headline banner was accompanied by photos of suburban streets and road signs. The question of terror threat was directly raised. The newspaper's first seven pages were devoted to reporting the story, with most reports describing the terror plot as 'alleged'. However, one wrote of 'the terrorist threat' as if an objective fact (McSmith and Judd, 2006), and another of 'the terrorist crisis' (McSmith, 2006). Similarly, the main editorial described 'people suspected of plotting' this specific incident, but then more generally about 'the threat to our societies', writing that 'the major terrorist threat today ... [is] cottage-industries of terror'. The editorial was clear:

> It is vital we recognise this reality. For our success in thwarting these attacks will rest largely on an accurate analysis of the nature of the threat we face. [...] What we have here is a home-grown terrorist threat ... unless we recognise this central truth ... the ranks of this generation of fanatics can only be expected to grow.
>
> (*The Independent*, 2006: 32)

With the newspaper's voice having announced the 'reality' and 'central truth' of the 'threat we face', on the opposite page, star columnist Robert Fisk suggested the very opposite. Writing from Beirut during the Israel–Lebanon conflict of 12 July–14 August, Fisk (2006: 33) appeared to attack his own newspaper's reporting:

> And I notice with despair that our journalists again suck on the hind tit of authority, quoting endless (and anonymous) 'security sources' without once challenging their information and the timing of [Deputy Commissioner of the Metropolitan Police] Paul [Stephenson]'s 'terror plot' discoveries or the nature of the details – somehow, 'fizzy drinks bottles' doesn't quite work for me.

The main authoritative voices – the reporting, the editorial, and the star columnist – in one issue of *The Independent* offered very different views on the nature of any terror 'threat'.

These debates are epistemological in nature. They concern the nature of reality and how we know that reality: 'knowledge that such-and-such is true' (Klein, 2005). The reporting and the editorial in *The Independent* presented a reality composed of a specific alleged threat and a more real general threat, while Fisk's scepticism towards the source of this knowledge implied that any propositions based on that knowledge were not connected to any reality.

The status of reality is similarly uncertain for audiences. In the ethnographic audience study we draw upon, for instance, there is a tendency among responses from Muslim interviewees that *either* they wish 'their side' of the War on Terror could be better represented in Western media *or* 'the true reality' be better represented. Al-Jazeera is welcomed because, compared to non-Arabic/Muslim channels, it is considered to perform these representative roles, offering a medium of sound and moving images that conveys *either* a particular reality – 'our reality from our news' – or a more accurate portrayal of reality (singular). For instance, in the following conversation between three working-class Muslim women in London, we find the dichotomy:

Hanan: ...there was that programme about Al Jazeera – when they showed a British soldier or something – and CNN got really angry and they called up Al Jazeera and said it's against Geneva conventions.

Jasmine: I'm not saying – I'm just saying that the truth is different to different people.

Sara: with Sky News they don't let you judge it to make the judgement yourself. With Al Jazeera they show you the whole truth and it's up to you to make the decision.

An epistemological distinction arises then: is what is at stake the revealing of a given reality (as Sara suggests), or is it not reality at stake but realities (as Jasmine suggests)? Is there a common world, or do we inhabit different worlds? Was John Reid's statement that politicians, reporters, and judges 'just don't get it' an indication that he thought his critics lived in 'a different world' or 'on a different planet'? Such divided perceptions about the status of reality are the very conditions for divided perceptions about how 'real' terror 'threats' are. The issue at hand, then, is to understand how it is that different perceptions of reality emerge, for only then can we see why different perceptions of security, threat, and terror exist.

The problem was clearly posed in Lippmann's *Public Opinion* (1922). He asked: How could there be viable national democracy in the United States, addressing national economic and foreign policy, when almost all citizens had little knowledge of life beyond their small communities? At a time before national television networks and newspaper distribution, when people rarely travelled far, citizens would lack common information and knowledge and thus be voting on issues they knew little or nothing about. Lippmann attacked those democratic theorists who assumed that a model of small-town democracy, where people knew most of the town's business, could be transposed to national level. Assembling a demos who shared a common reality would be, for Lippmann, an expensive technical exercise. His solution was the creation of social science research institutes to deliver both national level data and defined policy 'objects' or issues, so that at least policymakers and journalists would be better informed and debates could focus on shared matters of concern.

The production of common world(s) takes place in a far more complex interaction order today, with accelerated flows of information, knowledge, and people, often on a global scale. Yet a first step to understanding this interaction order is to recognise that, for citizens, it is constituted by certain discursive realities. Recall in our Introduction the notion of discourse as a particular system with rules and roles that lead to the delineation of what is 'say-able' within the discourse and that such discourses give meaning to objects and subjects. These sets of meanings a discourse gives can be considered to constitute, to varying extents, 'reality' for individuals. The audiences' study indicates that citizens' perceptions of threat and security are constituted by a *political* discursive reality, a *media* discursive reality (made up of news and non-news), and an *experiential* discursive reality. Each discursive reality acts as a prism, through which some things are visible and others are not, or things are *seen as* this or that (Wittgenstein, 2002). The effect is the creation of a perspective upon an event or thing (in Figure 8.1, perspective is marked 'P').

Changes to each discursive reality – new government policies, a shocking news report, or a racial attack in a local community – contribute to changing perceptions. Each overlaps and affects the other, for instance, when news media report government policy or the nearby racial attack, or the racial attack is linked to political motivations. And over time, a qualitative change in one may affect the characteristics of another. As we have argued in earlier chapters, aspects of social and political life have been increasingly 'mediatised' in the past decade or two, i.e. embedded in the mediascape. Think of the CNN effect: the capacity of media coverage of war to shape war that became apparent with CNN's coverage of the 1991 Gulf War, such that war and media became almost co-constitutive or mutually dependent. Now that the media is more self-reflexive about its role in constituting social, political, and indeed military affairs, this awareness feeds back into

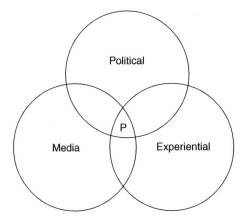

Figure 8.1 Discursive realities.

media practices. The relation between the three discursive realities, then, is complex and continually negotiated by media practioners, political actors and indeed citizens.

Each discursive reality may shift at different speeds, producing on occasion a parallax effect producing lags and disjunctures in perceptions between actors.[3] As different realities shift at different speeds – including sudden ruptures such as 9/11 – it is not surprising that different perceptions of terror, threat, and security are produced. This takes us to the second step in understanding the operations of today's interaction order, the importance of time.

Temporality

The speed at which the three discursive realities shift contributes to the uncertain and diverse perceptions of threat, terror, and security held by citizens, journalists, politicians, and security forces today.

In this section, we examine two temporal phenomena salient to the new security environment. The first is the nexus of normality and rupture. The second is the nexus of patience and urgency.

As we have documented in this book, the new security environment is marked by a series of critical, spectacular catastrophes, such as 9/11, Hurricane Katrina, and the 7/7 bombings. These catastrophes both stand out as ruptures to 'normalcy' and, for some, imply a 'new normal'. 9/11 is the exemplar. The event was interpreted as an unprecedented breach and an event that constituted a break in the course of human history. Recall in the aftermath pronouncements such as 'nothing will ever be the same', 'there can be no more humour', 'there can be no more novels', and so on.

It is in such catastrophic moments that we are confronted by 'the real', argues Zizek (1994). In his analytical schema, our lived, social, symbolic reality stands in relation to that which is repressed, what cannot be symbolised – that which he terms 'the real'. The latter may be an underlying antagonism in society, some 'traumatic kernel' we avoid considering (Wright and Wright, 1999: 79). And standing above this relation between symbolic reality and 'the real' are ideologies, whose purpose is to mask the divide in our reality. One does not have to fully align with Zizek's Lacanian perspective to appreciate how this schema can add to our understanding of recent catastrophes. US citizens were confronted with certain aspects of 'the real' that were backgrounded in their prior normality or symbolic reality. Television coverage of the event brought immediate, live footage of death (as discussed in Chapter 6), and it brought a reminder that the United States is not separated from world affairs, that 'war' is something that happens on US soil too.

The question thereafter was, 'How should such a rupture be managed?' The event could be reconciled with certain aspects of an ideology of American exceptionalism: the United States as innocent, attacked because others envied 'our freedoms', that it was manifest destiny that the US had been chosen by God to spread those freedoms through action overseas, and so on. Yet the possibility of *another* rupture posed a problem. As Grusin writes:

> Insofar as 9/11 has been called the 'first live global media event', for the United States it might also be seen to mark the *last* live global media event, or at least U.S. media seemed to want to make it such in its obsession with premeditating the future in the months that followed. [That is,] the United States seeks to try to make sure that it never again experiences live a catastrophic event like this that has not already been mediated.
>
> (Grusin, 2004: 21)

9/11 as a rupture caught America off guard, eliciting a 'cultural hesitation about immediacy', Grusin writes (2004: 22). It would be far more reassuring, paradoxically, if television and other media anticipated possible future threats to pre-empt the possibility of being caught off guard again – even if this means depicting normality as essentially insecure and dangerous and the next major attack as never far away (temporally or spatially).

Hence, and in sum, Grusin argues that the nexus of rupture and normality is managed through premediation, whereby television plays an important role in containing the terror of future attacks by anticipating – or speculating on – their nature, timing, and location. Later in this chapter we will see whether British audiences' consumption of news media since 9/11 reflects Grusin's thesis or whether insecurity is managed in different ways. Ξ A second temporal nexus in the new security environment, though perhaps also a permanent feature of representative democracy, is that between urgency and patience. As Barnett argues, the action and responsibilities associated with decision-making in a democracy are characterised by the interplay between these two temporal registers (Barnett, 2004: 507). On the one hand, there are occasions when we as a political community, often via our elected representatives, need to arrive at urgent, binding decisions. On the other hand, building consent for decisions often entails slow negotiation, particularly when disagreement exists on the nature of the very problems at hand. The frustration expressed by John Reid, British Home Secretary, that his ability to make and implement decisions is impeded by those who 'don't get it', suggests an elected politician who feels he lacks sufficient time for the painstaking argumentation involved in winning consent for radical policy changes. Given his definition of the imminent threat of 'unconstrained international terrorists' and the responsibility of his office to keep citizens safe above all else, the need to slow down, take dissenting opinions into account, and allow himself to be taken into account, may appear misplaced. Bruno Latour (2003: 143) writes of frustrations with this aspect of politics:

> When one says that someone or something is 'political', one signals above all this fundamental disappointment, as if it were no longer possible to move forwards in a straight line, reasonably, quickly, efficiently, but necessary to 'take into account', 'a whole lot of' 'extra-rational factors' of which one fails to clearly understand all the ins and outs but which form an obscure, soft, heavy, round mass that sticks to those with the best intentions and, judging by what they say, seems to slow them down. The expression 'that's political' means first and foremost 'it doesn't move straight', 'it doesn't move fast'; it always implies that 'if only we didn't have this load, we'd achieve our goal more *directly*'.

In the ethnographic audience research we find that while interviewees evaluated policies (indefinite detention, shoot-to-kill policing, pre-emptive strikes, and preventative war) in terms of the justness or efficacy of the policy, they also responded to the temporal aspect of these policies. Consider the following exchange with John, a builder in Swansea:

> John: Before we went to war with Iraq, police weren't carrying guns in their country, as they do now, they'll be carrying guns now for evermore. That's it! It'll always be a thing now! You've got to not forget now that time was on their side, not on our side!
>
> Interviewer: Whose side? The terrorists?
>
> John: Yes.
>
> Interviewer: Why's that?
>
> John: Well, they're in no rush; they'll do their business when they're ready. They're not going to stop.
>
> Interviewer: So do you think our country is a more insecure place because of it?
>
> John: Well, these people set themselves up and they do something when it's right for them, no hurry. We're in a hurry to get the war over with. When are the troops going to come home? They'll never come home! Never!

John emphasises the temporal aspect of the War on Terror. Britain is changed 'for evermore', now that police carry guns. Meanwhile, he identifies a disparity between the urgent nature of the security problem for the British government and both the terrorists' luxury of patience and the necessity of keeping British troops in Iraq indefinitely. It is also interesting that John connects British intervention in Iraq with terrorist threats in Britain.

Following the police killing of Brazilian plumber Jean Charles de Menezes in August 2005, interviewees expressed surprise by what appeared a shoot-to-kill policy. The speed of policy makes it difficult for citizens to keep up, opening a gap of incomprehension and incredulity. As one 15-year-old girl in East London comments (italics added):

> Shahed: What I don't understand is...9/11, that's what happened. The year after that, all this time, during this time he was really focused on Bin Laden how to get him. *Suddenly* he's gone toward Saddam Hussein. George Bush goes towards Saddam Hussein. That's what I really don't understand.

Security policy in this period featured the primacy of urgency over patience, it has been argued elsewhere (Moss and O'Loughlin, forthcoming). So, if citizens did *not* accept government definitions of terror threat, or accepted the risk as manageable and no reason to alter 'normalcy', then the lack of a well-argued and coherent security policy would be exposed. The persuasive effect of the government's cloud of justifications of the Iraq war in 2003 was negated, to some extent, by the absence of coherent justification over time. For example, in the following extract two 15-year-old girls in East London described the changing justifications of the Iraq war (italics added):

Interviewer: Speaking of that, what were your views about the war? Were they the same or did they change?

Angela: I think they changed. We went in there to get weapons of mass destruction but it kind of turned into getting rid of Saddam 'cause they found out there wasn't really any weapons.

Abby: I think that was never really the reason. They all had their own reasons, their own motives and *they were constantly trying to find new reasons* to try and support it. Most people argued that if they did it to stop Saddam Hussein there are a lot of other even worse dictators in the world they could have got as well and why are they choosing Saddam Hussein?

Angela: Exactly. There are a lot of coincidences there, they have ulterior motives.

The girls' perception of inconsistent policy justifications opened a space, such that they doubted the political representative's motives, casting doubt on the credibility of their policies.

We have suggested in this section that certain temporal registers, normality/rupture and urgency/patience, will bear upon shifting perceptions of security and terror. Let us now see how these tempos 'play out' as we identify and explore the discursive realities of citizens in some detail.

Perceptions of security in everyday lives: pen portraits

In this section, we identify the discursive realities that determine individuals' perceptions of threat, terror, and security. We draw on an ethnographic audience data to suggest how these different discursive realities operate and how they 'push' and 'pull' against one another to form a dynamic interaction order. We present this through a series of 'pen portraits' of individuals, families, and groups based on their discussions with our interviewers.[4] Rather than present separate analyses of how political, then media, then experiential realities contributed to interviewees' perceptions, we feel pen portraits illuminate the importance of the interaction of the three discursive realities in producing perceptions of 'real' threats.

Each pen portrait highlights something salient to our examination of the perceptions of threat, terror, and security in the interaction order. The first three raise the issue of the 'reality' of events and the relation between reality and proximity. Portraits 4 and 5 focus on the interaction of media and religious beliefs. Finally, portraits 6 and 7 explore the relation between media representations of Islam and terrorism and the potential racist 'backlash' against Muslims in local communities in Britain.

Pen portrait 1. Luke

Luke is a 21-year-old student and Muslim convert living in Edinburgh. He talked to the interviewer about his attendance at the 'Central' mosque in Edinburgh and an occasion when friends there discussed the need to avoid talking about terrorist threats in case anyone overhearing them might report them to the police. The War on Terror was certainly proximate to his life. As he said, 'I know the Algerian guy...at the mosque that was arrested for making sweets in his house'. This refers to the arrest on 12 February 2002 in Edinburgh of nine Algerian men on terrorism charges. (The charges were later dropped.) Luke's primary insecurity was government security policy. He expressed his agreement with the *Power of Nightmares* thesis (see Chapter 7), suggesting to the interviewer that governments today have no ideological mission so are 'using this [general terror threat] as a kind of...tool of power'.

Luke told the interviewer he did not feel threatened by terrorism, and challenged the notion of a clash of civilisations. Asked if he was worried about a polarisation between Western democracy and Islam, he replied:

> That it's polarised? Why would that worry me, the idea of the clash of civilisations worry me? Well I think the idea of clash of civilisations is too polemic to be real. I don't think it really exists you know, I don't think those sort of ideas have any real power.

Luke's justification for disputing the 'reality' of the discourse was his experience, both of living in Britain and of travelling in the Middle East, and his political knowledge. He displayed a high degree of political literacy and told the interviewer he consumed Western and Arabic news sources through radio, television, press, and the Internet. Used to searching for and analysing (comparatively) this range of news sources, for Luke, the world is too complex to be adequately described by a 'polemic'.[5] Instead of viewing the interaction order as defined by fixed discourses, Luke viewed political–media–citizen relations as malleable. He continues to talk about the clash of civilisations thesis:

> I think to be worried about it is very negative. I think you should more try to change that. And you can change that by just making people think about, erm, Muslims not as Muslims but as Ali, Mohammed, Hussain, you know, as people, and bridging those gaps.

From this first portrait we see how citizens, who draw upon their own knowledge and experience, challenge the terms and parameters of public political debate. Luke would prefer to see a patient process of bridging gaps in political relations than further urgent security policies and polemic discourses.

Pen portrait 2. George and Lynne

George and Lynne are a married couple with teenage children. They also live in Edinburgh. George is a senior manager in a financial organisation and Lynne is a housewife who commits time to charity work on poverty and fair trade issues. Both vote Labour and support Tony Blair. An interesting episode occurred in their lives around the G8 summit in July 2005 that took place in Scotland and which coincided with the 7/7 London bombings. The G8 summit was a global event that was – on a spatial axis – local to George and Lynne, and they expressed strong but opposing reactions to what happened. Exploring these reactions tells us more about the interaction order.

As riots occurred in the streets of Edinburgh, Lynne had felt excited, she told the interviewer. Lynne was ready to go on a 'Make Poverty History' march, consistent with her interest in the political issues to be debated at the G8 summit. Seeing police in the streets of her city, she comments:

> It was just – it was everywhere, it was kind of round about, in rather surreal ways . . . So I felt a bit involved but on the periphery . . . I think I was more interested in that the bombings . . . I don't remember feeling threatened or can't – I don't really remember anything specific about it actually.

Entangled emotionally, politically, and physically in the events in Edinburgh, Lynne devoted little attention to the London bombings and did not feel threatened by them. Nor did she feel insecure in Edinburgh, despite feeling 'involved'. Her husband experienced the events very differently. For George, news had been something that happened 'out there'. But on this day, protestors besieged his bank. George was not at the bank, but he became horrified as he spoke on the phone to his staff and learned how threatened they were. News became 'real', for George (emphasis added):

> I had staff who – remember the street that was blocked off, I can't remember the name of it [...] one of the buildings – we had people in and I was on the phone to one of my managers who works for me and he was literally saying there is people trying to climb in the window, you know there's mounted police with batons drawn, there's big crowds, we've been told 'don't leave the building'. So *it became very real, extremely real, far too real for me* and eh so a certain extent I watched some of the news coverage (Lynne: I watched a lot) em but I actually almost found it too personal. Didn't like watching it and didn't watch it as much regarding the G8 and the Edinburgh situation.

In fact, then, the news became *too* real for George, and he responded by turning away. As the manager responsible for the safety of his staff, he was implicated in the events. Experiencing the event through television news and telephone contact with those at the scene, the interaction order was very intense for George and he experienced this as a reality overload from which he preferred to turn away.

Pen portrait 3. Young mothers in East London

The sudden insecurity felt by George raises the question of whether viewers ever choose to keep news at a distance. In another interview, Ella, a friend of George and Lynne, mentions that she avoids news about global warming:

> I mean it is a bit of blotting out just to be able to get on with life and not to be permanently worried.
> There's enough to worry about near without having to worry about that as well.

Ella is exercising some control over her engagement with news, even if she appears aware that that she is avoiding the issue that news could relay to her. We find the same behaviour in other interviewees, in particular young mothers. In a focus group with four white twenty-something women in East London, each accounted for their habit of keeping potential anxieties at a distance. The interviewer asked if they were worried about any threat of terrorism:

> Aisha: At first it's like 'what's gonna happen?' We're hearing things on the news every day so 'what are we gonna do?' but on the other hand we've had IRA terror threats for years.
>
> Gemma: Exactly you've got to live your life...Every time you go to Spain there's always some bomb that goes off like in Madrid airport or something like that so you just can't...
>
> Interviewer: So you don't think, and I'm asking this to you as individuals, that the chances of an Al Qaeda attack are realistic?
>
> Aisha: No, I actually do.
>
> Jody: They may be a threat but it's not something you spend your whole life thinking about.
>
> Interviewer: You don't worry about it?
>
> Gemma: No, not really, you can't or you'd never leave your front door.

The young women identify a trade-off between worrying about threats and the quality of their everyday lives and decide upon preserving their quality of life. This decision must be seen within the context of a media ecology (Cottle, 2006) that surrounds them with threats. Despite a general scepticism towards news media, the women ultimately treat these threats as real. In the following extract, we see how concern with personal security and paedophilia are issues that Aisha appears to negotiate at a routine level.

> Aisha: When you see a package...that could be Al Qaeda anyhow. But you read something everyday. Paedophiles; if you've got children you are worried about this kind of thing. If you go to the toilet in McDonald's you've got to keep your eyes open and that's a natural every day fear you're gonna have every day anyway.
>
> Interviewer: So for you you'd say that the paedophile fear would be one of the fears that you've felt quite strongly?
>
> Aisha: Absolutely, every time I hear about it it's one of those things that I can't even bear to think about. You have to block it out of your head really quickly.
>
> Interviewer: So it is a fear that you think is very real?

Aisha: Ha?

Interviewer: So the stuff you hear about paedophiles in the news, you think it's all true?

Aisha: Yes. Absolutely.

Gemma: I agree.

Aisha: Especially with all the internet and everything it's getting worse – well, I don't know if it is because I don't know how it was before. It may be something that people are more honest about now and the media, even themselves, can be more honest about because it might have been a bit of a taboo for them before. I don't know if it is more rife today, I just know with the internet and everything it is a lot easier for it to be done. Your child can be at home and be a victim of a paedophile and that's from home.

What seems particularly at stake for these interviewees is ontological security. Ontological security refers to our familiarity and trust towards the world around us, formed by acting in and upon that world in our daily routines and social life such that life becomes manageable (Giddens, 1984). Increased media coverage of a range of issues, whether global warming, paedophilia, or terrorism, intrudes upon their 'peace of mind'. Viewers must negotiate their consumption of this coverage, making a trade-off between peace of mind and staying informed. News coverage offering premediation – news that identifies and speculates on future security threats – may be rejected by viewers since it offers a 'normalcy' of perpetual anxiety. There are other ways to manage insecurity, including turning the television off.

Seeing how viewers exercise this capacity to control their consumption within the context of their everyday lives sheds light on how and why viewers understand the 'reality' of terrorist threats. No matter the objective status of threat that political leaders speak of; citizens are aware of what they can 'deal with' in their lives, and if something is 'too real', as George put it, they may prefer to 'block it out' than accept or confront it. Indeed, the modulation of terror is performed by consumers of media as well as media producers.

The next two pen portraits explore the relation between media coverage of security issues and citizens' religious beliefs.

Pen portrait 4. Ruby and Rhamat

George and Lynne had an intensive moment within the interaction order, but there may also be *extensive* features to audiences/citizens'

engagements within the intersection of media, politics, and immediate experience. For instance, their interaction with news media may
involve an indirect but long-term engagement with an issue. Political, media, and experiential 'discursive realities' often have enduring
features. Through interviews with Ruby and Rhamat, for instance, we
see a relation between memory and media templates that contributes
to Ruby and Rhamat's perceptions of security events and terror (indeed
this connects to our discussion of 'media templates' in Chapter 2).

Ruby and Rhamat are a Sunni Muslim mother and daughter again
living in Edinburgh. Ruby is in her fifties and unemployed, and Rhamat
is in her mid-twenties and on a professional graduate scheme. The
interviewer showed them a number of still images from newspaper
coverage of the 7/7 London bombings of July 2005. For Ruby, images
blur across newspapers and television. She is unsure where she saw
images and attributes this to the rapid turnover of images on television
news bulletins. The interviewer asks Ruby if she has seen images like
these before:

> Ruby: I think when you reflect back – not specific ones of this
> but images of September 11th, but I suppose that was the most
> horrendous thing, that was worse.
> Interviewer: So these remind you of those images?
> Ruby: Yeah but that was on a larger scale, that was just horrendous –
> even [a] whole building, such a huge, huge building, the whole
> building came down, destruction and uproar and pandemonium I
> suppose.

Images of 7/7 evoke thoughts of 9/11. But note the important 'I
suppose' at the end of Ruby's comparison. She is inferring how the experience might have been. The mediation of television invites this; apart
from exceptions such as the experience of George and Lynne within the
G8 protest, we can never be there. Later in the interview Ruby mentions
she saw a documentary about the plane flights of 9/11 – a reconstruction based on the phone calls made to families on the day. Again she
attempts to bridge the distance between herself and those involved, or
put herself in their position, saying it was 'quite frightening what the
passengers must have gone through'. Rhamat appears to connect to the
incident through the documentary's personalisation of events:

> Rhamat: It's really interesting, I don't know, because I'm such a strong
> believer and it was interesting what each member of the family was

saying about their – whoever they'd lost on that plane – they were very – 'if you knew him you'd find out he was very strong, he would never give up'. It was so scary how each one of them said 'he was a black belt in this' and 'he was a martial – he was strong in this'. I thought you know I really believe that God...he wouldn't wish this upon anyone...you know this kind of thing, he would make sure that people were strong enough to cope, tolerate it you know, have the strength to tolerate it.

Ruby: Well that's what we believe, yeah.

Rhamat: I really believe that yeah. He wouldn't have just chosen anyone to be on that plane. They were able to – well they fought back you know.

Ruby and Rhamat interpret the re-mediation of the events of 9/11 through their particular religious prism, in the process re-confirming their beliefs. It appears they negotiate the media 'discursive reality' that portrays shocking events such as 9/11 by recourse to the certainties of their religious 'discursive reality'. Through that prism, Ruby and Rhamat are able to cope with such shocking events. Their ontological security is maintained.

Pen portrait 5. Tower Hamlets teenagers

Focus groups with Bengali-Muslim teenagers in Tower Hamlets, East London, revealed more about the complex interactions between political, media, and experiential discursive realities. As for Ruby and Rhamat, religious belief bears strongly upon interpretations of security events. As Al-Ghabban (2007) notes in his analysis of these focus groups, a conflation of circumstances leads many of the teenagers to interpret events through a fatalistic – even apocalyptic – prism. Consider the following extract in which the teenagers discuss the significance of the Asian tsunami of 2004:

Habiba: It's a wake-up call for the world, innit?

Interviewer: What d'you mean?

Rumena: Like the end of the world is coming.

Habiba: Like you don't have much time, do you? The wave just showed people that you might just die *next day* [her emphasis].

Interviewer: So how does that make you feel about life then, when you say it like that?

Habiba: It's coming to an end.

Rumena: There's signs in different ways that I can see it. There's signs.
   Signs in religious terms and signs in the world terms.
Habiba: The war in Iraq, it's just like the Third World War, innit?
Interviewer: So you're saying the war in Iraq is 'a sign'?
Rumena: A lot of people are dying in the world for no reason. [...]

As they continue, note how their conversation oscillates between the global and the local, and between human conflict and natural disaster, as if everything were connected within a single, complex interaction order (or disorder)[6]:

Habiba: Because the world's more advanced, all the things are more...
Rumena: [overlapping] It was probably safer twenty years ago, than it
   is now.
Habiba: All the ammunition they have now and [...]
Rumena: Crime.
Habiba: If you think about the East End, say for example, where we
   live, you know. Crime's just increasing so fast.
Interviewer: What else makes you think that the world's a scarier
   place?
Habiba: The war in Iraq.
Interviewer: And what else?
Rumena: The Tsunami...
Habiba: Yeah.

The teenagers appear to depict a world in which forces 'out there' control events leaving them in an entirely passive position, left only to notice 'signs' and be prepared for a sudden death. Al-Ghabban argues that, in fact, a fatalistic position is consistent with the politico-religious, media, and experiential 'discursive realities' that we argue structure perspectives of the interaction order:

One can see how a social context of poverty and disempowerment in conjunction with media discourses about an impending terrorist attack and quasi-religious convictions about fate, death and 'judgement day' don't simply interact loosely but lock into, or are forcibly articulated with one another.

(Al-Ghabban, 2007)

The three discursive realities reinforce one another. One cannot identify a single factor explaining why these teenagers hold such apocalyptic worldviews (e.g. 'Islam'). It is the particular configuration of discursive realities that result in any perception of threat, terror, and insecurity.

Our final two pen portraits scrutinise an element of the contemporary interaction order that alarmed both white secular/Christian interviewees and Muslim interviewees: the relation between media coverage of Islam and terrorism and the possibility of a racist 'backlash' against Muslims in Britain.

Pen portrait 6. Muslims in northern industrial towns

In our first pen portrait, we saw how Luke rejected the 'power' of the 'clash of civilisations' discourse. Yet the ethnographic data contained evidence that this discourse is experienced by interviewees as instantiated or realised, and on many occasions. A series of focus groups with Muslim men and women living in several industrial towns in Yorkshire and Lancashire reveal how news media and state security practices are felt to 'reach into' their lives such that it appears Muslims are being victimised.[7] For instance, while complaints of media misrepresentation of Muslims and Islam were voiced before the 7/7 London bombings, in the period following the bombings interviewees perceived an intensification of this misrepresentation such that it became inescapable. In the following extract, Asim, a 29-year-old solicitor in Bradford, offered his view of post-7/7 media coverage and connected it to how he was perceived by non-Muslims:

> Asim: As for the media coverage, it was just a free for all, for them to have their field day or field month or field year against Islam, which has been building up slowly slowly since September 11. But now it's been made more relevant to the British people, because it was always something that happened elsewhere but now it's something that happened on your own doorstep, and it's, I mean, really the media have unleashed every bit of hatred they've got within them, every bit of misrepresentation or scare mongering. You can actually feel it now. You can feel the way the attitudes of people have changed towards you. If you work with non-Muslim people who are really quite indifferent to us, at one point we were just a different colour a different name a different set of...but I think you're looked at evil, suspicious...

7/7 acted as a catalytic event, from Asim's account, amplifying insecurity for Muslims as news media unleashed 'every bit of hatred they've

got' that had previously been contained. For many Muslim interviewees, their suspicion of an intrinsically anti-Muslim news media was
confirmed by the reporting of the 7/7 bombings:

> Khan: When we found out we were at work, at reception, plasma
> screen, everyone was crowding round...one thing I was quite
> shocked about was almost as soon as the information was coming
> in, 'cause I think they said initially it was a power surge, but then
> as soon as they said it was a bomb, straight away kind of said
> 'Muslim radical', which I thought was a bit [unfair] since nobody
> had [known] straight away, I found [this] a bit weird...

The media surround or ecology was experienced as hostile. Equally,
the state was experienced as reaching into Muslim lives. Asim again
offers his perspective:

> [T]here is a great deal of suspicion out there: stop and search. Now that's
> interesting because working in criminal litigation you come across a
> lot of youngsters from an ethnic minority and it's a recurring theme
> that comes again and again, not that we're stopped because we're
> Pakistanis anymore but we're stopped because we're Muslims. There's
> a lot of people saying that, and it's alright one little idiot saying that
> to you and you just brush him off but then when fifty of them say
> that to you start to think, 'hold on maybe they're right'. You get a
> lot of people being picked up for the most trivial offences and then
> that being an excuse to look through the car, and 'actually we'd like
> to have a look at your house as well'. You know the craziest thing is
> that these people are not even in the slightest way religiously inclined,
> they're just street kids who haven't got the foggiest about religion.

The state was experienced as reaching into their communities and
their homes, and was a presence while travelling – tales of perceived
discrimination at airport customs were frequent.

As we might expect, interviewees responded differently to the
'surround' of media and state depending on the particular configuration of political, media and experiential 'discursive realities' in their
lives. Some Muslims interviewed who complained about media misrepresentation believed that engagement with the political culture was the
only way to change that culture. Critical of existing Muslim political
'representatives' who are 'in their own bubble', a group of three Muslim
women in Oldham express a relatively politicised subjectivity:

Bina: Some people think you've just got to work that extra harder now, just got to wake up and work that much more, to get rid of these misconceptions...

Sofie: I think that's the one thing that has [...] been a good thing for the Muslim community. It's got us off our backsides to do something, so all these years, all these things have happened [...]

Reshma: We've isolated ourselves.

Sofie: Exactly, you know, our own communities.

Interviewer: It's like forcing us to engage

Sofie: Yeah and that's a good thing.

They had been involved in government consultations but were looking for other forms of engagement. Strategies for engagement was a recurring theme among younger Muslims. Discussions focused on the relative merits of becoming a journalist in the 'mainstream' political culture or launching specifically Muslim news media and of joining an existing 'mainstream' political party or wondering whether only a specifically Muslim party could offer adequate representation. Many interviewees suggest that engagement with the existing liberal media and liberal political culture, albeit in new and more vigorous ways, would better realise their goals than separate Islamic media or parties. This has implications for how we consider the ongoing battle for legitimacy. It appears these interviewees felt incumbent politicians and government policies lacked legitimacy, but the political system itself *could still be* the arena for generating legitimate policies.

But there were also instances of disengagement and a turning away from the political culture. Masood, a businessman of Pakistani Muslim origin living in Edinburgh, described an experience when he, his wife, and his children were detained at customs, an experience that altered his perceptions of Britain as a 'liberal', 'tolerant' society (Qureshi, 2006; see also Qureshi, 2007). 'There was a time I would have been prepared to die for this country', he said. Masood expressed a notion labelled 'myth of return': he and his wife had kept assets in Pakistan because they felt life for Muslims in Britain was precarious and insecure. This extreme insecurity was not isolated: Muslim interviewees in Oxford and Lancashire also spoke about the 'myth of return'. Thus, while racism and media misrepresentation were triggers for political engagement for some interviewees, others considered leaving the country altogether.

Such responses can be subsumed within a tendency among Muslim interviewees to 'second guess' non-Muslim (usually white) perceptions of Muslims. Yet an examination of the role of media and security policy in the perceptions of insecurity – and in particular a racist backlash against Muslims – must also explore non-Muslim perspectives. Let us turn to these next.

Pen portrait 7. Debbie and Florence

Debbie and Florence are working-class women in their twenties living in Swansea, Wales. Their main sources of news media are GMTV in the morning and two newspapers, their local *Evening Post* and the *Daily Express*. They expressed a feeling of being distanced from and bored by politics. Their perspective on Islam and a racist backlash against Muslims in their own communities is a revealing counterpoint to pen portrait 6. The two women repeatedly asserted their own tolerance, Debbie saying 'Live and let live, that's my motto', but there is no doubt that Muslims are an unknown other:

> Interviewer: Have you ever met anyone from that religion?
> Florence: No not really. I've got nothing against them, I don't mind any religion, I would talk to any religion. I wouldn't...I couldn't be nasty to people. You know they say the asylum seekers are coming in and having this and that. I couldn't be nasty to them.
> Debbie: (inaudible) it's just how it is. Their life is as (inaudible) as ours at the end of the day. To be fair, I can imagine, when you see all the people taunting them and chucking things and that.
> Interviewer: Do you see that?
> Debbie: No, well, it might be on the news and you read the paper.

Spontaneously, a connection is made between Muslims and asylum seekers, and asylum seekers 'having this and that' with the implied zero sum trade-off that others must be losing. Florence says of those resentful towards asylum seekers, 'they think we're getting a raw deal'. 'They' seem a generalised local opinion from which Debbie and Florence distance themselves. Later, however, Florence also connects asylum seekers to terrorism, saying 'you know they're going to do something like blow us up!' The interviewees talk of their fear of Muslims in Islamic dress:

> Florence: When they're dressed in black like that, you know, I don't understand that, why they wear all that? For what reason? They wear all that charade!
> Debbie: Yeah, and that's a bit frightening! In itself, isn't it? You see someone coming towards you on the bus or whatever, and they were wearing a big coat and mask and all, and you can't see

them, can you, you can't see their faces. That's what I don't like really.

Debbie and Florence explain local negative feeling towards Muslims within a broader context of a loss of community. Debbie compares her mother's tales of knowing 'everyone' in Swansea to the 'all languages and nationalities' that now make up the population, saying it has 'all gone to ruin, with everything'. Here, 'everything' includes street crime and economic insecurity alongside a decline of community cohesion. For individuals like Debbie and Florence, this configuration of discursive realities may become self-reinforcing. With little political engagement, a media discursive reality informed by the anti-immigrant *Daily Express*, and an experiential reality dominated by loss of community and a range of insecurities, it may make a certain sense to look for sources of blame. This may explain why blame is often put on the stranger – the unknown, threatening other (Dench et al., 2006). Yet Debbie and Florence appear extremely curious about Islam as a religion, and in particular the position of women – Debbie mentions 'I go through town...you see the women too frightened to look at you...And yet the men can walk and do what they please!' Personal contact with Muslims might alleviate the fears and suspicions held by Debbie and Florence, disrupting the existing configuration of discursive realities.

An interview with two more working-class white women in Swansea elicited similar ambiguities. Hayley and Claire, playgroup workers, describe the complex interaction order between local minorities, the 2003 Iraq war, media portrayal of Muslims, and the possibility of future terrorist attacks by Muslims. In doing so, they arrive at a pessimistic logic:

> Hayley: I don't know. I think that now in some ways I'm more aware of like Muslims...I do take more notice of them now, and like where they are and stuff.
>
> Interviewer: Why's that?
>
> Claire: It's like a cliché isn't it? The Indians running the corner shop! [...]
>
> Hayley: And yeah, because their religion is being, is so portrayed in a bad way...they're likely to lash out more. If you're being treated bad, it causes you to react to it. If you were left alone, everyone would just, like, live. But because everything's been made so much worse now, with the war, 'all Muslims are bad, blah blah blah',

they're much more likely to go 'well actually we're not, pay attention to us!'
Claire: And that's going to make things worse, and they could do
some worse stuff.

In pen portrait 6, we saw how some young Muslims aspired to
challenge perceived media misrepresentations and make the white
majority pay attention to a positive Islam. Yet Hayley and Claire
suggest the interaction order leaves room only for further conflict,
that negative news media portrayal will provoke Muslims to respond
aggressively.

In sum, these pen portraits have illuminated the diverse processes by
which citizens' perceptions of terror, threat, and security are formed.
We have seen how shifting discursive realities can combine or conflict,
pull together or pull apart, on temporal and indeed spatial axes. We
have also seen how citizens' engagement with news media and representations of threats must be viewed as a situated process. Citizens must
routinely decide how much 'reality' they can cope with, as they seek
to preserve their ontological security. The modulation of threat is done
by consumers of news media as well as producers. In light of this, we
hope to have contributed to an understanding of why such differing
perceptions of terror threat exist.

The modulation of terror and the prospects for democracy

At first glance, it would appear that media-driven transformations of the
interaction order imperil democracy. This is particularly the case if we
assume that a viable democratic system must overlap with a coherent
national public sphere.[8] The consumption of media is fragmenting due
to the proliferation of news channels and Internet sites. Even if citizens
choose to stick to a limited range of news sources, they cannot but be
aware of the existence of a diverse news 'menu'. Production too appears
to fragment. New technologies allow 'democratic' news production in
the form of blogging, 'citizen journalists' offering cameraphone footage
from disaster zones, and terrorists' hostage videos. The trend is towards
a situation whereby anyone can put anything 'out there' into what
becomes a global public sphere. Given the apparent tendency towards
niche channels and audiences, and the transnational nature of much
media production and consumption, what chance for national public
debates? No wonder McNair titles his recent book on media and democracy *Cultural Chaos* (McNair, 2006). To return to Lippmann's remarks

on the difficulty of assembling a demos, what chance for a 'common world' where similarly informed citizens can debate matters of shared concern and generate consent for government policies?

The battle for legitimacy becomes more complex and difficult. One consequence of the fragmentation of media production and consumption is that any governmental or political discourse becomes 'exposed' to an unprecedented extent. The following quote is from an unnamed aide to President George W. Bush, in 2002, before the Iraq war. He is speaking to *New York Times* journalist Ron Suskind (2004):

> The aide said that guys like me were 'in what we call the reality-based community', which he defined as people who 'believe that solutions emerge from your judicious study of discernible reality'. [...] 'That's not the way the world really works anymore', he continued. 'We're an empire now, and when we act, we create our own reality. And while you're studying that reality – judiciously, as you will – we'll act again, creating other new realities, which you can study too, and that's how things will sort out. We're history's actors . . . and you, all of you, will be left to just study what we do'.

This hubristic drive to author world history, the notion of straightforwardly ordering global order, look slightly misjudged in the light of Abu Ghraib, Guantanamo Bay, Fallujah, Haditha, daily killings in Iraq, and other contradictions of the 'reality' the US administration may have wished to create. This may seem an extreme example, but our point is that the very idea of an authoritative voice, of watertight knowledge, whether in the pronouncements of major television networks and 'paper of record' press, or by our political and military leaders and officials, is problematised. Moral high ground is very difficult to achieve and sustain in an age of fact-checking bloggers and mobile cameraphones. Indeed, leaders often know their statements will offend some part of their public and that counter-statements will emerge. Provoking a minority becomes an occupational hazard, perhaps even a strategy. An instance of the panic this brings politicians occurred in Britain during the 2005 General Election campaign, when a Conservative candidate sent out leaflets with different messages to white and Asian communities in his constituency. Charter (2005) writes, 'Humfrey Malins, the Tory candidate in Woking, wrote in Urdu to Muslim voters asking for support over his record on helping with visas and visits, while predominantly white areas received a tough message on reducing immigration'. It is as if Malins had given up on the notion of a single demos.

Against this backdrop, the analysis presented in this chapter has demonstrated why it is that politicians' public pronouncements on the existence and nature of terror threats are likely to receive diverse responses from citizens. Shifting discursive realities from citizens' perspectives on terror, threat, and insecurity, and these discursive realities shift at different tempos, pushing and pulling against one another, which can have the effect of reinforcing or disrupting those perceptions. The 'reality' of terror threats may seem very different as a result of this process. And while political and religious beliefs bear upon perceptions of reality and security, so does the preservation of peace of mind. Citizens are in a position of actively managing their own perceptions of security, vis-à-vis their consumption of media and engagement with politics and events, and it may be that government definitions of terror threats are not always reconcilable with ontological security.

If this analysis has alerted us to the difficulty of achieving a 'common world', we nevertheless wish to close this chapter by refuting the notion that political disconnection and a 'legitimacy deficit' are a necessary or enduring consequence. It is clear that all the interviewees shared certain same matters of concern. *Everybody* had an opinion about Iraq and terrorism. And yet, everybody had a different perspective and could turn to different sources of knowledge. Fragmentation of media production and consumption may reinforce tendencies towards diverse opinions, but provided these opinions are about shared matters of concern, this is surely a condition for democratic engagement. The problem, then, is achieving a democratic system to which all citizens feel they *can* connect when they see fit, such that certain perspectives are not *a priori* excluded. As we saw earlier in the chapter, some older Muslim interviewees responded to what they perceived to be a culture of media misrepresentation, inadequate political representation, and a resulting anti-Muslim backlash in their everyday lives, by expressing a 'myth of return' notion. Their insecurity compelled them to consider leaving Britain. However, more optimistically, a number of younger Muslim interviewees talked about vibrant debates and activity amongst their peers concerning strategies to engage with and become represented within British media and democracy. They wished to bring their political beliefs, their often-transnational and multilingual media diet, and their particular local experiences to bear upon national debates and policymaking processes. Discourses such as 'clash of civilisations' were not 'real' but polemics to be undermined through patient efforts to explain and bridge positions.

We have referred to television throughout this book as a renewed media. And one test of democratic institutions is their capacity for renewal. Fragmented media practices and diverse, shifting realities are not inconsistent with political engagement. In fact, it may be that after decades of increasing political disconnection, it will be around security issues that the demos can be re-assembled and democracy renewed.

9
The Irresolution of Television

Television news discourse is in crisis. The technological and textual transformations in twenty-first century television are inseparable from the post-9/11 environment of insecurity. Television's economy of liveness and visually intensive interaction order is at the centre of new media and security ecologies that have marked the new century. The relationship between television and terror in this period is subject to a process we label 'media renewal'. This is the process in which television in particular appropriates 'news content' and constructs the existence of news as if contingent upon the medium itself. This is not just to say that television news is reflexive in shaping the stories upon which it reports and that the medium remediates (refashions) other media (Bolter and Grusin, 1999) but that it also 'renews' itself through its constant discursive self-attention and verbal and graphic self-consciousness. In this way, renewal functions to promote television's constative (authenticating and validating) presence in the interaction order, continually seeking new parts for itself in the script of the moment. And it is these scripts which are increasingly more adventurous as television seeks to function as author, historian, and prophet, simultaneously transcending and filling time (and place).

The crisis of television news discourse develops from the contradictions in the medium's destabilising/stabilising regime. Television news chases its tail and then determinedly holds up and scrutinises this same process as a measure of its own success. For instance, Luhmann (2000: 39) argues, 'The mass media seem simultaneously to nurture and to undermine their own credibility. They "deconstruct" themselves, since they reproduce the constant contradiction of their constative and their performative textual components with their own operations'. While we do not embrace Luhmann's (2000) wholesale reduction of the 'system' of the mass media to the 'autopoietic' (self-producing and self-contained) operations of technical codes, the internal workings and contradictions that he identifies in the workings of television contribute to what we have explored here as media renewal. Let us elaborate.

As Mellencamp (2006: 128) states, 'With its strategy of creation/ contradiction/cancellation, TV is the outbreak and the protective action'. We have argued that television news modulates between these functions. It is unable to stem the terrorism that exploits its own connectivity, yet as a system it nonetheless has a regulatory mechanism – constitutive of and subject to an interaction order. For all the technological shifts embedded in the huge social, cultural, and political transformations over the past quarter of a century, it is this system that has become even more *attuning of* and *attuned to* the rituals and routines of its publics.

Ultimately, television news has to contain and render familiar and safe the terrors that it imagines and delivers, for if it did not do so it could render itself obsolete, unable to attract and maintain the audiences who largely collude in the safety of sanitisation and massive selectivity, as enforced by the medium's 'standards of taste and decency'.

The tensions in public and political discourses as to the viability, legitimacy, and 'progress' of the War on Terror are not merely reflected or refracted in media representations, but are actually inextricably bound up in the *pre*sentation of the electronic media (Lash, 2002: 71). Television news today has a very powerful capacity to predict, pre-empt, and even pre-meditate events, ushering in and regulating a climate of insecurity and terror. It is the 'oxygen' – or rather the pivotal 'actor' – in the connectivity that is required both by terrorists in disseminating terror and by those who proclaim to be engaged in fighting terror (either through assuaging or exacerbating threats depending on which serves their particular political and military objectives).

To summarise: the crisis in news discourse identified here results from a fundamental binary or contradiction in the operations of television news in the post-9/11 era.

Firstly, television news amplifies (and conflates) different threats and insecurities (economic, human, environmental) in a number of intersecting ways. It does this through the following:

- Promoting immediacy, intimacy, and visuality as core criteria for determining news agendas. This economy of liveness and connectivity coupled with the textual and graphic enhancements of 'televisuality' is the most effective global delivery system for terror events and discourses – and counter-discourses. In this way, it is not an exaggeration to state that the medium has become 'weaponised'. Television is not merely an instrument of war but an actual constituent of terrorism today.

- The expanded 'media vector' (the temporal and spatial tools, dimensions, and reach of television and other media) AND the expanded 'terror vector' (the fact that 'the price of terrorism has been brought down to zero' (Durodie, 2006)[1] intersect to effect new dimensions of coverage. This results in expanded news and informational space which serve to encourage an exponential growth in speculative public discourses (by journalists, 'experts', academics, pressure groups) on the nature of existing and potential security threats, their conflation, and potential responses by government and military forces. Conversely, this speculative, expansive chatter also diminishes the significance of responses, as each becomes part of a surfeit of information, images, and 'opinion' (see below).

Secondly, television news contains and assuages threats and insecurities through the following:

- *Repetition*: TV news's economy of liveness is matched by its compulsion to repeat, recycle, and reframe. Indeed, the value attributed to the footage of events selected for broadcast – owing to their greater dramatic immediacy and intimacy – is also one of the criteria for their re-selection and reuse. In fact, the notion of 'shock value' is a matter of ever-diminishing returns.
- *Fitting new stories into pre-existing templates that viewers are familiar with*: This might be considered to reduce uncertainty and provide reassurance as to likely and knowable outcomes. The archive is one of television's accumulating constative mechanisms, and it is increasingly accessible and retrievable.
- *Sanitising the violent 'excesses' of conflict and warfare*: Television news is subject to an economy of 'taste and decency' and to presumptions as to the sensitivities of audiences. Television, and television news in particular, is thus condemned by the thresholds (of its own producers, policymakers, and by audiences) that curtail the extent to which it can fully expose the worlds it connects and represents.

Hence, television news modulates between bringing the world's wars and catastrophes into the West's horizon of responsibility, while simultaneously blocking them from clear view. However, a corollary if not a consequence of the shifts of media renewal that we have identified is in the diminished usefulness and effectiveness of some of the traditional modes and methods of enquiry associated with televisual texts. In the opening chapter, we situate our approach in the context of these dominant and not-so-dominant schools of thought. Whereas once Media Sociologists pursued the Holy Grail of locating or differentiating graduations of 'meaning' in media texts, their receivers, and their producers, media renewal has ushered in a rather different set of challenges for those seeking a critical interpretative view of twenty-first century mass media.[2]

One of these challenges is how to engage with the issue of the surfeit or satiation of images, information, and that which is promoted as opinion. These appear to block or weaken what were once easily identifiable (or at least presumed) *collective* responses of shock to scenes of violence, atrocity, and warfare. For instance, Nicholas Mirzoeff (2005: 14) draws on Hannah Arendt's phrase to argue that a 'banality of images' results from their excess in the contemporary mediascape: 'the very awareness of the input of the viewer in creating meaning has paradoxically weakened that response. For if all meanings are personal response, the argument goes, then no one meaning has higher priority'. Television news today actually pursues and presents as 'news' a feedback loop of 'meaning' through a contradictory aggregation and disaggregation of responses to events. It obsesses over polls and surveys, claiming if not inferring to be identifying collective 'public opinion',[3] yet in covering and constructing those same events, TV news frequently incorporates the input of 'witnesses', bystanders, or just passers-by. The criterion for their selection often appears to be nothing more than their availability. The aggregation and disaggregation is further developed as viewers are directed to participate in surveys and invited to contribute their personal comments in response to articles, issues, and events, which are read out by presenters, and also appearing online as fragmented blogs, affording stories an extended present on the Web. Under the guise of interactivity, news texts thus reflexively incorporate a mass of concentrated and diffused 'opinion', becoming weighed down and diminished by its pursuit of its own impact while simultaneously weakening or devaluing public response.

Confidence in news texts has been eroded as television has become an increasingly central and immediate vehicle for the battle over the legitimacy of actions and of policy agendas in the War on Terror (Gow and Michalski, 2007). In this environment, featuring as it does the extension of local, national and global discourses on news events via the Web, we find that news reports of terror- and security-related events are potentially subject to more immediate and extensive challenge and counter-challenge. For instance, it is difficult to imagine how the impact of the footage of the bodies of children being carried from the rubble of Qana in southern Lebanon on 30 July 2006 could be contained or 'spun' by those supportive of the Israelis who had carried out this attack. Yet, this was precisely what did happen, with claims that some of the bodies of the children killed at Qana were carried back-and-forth in front of the cameras by men 'who weren't rescuers', implying that the present-ation of the incident (if not even the attack itself) had been staged as part of Hezbollah propaganda to undermine the Israeli military strategy. These allegations were made initially by bloggers but were then cited by mainstream news organisations. For instance, on BBC2's *Newsnight* programme on 31 July 2006, Tim Whewell interviewed Richard North, a conservative internet blogger, who claimed that the Qana disaster scene was more akin to a 'theatre set': 'not a record of a rescue but one of a vast, grotesque theatre, staged to maximise, to milk as much sympathy, as much empathy, and as much shock, out of the situation as possible'.

It is not just the content of North's claim that is significant, but that it is indicative of two trends: firstly, that there is a growing scrutiny of news images and the narratives constructed around them and a consequential growing mistrust of images which may quickly appear across a range of media. For example, Reuters sacked the Lebanese freelance photo-grapher Adnan Hajj once it was discovered that he had 'doctored' two photographs used by the news organisation. The published images were 'enhanced' with additional and darker smoke rising from the aftermath of an Israeli attack on Beirut and additional flares added to an Israeli jet in the sky.[4] Secondly, North's claim is indicative of the manner in which bloggers may become increasingly influential, although by no means dominant, in shaping the news agenda of mainstream media.

A final challenge concerns the role of audiences in modulating terrifying news. Our analysis suggests that while television struggles through its uneven oscillations between amplification and contain-ment of human, environmental, and economic insecurities, audiences are to some extent free to engage with news on their own terms, and in their own times. In managing and modulating their own intake of news about terrorism and war, citizens have diffuse and complex rela-tions with, and within, television's interaction order. They face several discursive realities – whether the reality of life at home, at work, in their communities, or the putative realities *pre*sented and relentlessly re-presented in media and political discourses. Hence, the nature of their responses, both to the crisis of news discourse and to today's increasingly securitised political discourses, is shifting and cannot be assumed. We have taken a small step forward in identifying how audiences' perceptions shift in relation to these discourses, to massive security events, and to everyday insecurities.[5] As the new ecology of images continues to transform over the next decade, understanding how viewers respond to – and shape – this environment (through their media consumption patterns, their political behaviour, and so on) is a critical issue that demands an interdisciplinarity from academics and their critical engagement with policy practitioners attempting to 'order' the War on Terror. While television news struggles with its own role, we must not lose sight of viewers' capacities to scrutinise and engage with media and political discourses in pragmatic and indeed novel ways; we hope that concepts such as modulation, media renewal, and interaction order offer some leverage for understanding how television, audiences, and security events will intersect in the coming years.

In sum, the radically enhanced connectivity of the digital world has afforded television and other news media unparalleled opportunity. Yet media renewal has brought about an inward gaze and a self-concern that has seriously diminished television's capacity to cope with the threats and challenges thrown up by that same connectivity. The defining features of television news in the digital age of terror, namely its economy of liveness, its new ecology of images, and its heightened partial reflexive scrutiny, have enabled the development of a new era of insecurity; an era that the medium is both constitutive of and trapped within.

Notes

1 Introduction

1. The distinctiveness of the function and role of the media in the 'post-9/11' period is still an emergent issue. For one of the first (and instructive) 'responses' in this respect, see Barbie Zelizer and Stuart Allan (2002) *Journalism After September 11*, London: Routledge.
2. The full title of the project is *Shifting Securities: News Cultures Before and Beyond the Iraq Crisis 2003*. The project was funded under the New Security Challenges programme run by the Economic and Social Research Council (ESRC) (Award Ref: RES-223-25-0063). The principal applicant was Marie Gillespie of The Open University. Gillespie supervised the audiences ethnography, in which the following carried out research: Ammar Al Ghabban, Habiba Noor, Awa Hassan Ahmed, Atif Imtiaz, Akil Awan, Noureddine Miladi, Karen Qureshi, Zahbia Yousuf, David Herbert, Sadaf Rivzi, Somnath Batabyal, Awa Al Hassan, and Marie Gillespie. The news media analysis was carried out by Andrew Hoskins and Ben O'Loughlin. The elite interviews were carried out by James Gow and Ivan Zverzhanovski at King's College, London. At the time of writing this book (summer 2006), full data from the third strand is not complete, so we omit findings from the elite interviews.
3. In her study *Spectatorship and Suffering*, Chouliaraki adopts a similar approach to deciding on texts to study. She refers to her approach as 'phronesis' (see Chouliaraki, 2006: 7–11).
4. We did the same for footage of the opening phase of NATO military intervention in the 1999 Kosovo war, but have not included that case study in this book.
5. Transana is free and open source qualitative analysis software for video and audio data developed at the University of Wisconsin-Madison Center for Education Research (http://www.transana.org).
6. There are, of course, other connotations, for instance security as a guarantee that a promise will be met.
7. These roles are by no means distinct. Experienced reporters may 'graduate' to a position of in-studio 'expert', for instance, while witnesses can become reporters (such as Salam Pax, the Baghdad Blogger).
8. In this book, we do not employ a narrative approach to studying media texts. For an overview of this approach, see Gillespie (2006b), and for an application of the approach to television news coverage of war and conflict, see Chouliaraki (2006).
9. Jay David Bolter and Richard Grusin (1999) develop a model of 'premediation': namely that the cultural significance of new visual media is acquired through their 'refashioning' of earlier media forms.
10. Cf. Marie Gillespie (2001) Audience Research Study, 'After September 11: TV News and Transnational Audiences' Project (http://www.afterseptember11.tv).

11. For analysis of media templates in relation to their shaping of the relation-ship between media and memory see Andrew Hoskins (2006) 'Temporality, Proximity, and Security: Terror in a Media-Drenched Age', *International Relations*, 20 (4): 453–66 and Hoskins (forthcoming) *Media and Memory*, London: Routledge.
12. Note that *Spooks* was renamed *MI-5* for North American audiences due in part to the racial connotation of the former term.

2 Television and time

1. See John Urry (2000: 113) for a clear outline of the central characteristics of clock-time.
2. Television today is neither an 'old' nor a 'new' medium; thus we employ the term 'renewed' to refer to the transformations of the electronic media – principally television and radio – that exist and transmit through other media in the digital age.
3. See Leon Kreitzman's (1999) *The 24 Hour Society*.
4. For a recent justification for use of the terms 'Western' and 'the West', see Gow (2005).
5. Gitlin selected the top ten best-selling novels in the United States according to the *New York Times'* lists from the first week in October in the years 1936, 1956, 1976, 1996, and 2001 and looked at four sentences from each book, the first ones beginning on pages 1, 50, 100, and 150 (2002: 98).
6. Gitlin offers no convincing explanation for the slight change in these trends from 1996 (as evident in the table) other than a countertrend to that of 'oversimplification' in the language of popular fiction (ibid.).
7. Helga Nowotny (1994: 4) argues that there has occurred an 'inexorable disap-pearance of the category of the future' to be replaced by that of 'the extended present', cf. Chapter 2, herewith.
8. Here we amend Caldwell's metaphor, who argues, 'Television has always been *textually messy* – that is, textural rather than transparent' (emphasis in original, 1995: 23).
9. cf. Nowotny. Barbara Adam draws on Nowotny's use of this term to argue, 'This suggests a porosity and permeability of the boundary between the present and the future, a blurring that makes it impossible to establish which time dimension we are dealing with' (1990: 141).
10. See Nowotny (1994) for an advanced critique of the idea of 'simultaneity'. For example, she argues, 'What passes over the screen in colourful succession is a parady of simultaneity: the events which are shown follow the rule of dramatic portrayal by a medium. They have little to do with the social reality from which they have been detached. Whether they are fiction or are to be seen from the point of view of simultaneity has become largely irrelevant to the observer' (1994: 30). See also note 6 of Chapter 1.
11. For a detailed discussion of the effects of 'real-time' television coverage on political decision-making, see Nik Gowing (1994) 'Real-Time Television Coverage of Armed Conflicts and Diplomatic Crises: Does It Pressure or Distort Foreign Policy Decisions'? Harvard University: The Joan Shorenstein Barone Centre on the Press, Politics and Public Policy, John F. Kennedy School of Government – Working Paper 94-1.

12. Cited in Boden and Hoskins (1995).
13. Instead, CNN relied upon still photographs of their correspondents in the al-Rashid hotel and various maps of the region; see Hoskins (2004a) for a discussion of the impact of this extended live audio-only transmission on television.
14. See, for example, Patricia Mellencamp (1990) 'TV Time and Catastrophe'.
15. See Nick Couldry's (2003) critical analysis of Dayan and Katz's model of media events and his proposed narrower redefinition of this term in relation to 'the myth of the mediated centre' (p. 67).
16. See Julian Borger (2006) 'It's Like Watching Two Different Wars', *The Guardian*, 2 August 2006, at http://commentisfree.guardian.co.uk/julian_borger/2006/08/post_279.html (accessed 8 August 2006).
17. Cf. Andrew Hoskins (2004) 'Television and the Collapse of Memory', *Time & Society*, 13 (1), 114.
18. See, for example, James Silver (2006) 'Unfriendly Fire From All Sides', *Media Guardian*, 31 July 2006, http://media.guardian.co.uk/pda/avantgo/story/0,,1833642-Top+10+media+stories,00.html (accessed 1 August 2006).
19. Ellis here cites a phrase coined by Trevor McDonald, for many years the anchor of ITV's *News at Ten*, who, he explains, 'utters this remark as a justification of the activity of television news', Ellis, 2002, p. 15, n. 6. Al-Qaeda also use this line as an excuse to bomb innocent Western civilians, arguing that these civilians have watched the news and not acted against the governments (Devji, 2005).

3 Hurricane Katrina and the failure of the 'CNN effect'

1. Cited in Boden and Hoskins (1995).
2. This discussion is necessarily brief and the reader is reminded of the larger literatures. On frames and framing, see Gitlin (1980), Entman (1993), Reese (2001), D'Angelo (2002), De Vreese (2003), Livingston and Bennett (2003), and Weaver et al. (2004). On indexing see Althaus et al. (1996) and Althaus (2003). On media effects, see Abercrombie (1996), Abercrombie and Longhurst (1998), and McQuail (2005).
3. Our critique of these approaches is informed by discussions of causality in Clegg (1989) and Hay (2002).
4. Readers may compare Entman's analysis with the Glasgow Media Group's (1985) study of television news framing of the Falklands War, in particular the sinking of the HMS Sheffield by Argentine forces and the sinking of the Belgrano by British forces.
5. See also Stuart Croft (2006) *Culture, Crisis and America's War on Terror*, Cambridge: Cambridge University Press, p. 275.

4 Talking terror: political discourses and the 2003 Iraq war

1. Once, international relations scholars referred to 'the' security dilemma as those situations in which two states with no reason to fight begin to feel mutually insecure merely because of the other's presence, leading to an arms

race that worsened the dilemma (Herz, 1950). Today's dilemma sees the governments pursue actions ostensibly supposed to increase the physical security of all of its citizens, but these actions appear to make some citizens within those countries feel victimised and more insecure.

2. For an excellent discussion of rhetorical clouding and why citizens read into politicians' statements their particular interests, see Lippmann, W. (1922) *Public Opinion*, New York: Harcourt, Brace and Company, Chapter XIII.

3. This dichotomy is somewhat simplistic. For a more complete and historical account of these debates, see O'Loughlin (2005).

4. The concept 'logic of equivalence' is taken from Stuart Hall's (1983, 1988) analysis of Thatcherism.

5. For further consideration of the sublime and international security and conflict, see the August 2006 special issue of *Millennium: Journal of International Relations*, 34: 3.

6. Noor's research is available at http://www.reproduce.blogspot.com/. Readers may wish to compare the news videos made by schoolchildren in New York and London.

5   Television's quagmire: the misremembered and the unforgotten

1. Mimi White and James Schwoch 'History and Television' at http://www.museum.tv/archives/etv/H/htmlH/historyandt/historyandt.htm (accessed 14 May 2006).

2. Ibid.

3. Todd Gitlin (2004) 'The Great Media Breakdown', http://www.motherjones.com/news/ feature/2004/11/10_402.html (accessed 23 January 2005).

4. This remark taken from the Prime Minister's 'statement to the nation' on 11 September 2001, available at http://news.bbc.co.uk/1/hi/uk_politics/1538551.stm (accessed 16 October 2002).

5. See http://www.thenation.com/doc/20021007/alterman (accessed 22 March 2006).

6. Jonathan Freedland, for example, identifies a splintering of the political bipartisan consensus in the United States some eight months after 9/11 ('The return of politics', *Guardian Weekly*, 30 May 2002, available at http://www.guardian.co.uk/GWeekly/Story/0,,724082,00.html) (accessed 24 November 2005).

7. George Soros (2006) 'A Self-Defeating War', available at http://www.huffingtonpost.com/george-soros/a-selfdefeating-war_b_30591.html.   First published in the *Wall Street Journal*, 15 August 2006 (accessed 16 September 2006).

8. Jonathan Raban (2006) 'September 11: The Price We've Paid', *The Independent Extra*, 8 September 2006, p. 5.

9. John Rentoul speaking on *Newsnight*, BBC2, 15 August 2006.

10. See, for example, Alison Landsberg (2004) *Prosthetic Memory: The Transformation of American Remembrance in the Age of Mass Culture*, who considers how new technologies can be 'liberating' in terms of the access afforded to the past by new generations.

11. On the myth of the US television news coverage of casualties during the Vietnam War, see Daniel Hallin (1986) *The "Uncensored War": The Media and Vietnam*, Oxford: Oxford University Press.

12. G. Thomas Goodnight, '"Iraq is George Bush's Vietnam": Metaphors in Controversy: On Public Debate and Deliberative Analogy', www.usc.edu/dept/LAS/iids/docs/Iraq_and_Vietnam.doc (accessed 24 June 2006).

13. Thomas L. Friedman (2006) 'Barney and Baghdad', *The New York Times*, 18 October 2006, at http://select.nytimes.com/2006/10/18/opinion/18friedman.html (accessed 20 October 2006).

14. Ibid.

15. O'Keefe, 'Bush Accepts Vietnam Comparison', *ABC News*, at http://abcnews.go.com/WNT/story?id=2583579 (accessed 20 November 2006).

16. See official transcript of White House press briefing, 19 October 2006, at http://www.whitehouse.gov/news/releases/2006/10/20061019-1.html (accessed 18 November 2006).

17. We are grateful to Marie Gillespie for this concept and for her insightful application of it in contributing to a genuinely multidisciplinary understanding of the impact or news texts in a media-saturated environment.

6   The distant body

1. For analysis of the uses and the representations of the Jarecke photograph up to the 2003 Iraq war, see Andrew Hoskins (2004) *Televising War: From Vietnam to Iraq*, London: Continuum.

2. See our previous chapter for a discussion of the 'Vietnam template'.

3. Peter Preston (2004) 'Writing the Script for Terror', *The Guardian*, 6 September 2004, p. 15.

4. The Rory Peck Trust aims to promote the safety and security of freelance news gatherers worldwide and to provide financial and moral assistance to the dependants of those who are killed, seriously injured, or imprisoned in the course of their work (See http://www.rorypecktrust.org).

5. Jonathan D. Moreno, 'The Medical Exam as Political Humiliation', *The American Journal of Bioethics*, 4 (2): W20.

6. Mark Boden (2004), 'The Lesson of Mogadishu', *WSJ Opinion Journal*, 5 April 2004, http://www.opinionjournal.com/editorial/feature.html?id=110004911 (accessed 17 July 2004).

7. *Channel 4 News*, broadcast 31 March 2004.

8. Section 1 of Ofcom's Programme Code does not appear to have changed since being published by its predecessor the Independent Television Commission (ITC) prior to 2004. Its 'general requirement' that was set out in legislation is as follows:

> Section 6(1) of the Broadcasting Act 1990 requires that the ITC does all it can to secure that every licensed service includes nothing in its programmes which offends against good taste or decency or is likely to encourage or incite to crime or lead to disorder or be offensive

to public feeling. Section 7(1)(a) requires the ITC to draw up a code giving guidance as to the rules to be observed with respect to the showing of violence, or the inclusion of sounds suggestive of violence, in programmes included in licensed services, particularly when large numbers of children and young people may be expected to be watching the programmes. Programme services are free to deal appropriately with all elements of the human experience but should avoid gratuitous offence by providing information and guidance to audiences, bearing in mind the expectations of those watching. Decisions on programme content will vary according to the time of day, nature of the channel and the likely audiences. This is true not only in respect of children but for audiences in general. Viewers are more likely to experience distress or offence as a result of strong material if they are taken unawares. (http://www.ofcom.org.uk/tv/ifi/codes/legacy/programme_code/pc_section_one) (accessed 15 December 2006)

9. See, for example, Nathan Roger (forthcoming) 'From Terry Waite to Kenneth Bigley: How Terrorists Use New Media to Promote Their Cause', in Sean Redmond and Karen Randell (eds) *The War Body on Screen*, London: Continuum.
10. Duncan Walker (2004) 'Who Watches Murder Videos'? BBC News online, 12 October 2004, http://news.bbc.co.uk/1/hi/magazine/3733996.stm (accessed 25 January 2005).
11. Claire Cozens (2004) 'Editors 'clean up' bomb photo', *The Guardian*, 12 March 2004, available at http://www.guardian.co.uk/international/story/0,,1168277,00.html (accessed 27 March 2004).
12. Susan Sontag (2002) 'Looking at War', *The New Yorker*, 9 December 2002, available at www.newyorker.com/archive/content/articles/050110fr_archive04?050110fr_archive04 (accessed 15 July 2003).
13. Philip Gourevitch cited in Philip Seib (2002: 13) *The Global Journalist: News and Conscience in a World of Conflict*, Oxford: Rowman & Littlefield Publishers, Inc.
14. The defining report was broadcast on BBC television news bulletins on 23 October 2004.
15. Sally Bedell Smith (2004) 'Famine Reports Show Power of TV', *The New York Times*, 22 November 2004, available at http://query.nytimes.com/gst/fullpage.html?res=9D04EEDF1638F931A15752C1A962948260&sec=&pagewanted=print (accessed 15 January 2005).
16. Ibid.
17. See Luke Harding (2005) 'Is Bush's Iraq Death Toll Correct', *The Guardian*, 14 December 2005, online at http://www.guardian.co.uk/Iraq/Story/0,,1666865,00.html (accessed 15 December 2005).
18. Gilbert Burnham et al. (2006) 'Mortality after the 2003 Invasion of Iraq: A Cross-sectional Cluster Sample Survey', *The Lancet*, published online 11 October 2006, http://dx.doi.org/10.1016/S0140-6736(06)69491-9 (accessed 11 October 2006). Note: this study was based on household interviews – not a body count – and was a follow-up to a report by the same group two years earlier.

19. The Iraq Body Count Project claims to be an 'ongoing human security project which maintains and updates the world's only independent and comprehensive public database of media-reported civilian deaths in Iraq that have resulted from the 2003 military intervention by the USA and its allies'. To account for discrepancies in figures of casualties reported by different sources, it updates both a 'minimum' and a 'maximum' of civilian deaths (http://www.iraqbodycount.org/).
20. *Iraq: The Hidden Story*, Channel 4, broadcast 8 May 2006.

7   Drama and documentary: The power of nightmares

1. We are aware that for a minority, politics *is* entertainment. For insiders, the thrill of the campaign race and the gossip around executive circles is as entertaining as any sports or soap operas. We follow van Zoonen's (2005: 10) use of 'entertainment' here as 'particular cultural genres and products' connected to popular culture and escapism.
2. Ostensibly powerless, but viewers can still turn off, turn over, or pause or skip if watching on tivo, Sky+, or video recording.
3. Their examination draws heavily on Castres (1977).
4. Indeed, in September 2006, the John Humphrys of the BBC Today radio programme agreed to go and report from the Red Zone in early 2007 for these reasons. See Luckhurst (2006).

8   Security and publics: democratic times?

1. The arguments in this chapter on temporality and common worlds are substantially similar to those presented in Moss and O'Loughlin (Forthcoming). We are grateful to Moss for letting us use insights derived from his theoretical groundwork.
2. The phrase, 'the enemy within' has a long history, and its deployment by *The Independent*, a newspaper critical of the Iraq war and much anti-terror legislation, raises questions. Was the newspaper being ironic, disputing the existence of an 'enemy within' and any associated 'paranoid' discourse (Hage, 2003). Yet its reporting and editorial identified the existence of an 'enemy within'.
3. Zizek (2006: 17) writes, 'The standard definition of parallax is, the apparent displacement of an object) the shift of its position against a background), caused by a change in observation position that provides a new line of sight'. He also writes of a parallax gap: 'the confrontation of two closely linked perspectives between which no neutral common ground is possible' (ibid: 4). This leads to a political parallax: 'the social antagonism which allows for no common ground between the conflicting agents' (ibid: 10).
4. The pen portrait format is taken from Qureshi (2007).
5. This critical engagement with and use of media contradicts the gloomy dystopian predictions of Paul Virilio. For Virilio, the capacity to access live news from anywhere (at the speed of light) turns the viewer into a '*citizen-terminal* soon to be decked out to the eyeballs with interactive prostheses

based on the pathological model of the 'spastic', wired to control his/her domestic environment without having physically to stir' (1997: 20).

6. To that extent, we align with Thrift's observations on recent trends in social theory: 'Space is no longer seen as a nested hierarchy moving from 'global' to 'local'. This absurd scale-dependent notion is replaced by the notion that what counts is connectivity' (Thrift, 2004: 59).

7. We draw here on arguments made here in unpublished work by the ethnographer Atif Imtiaz on the Shifting Securities project.

8. Such an assumption is contested by cosmopolitan theorists following Ulrich Beck's suggestion that globalisation renders political categories based around the nation 'zombie categories'. For such work applied to studies of media and audiences, see Robins and Aksoy (2005) 'Whoever Looks Always Finds: Transnational Viewing and Knowledge Experience'.

9   The irresolution of television

1. Bill Durodie, speaking on *Newsnight*, BBC2, broadcast 18 August 2006.

2. This is not to suggest the paradigms of Media Sociology and Media Studies have been rendered obsolete, but that they do not seem particularly 'fit for purpose', in that they have not, and it seems cannot, develop at a pace adequate to that of their subject matter, namely what is called variously 'new media'.

3. Witness the British media's excitement at being able to cover the creation of a citizen e-petition in February 2007, and thus 'connect' to citizen–audiences.

4. See Patrick Barkham, 'Spot the Difference', *Media Guardian*, 14 August 2006, p. 3.

5. We must reiterate how grateful we are to the ethnographic researchers named earlier for generating this data.

Bibliography

Abercrombie, N. (1996) *Television and Society*, Cambridge: Polity Press.

Abercrombie, N. and Longhurst, B. (1998) *Audiences – A Sociological Theory of Performance and Imagination*, London: Sage.

Adam, B. (1990) *Time and Social Theory*, Cambridge: Polity Press.

Adam, B. (1995) *Timewatch: The Social Analysis of Time*, Cambridge: Polity.

Albertsen, N. and Diken, B. (2001) 'What is the Social?' http://www.comp.lancs.ac.uk/sociology/soc033bd.html (accessed 12 January 2003).

Al-Ghabban, A. (2007) 'Global Viewing in East London: Multi-ethnic Youth Responses to Television News in a New Century', *European Journal of Cultural Studies*, special issue on 'Media, Diasporas and the Politics of Security'.

Allan, S. (1999) *News Culture* Maidenhead: Open University Press.

Althaus, S. L. (2003) 'When News Norms Collide, Follow the Lead: New Evidence for Press Independence', *Political Communication*, 20: 4.

Althaus, S. L. et al. (1996) 'Revising the Indexing Hypothesis: Officials, Media, and the Libya Crisis', *Political Communication*, 13, 407–421.

Appadurai, A. (1996) *Modernity at Large: Cultural Dimensions of Globalization*, Minneapolis: University of Minnesota Press.

Appy, C. G. (2006) *Vietnam: The Definitive Oral History Told from All Sides*, Ebury Press.

Baldwin, S. (2003) 'This is the Longest Day of My life', *Politics and Culture*, 3, http://aspen.conncoll.edu/politicsandculture/page.cfm?key=260 (accessed 18 November 2006).

Barkham, P. (2006) 'Spot the Difference', *The Guardian*, Media, 14 August, p. 3.

Barnett, C. (2003) *Culture and Democracy: Media, Space and Representation*, Edinburgh: Edinburgh University Press.

Barnett, C. (2004) 'Media, Democracy and Representation: Disembodying the Public', in Barnett, C. and Low, M. (eds) *Spaces of Democracy: Geographical Perspectives on Citizenship, Participation and Representation*, London: Sage.

Bauman, Z. (2006) *Liquid Fear*, Cambridge: Polity Press.

Beckett, A. (2004) 'The Making of the Terror Myth', *The Guardian*, 15 October, http:// www.guardian.co.uk/print/0„5039836-111274,00.html (accessed 12 October 2006).

Bell, A. (1991) *The Language of News Media*, London: Blackwell.

Bell, A. (1995) 'News time', *Time and Society* 4 (3), 305–328.

Bell, A. (1998) 'The Discourse Structure of News Stories', in Bell, A. and Garrett, P. (eds) *Approaches to Media Discourse*, Oxford: Blackwell Publishers Ltd, pp. 64–104.

Bennett, W. L. (1990) 'Towards a Theory of Press-State Relations in the United States', *Journal of Communication*, 40: 103–125.

Bennett, W. L. and Paletz, D. L. (1994) *Taken by Storm: The Media, Public Opinion, and U.S. Foreign Policy in the Gulf War*, Chicago: University of Chicago Press.

Bentham, J. (1995) *The Panopticon Writings*, Miran Bozovic (ed.), London: Verso.

Bergen, P. (2005) 'Beware the Holy War', The Nation, 20 June, http://www.thenation.com/doc/20050620/bergen (accessed 12 November 2006).

Bhaskar, R. (1978) *A Realist Theory of Science*, Brighton: Harvester.

Bhaskar, R. (1989) *Reclaiming Reality*, London: Verso.

Boden, D. (1991) 'Reinventing the Global Village: Communication and the Revolutions of 1989', unpublished manuscript, Department of Sociology, Lancaster University.

Boden, M. (2004) 'The Lesson of Mogadishu', *WSJ Opinion Journal*, 5 April 2004, http://www.opinionjournal.com/editorial/feature.html?id=110004911 (accessed 17 July 2004).

Boden, D. and Hoskins, A. (1995) 'Time, Space and Television', unpublished paper presented at 2nd Theory, Culture & Society Conference, 'Culture and Identity: City, Nation, World', Berlin, 11 August 1995.

Boltanski, L. (1999) *Distant Suffering: Morality, Media and Politics* (translated by Graham Burchell), Cambridge: Cambridge University Press.

Bolter, J. D. and Grusin, R. (1999) *Remediation: Understanding New Media*, London: The MIT Press.

Bourdon, J. (2000) 'Live Television Is Still Alive: On Television as an Unfulfilled Promise', *Media, Culture & Society*, 22 (5): 531–556.

Bourke, J. (2004) *Al-Qaeda: Casting a Shadow of Terror*, London: I.B. Tauris.

Braun, D. and Busch, A. (eds) (1999) *Public Policy and Political Ideas*, Cheltenham: Edward Elgar.

Broe, D. (2004) 'Fox and Its Friends: Global Commodification and the New Cold War', *Cinema Journal*, 43 (4): 97–102.

Bucy, E. P. (2002) 'Audience Responses to Traumatic News: Processing the World Trade Centre Attacks', Harvard Symposium on 'Restless Searchlight: The Media and Terrorism', JFK School, 29 August.

Burke, J. (2003) *Al-Qaeda: Casting a Shadow of Terror*, New York: IB Tauris.

Burnham, G. et al. (2006) 'Mortality after the 2003 Invasion of Iraq: A Cross-Sectional Cluster Sample Survey', *The Lancet*, 11 October, http://dx.doi.org/10.1016/S0140-6736(06)69491-9 (accessed 11 October 2006).

Caldwell, J. T. (1995) *Televisuality: Style, Crisis, and Authority in American Television*, New Brunswick: Rutgers University Press.

Campbell, D. (2004) 'Horrific Blindness: Images of Death in Contemporary Media', *Journal for Cultural Research*, 8 (1): 55–74.

Carr, M. (2006) *Unknown Soldiers: How Terrorism Has Transformed the Modern World*, London: Profile Books.

Castells, M. (1996) *The Rise of the Network Society: Volume I of the Information Age. Economy, Society and Sulture*, Malden, MA: Blackwell.

Castells, M. (1997a). *End of Millennium: Volume III of the Information Age. Economy, Society and Culture*, Malden, MA: Blackwell.

Castells, M. (1997b). *The Power of Identity: Volume II of the Information Age: Economy, Society and Culture*, Malden, MA: Blackwell.

Castres, P. (1977) *Society Against the State*, New York: Urizen.

Charter, D. (2005) 'The Two Faces of Top Tory's Migrant Campaign', *The Times*, 23 April.

Chibnall, S. (1977) *Law and Order News: An Analysis of Crime Reporting in the British Press*, London: Tavistock.

Chouliaraki, L. (2005) 'Spectacular Ethics: On the Television Footage of the Iraq War', *Journal of Language and Politics*, 4 (1): 43–59.

Chouliaraki, L. (2006) *The Spectatorship of Suffering*, London: Sage.

Clegg, S. (1989) *Frameworks of Power*, London: Sage.

Columbia Journalism Review (2004) 'Brits vs. Yanks: Who Does Journalism Right?', May/June, Issue 3.

Cooper, M. (2006) 'Pre-empting Emergence: The Biological Turn in the War on Terror', *Theory, Culture and Society*, Vol. 23, No. 4, 113–135.

Cottle, S. (2006) *Mediatized Conflict: Developments in Media and Conflict Studies*, Maidenhead: Open University Press.

Couldry, N. (2003) *Media Rituals: A Critical Approach*, London: Routledge.

Cozens, C. 'Editors 'Clean Up' Bomb Photo', *The Guardian*, 12 March 2004, available at http://www.guardian.co.uk/international/story/0,,1168277,00.html (accessed 27 March 2004).

Croft, S. (2006) *Culture, Crisis and America's War on Terror*, Cambridge: Cambridge University Press.

Crowther, P. (1998) 'The Sublime', in E. Craig (ed.) *Routledge Encyclopedia of Philosophy*, London: Routledge, http://www.rep.routledge.com/article/M040 (accessed 29 October 2006).

Curtis, A. (2005) 'Creating Islamist Phantoms', *The Guardian*, 30 August, http://www.guardian.co.uk/print/0,,5273306-103677,00.html (accessed 18 November 2006).

Daalder, I. N. and Lindsay, J. M. (2003) *America Unbound: The Bush Revolution in Foreign Policy*, Washington, DC: Brookings.

D'Angelo, P. (2002) 'News Framing as a Multi-paradigmatic Research Program: A Response to Entman', *Journal of Communication*, 52 (4): 870–888.

Davis, D. (2006) 'Future-War Storytelling: National Security and Popular Film', in Martin, A. and Petro, P. (eds) *ReThinking Global Security: Media, Popular Culture and the "War on Terror"*, New Brunswick, NJ: Rutgers University Press, pp. 13–44.

Dayan, D. and Katz, E. (1992) *Media Events: The Live Broadcasting of History*, Harvard: Harvard University Press.

Deleuze, G. and Felix, G. (1987) *A Thousand Plateaus: Capitalism and Schizophrenia* (translated by Brian Massumi), Minneapolis: University of Minnesota Press.

Deleuze, G. and Guattari, F. (2000) *Anti-Oedipus: Capitalism and Schizophrenia*, London: Athlone Press.

Dench, G. et al. (2006) *The New East End: Kinship, Race and Conflict*, London: Profile Books.

Denzau, A. T. and North, D. C. (1994) 'Shared Mental Models: Ideologies and Institutions', *Kyklos*, 47: 1.

Derrida, J. (1978) *Writing and Difference*, London: Routledge.

Devji, F. (2005) *Landscapes of the Jihad: Militancy, Morality and Modernity*, London: C. Hurst & Co.

De Vreese, C. H. (2003) *Framing Europe: Television News and European Integration*, Amsterdam: Aksant.

Dillon, M. (2007) 'Governing Terror: The State of Emergency of Biopolitical Emergence', *International Political Sociology*, 1: 7–28.

Durodie, B. (2006) *Newsnight*, BBC2, broadcast 18 August 2006.

Ellis, J. (1992) *Visible Fictions: Cinema, Television, Video* (Second Edition), London: Routledge.

Ellis, J. (2002) *Seeing Things: Television in the Age of Uncertainty*, London: I.B. Tauris & Co. Ltd.

Entman, R. W. (1993) 'Framing: Toward Clarification of a Fractured Paradigm', *Journal of Communication*, 43 (4): 51–58.

Entman, R. W. (2004) *Projections of Power: Framing News, Public Opinion, and U.S. Foreign Policy*, Chicago: The University of Chicago Press.

Fairclough, N. (1992) *Discourse and Social Change*, Cambridge: Polity Press.

Farr, J. (1989) 'Understanding Conceptual Change Politically', in Ball, T. et al. (eds) *Political Innovation and Conceptual Change*, Cambridge: Cambridge University Press.

Fenton, T. (2005) Bad News: The Decline of Reporting, the Business of News, and the Danger to Us All, New York: Harpercollins.

Ferrarotti, F. (1990) *Time, Memory, and Society*, Westport: Greenwood Press.

Feuer, J. (1983) 'The Concept of Live Television: Ontology as Ideology', in Kaplan, A. E. (ed.) *Regarding Television, Critical Approaches – An Anthology*, Los Angeles: University Publications of America, Inc., pp. 12–22.

Fisk, R. (2006) 'If You Want the Roots of Terror, Try Here', *The Independent*, 12 August, p. 33.

Foucault, M. (1978) *The History of Sexuality: An Introduction*, Harmondsworth: Penguin.

Foucault, M. (1980) *Power/Knowledge: Selected Interviews and Other Writings, 1972–77*, Gordeon, C. (ed.), Brighton: Harvester.

Foucault, M. (1985) *The Use of Pleasure*, Harmondsworth: Penguin.

Foucault, M. (1986) *The Care of the Self*, Harmondsworth: Penguin.

Foucault, M. (1989) *The Archaeology of Knowledge*, London: Routledge.

Francoli, M. (2007) 'The Big Blog', in Josh Greenberg and Charlene Elliott (eds) *Communication in Question: Canadian Perspectives on Contentious Issues in Communication Studies*, Thomson-Nelson (forthcoming).

Freedland, J. 'The Return of Politics', *Guardian Weekly*, 30 May 2002, http://www.guardian.co.uk/GWeekly/Story/0,,724082,00.html (accessed 24 November 2005).

Friedland, R. and Boden, D. (ed.) (1994) *NowHere: Space, Time and Modernity*, Berkeley, University of California Press.

Friedman, J. (2002) 'Attraction to Distraction: Live Television and the Public Sphere', in Friedman, J. (ed.) *Reality Squared: Televisual Discourse on the Real*, London: Rutgers University Press, pp. 138–154.

Friedman, T. L. (2006) 'Barney and Baghdad', *The New York Times*, 18 October 2006, at http://select.nytimes.com/2006/10/18/opinion/18friedman.html (accessed 20 October 2006).

Galtung, J. (1998). High Road, Low Road: Charting the Course for Peace Journalism. *Track Two*, 7, 7–10.

Galtung, J. and Ruge, M. H. (1965) 'The Structure of Foreign News: The Presentation of the Congo, Cuba and Cyprus Crises in Four Foreign Newspapers', in Tunstall, J. (ed.) (1970) *Media Sociology: A Reader*, London: Constable, pp. 259–298.

Garfinkel, H. (1967) *Studies in Ethnomethodology*, Cambridge: Polity Press.

Garfinkel, H. (edited and introduced by Rawls, Anne W.) (2002) *Ethnomethodology's Program: Working Out Durkheim's Aphorism*, Lanham, Boulder, New York, Oxford: Rowman & Littlefield Publishers, Inc.

Giddens, A. (1984) *The Constitution of Society*, Cambridge: Polity.

Gilboa, E. (2005) 'Global Television News and Foreign Policy: Debating the CNN Effect', *International Studies Perspectives*, 6, 325–341.

Gillespie, M. (2006a) 'Security, Media, Legitimacy: Multi-ethnic Media Publics and the Iraq War 2003', *International Relations*, 20 (4): 467–486.

Gillespie, M. (2006b) 'Narrative Analysis', in Gillespie, M. and Toynbee, J. (eds) *Analysing Media Texts*, Maidenhead, UK: Open University Press.

Gillmor, D. (2006) *We The Media: Grassroots Journalism, By the People, For the People*, Sebastapol, CA: O'Reilly Media, Inc.

Gitlin, T. (1980) *The Whole World is Watching – Mass Media in the Making and Unmaking of the New Left*, London: University of California Press.

Gitlin, T. (2001) *Media Unlimited: How the Torrent of Images and Sounds Overwhelms Our Lives*, New York: Metropolitan Books.

Gitlin, T. (2004) 'The Great Media Breakdown', http://www.motherjones. com/news/feature/2004/11/10_402.html (accessed 23 January 2005).

Glasgow Media Group (1985) *War and Peace News*, Milton Keynes: Open University Press.

Goffman, E. (1972) *Relations in Public: Microstudies of the Public Order*, Harmondsworth: Penguin Books Ltd (first published 1971 in the United States by Basic Books Inc.).

Goffman, E. (1981) *Forms of Talk*, Philadelphia: University of Pennsylvania Press.

Goodnight, G. T. '"Iraq is George Bush's Vietnam": Metaphors in Controversy: On Public Debate and Deliberative Analogy', http://www. usc.edu/dept/LAS/iids/docs/Iraq_and_Vietnam.doc (accessed 24 June 2006).

Gow, J. (2005) *Defending the West*, Cambridge: Polity.

Gow, J. and Michalski, M. (2007) *War, Image and Legitimacy: Viewing Contemporary Conflict*, London: Routledge.

Gowing, N. (1994) 'Real-Time Television Coverage of Armed Conflicts and Diplomatic Crises: Does it Pressure or Distort Foreign Policy Decisions'? Harvard University: The Joan Shorenstein Barone Centre on the Press, Politics and Public Policy, John F. Kennedy School of Government, Working Paper 94-1.

Grusin, R. (2004) 'Remediation', *Criticism*, 46 (1): 17–39.

Hage, G. (2003) *Against Paranoid Nationalism*, London: Merlin Press Ltd.

Hall, S. (1983) 'The Great Moving Right Show', in Hall, S. and Jacques, M. (eds) *The Politics of Thatcherism*, London: Lawrence and Wishart.

Hall, S. (1988) *The Hard Road to Renewal*, London: Verso in association with *Marxism Today*.

Hallin, D. C. (1986) *The 'Uncensored War': The Media and Vietnam*, Oxford: Oxford University Press.

Hallin, D. C. (1993) *We Keep America on Top of the World: Television Journalism and the Public Sphere*, London and New York: Routledge.

Harding, L. (2005) 'Is Bush's Iraq death toll Correct', *The Guardian*, 14 December, online at http://www.guardian.co.uk/Iraq/Story/0,,1666865,00.html (accessed 15 December 2005).

Hay, C. (2002) *Political Analysis: A Critical Introduction*, Basingstoke: Palgrave.

Herman, E. S. and Chomsky, N. (1988) *Manufacturing Consent: The Political Economy of the Mass Media*, New York: Pantheon Books.

Herz, J. H. (1950) 'Idealist Internationalism and the Security Dilemma', *World Politics*, 2 (2), 157–180.

Hobsbawn, E. (1962) *The Age of Capital: 1848–1875*, London: Weidenfeld & Nicholson.

Hoskins, A. (2001) 'Mediating Time: The Temporal Mix of Television', *Time & Society* 10 (2/3): 333–346.

Hoskins, A. (2004a) 'Television and the Collapse of Memory', *Time & Society*, 13(1): 109–127.

Hoskins, A. (2004b) *Televising War: From Vietnam to Iraq*, London: Continuum.

Hoskins, A. (2006) 'Temporality, Proximity, and Security: Terror in a Media-Drenched Age', *International Relations*, 20 (4): 453–466.

Hoskins, A. (forthcoming) *Media and Memory*, London: Routledge.

Howarth, D. (1995) 'Discourse Theory', in Marsh, D. and Stoker, G. (eds) *Theory and Methods in Political Science*, Basingstoke: Macmillan.

Howarth, D. (2000) *Discourse*, Buckingham: Open University Press.

Howarth, D. et al. (eds) (2000) *Discourse Theory and Political Analysis*, Manchester: Manchester University Press.

The Independent (2006) 'Less a Global Arc of Extremism than Proof of Alienation Closer to Home', 12 August, p. 32.

Jackson, R. (2005) *Writing the War on Terrorism: Language, Politics and Counter-terrorism*, Manchester: Manchester University Press.

Jalbert, P. L. (1999) 'Critique and Analysis in Media Studies: Media Criticism as Practical Action', in Jalbert, P. L. (ed.) *Media Studies: Ethnomehodological Approaches*, Lanham: University of Press of America, pp. 31–51.

Jeffries, S. (2005) 'The film US TV Networks Dare Not Show', *The Guardian*, 12 May, http://film.guardian.co.uk/cannes2005/story/0,15927,1481970,00.html (accessed 17 November 2006).

Johnson, P. (2006) '10 Years Later, Fox News Turns up the Cable Volume', USA Today, 10 January, http://www.usatoday.com/life/television/news/2006-10-01-fox-news_x.htm.

Johnson-Cartee, K.S. (2005) *News Narratives and News Framing: Constructing Political Reality*, Lanham: Rowman & Littlefield Publishers Inc.

Joseph, J. (2006) 'Here is the Lack of News from Iraq…', *The Times*, 9 May, http://www.timesonline.co.uk/article/0,,26430-2170892,00.html (accessed 17 November 2006).

Kagan, R. (2002) 'Power and Weakness', *Policy Review*, 113, http://www.policyreview.org/jun02/kagan.html (accessed 17 November 2006).

Kagan, R. (2004) *Of Paradise and Power: America and Europe in the New World Order*, New York: Knopf.

Kagan, R. and Kristol, W. (1996) 'Towards a Neo-Reaganite Foreign Policy', *Foreign Affairs*, 75 (4), 18–32.

Kagan, R. and Kristol, W. (2001) 'A National Humiliation', *The Weekly Standard*, 16–23 April, 11–15.

Kepel, G. (2004) *The War for Muslim Minds*, London: Belnap.

Klein, P. D. (2005) 'Epistemology'. In Craig, E. (ed.) *Routledge Encyclopedia of Philosophy*. London: Routledge, http://www.rep.routledge.com/article/P059 (accessed 22 August 2006).

Koehler, R. (2005) 'Neo-Fantasies and Ancient Myths: Adam Curtis on the Power of Nightmares', *Cinema Scope*, 23 (7) 2, http://www.cinemascope.com/cs23/int_koehler_curtis.htm (accessed 17 November 2006).

Kreitzman, L. (1999) *The 24 Hour Society*, London: Profile Books Ltd.

Kress, G. R. and van Leeuwen, T. (2001) *Multimodal Discourse*, London: Arnold.

Laclau, E. and Mouffe, C. (1985) *Hegemony and Socialist Strategy*, London: Verso.

Landsberg, A. (2004) *Prosthetic Memory: The Transformation of American Remembrance in the Age of Mass Culture*, New York: Columbia University Press.

Lash, S. (2002) *Critique of Information*, London: Sage.

Latour, B. (2003) 'What If We Talked Politics a While?', *Contemporary Political Theory*, 2 (2), 143–164.

Law, J. (2005) *After Method: Mess in Social Science Research*, Abingdon, UK and New York: Routledge.

Layoun, M. N. (2006) 'Visions of Security: Impermeable Borders, Impassable Walls, Impossible Homelands?', in Martin, A. and Petro, P. (eds) *ReThinking Global Security: Media, Popular Culture and the 'War on Terror'*, New Brunswick, NJ: Rutgers University Press, pp. 45–66.

Lehman, I. A. (2004) 'Exploring the Transatlantic Media Divide over Iraq: How and Why U.S. and German Media Differed in Reporting on U.N. Weapons Inspections in Iraq: 2002–2003', The Joan Shorenstein Center on the Press, Politics and Public Policy, Working Paper Series, 2004#1.

Lewis, J. (2005) *Language Wars: The Role of Media and Culture in Global Terror and Political Violence*, London: Pluto.

Lippmann, W. (1922) *Public Opinion*, New York: Harcourt, Brace and Company.

Livingston, S. (1997) 'Clarifying the CNN Effect: An Examination of Media Effects According to Type of Military Intervention', Joan Shorenstein Center, Harvard University, Research Paper R-18.

Livingston, S. and Bennett, W. L. (2003) 'Gatekeeping, Indexing, and Live-Event News: Is Technology Altering the Construction of News?', *Political Communication*, 20: 4.

Livingston, S. and Eachus, T. (1995) 'Humanitarian Crises and U.S. Foreign Policy: Somalia and the CNN Effect Reconsidered', *Political Communication*, 12, 413–429.

Livingstone, S. (ed.) (2005) *Audiences and Publics: When Cultural Engagement Matters for the Public Sphere*, Bristol: Intellect Press.

Luckhurst, T. (2006) 'Humphrys Goes to War', *The Independent on Sunday*, Business section, pp. 14–15.

Luhmann, N. (2000 [1996]) *The Reality of the Mass Media* (translated by Kathleen Cross), Oxford: Polity Press.

Marriott, S. (1995) 'Intersubjectivity and Temporal Reference in Television Commentary', *Time & Society*, 4(3), 345–364.

Marriott, S. (1996) 'Time and Time Again: 'Live' Television Commentary and the Construction of Replay Talk', *Media, Culture & Society*, 18 (1): 69–86.

Marriott, S. (1997) 'The Emergence of Live Television Talk', *Text* 17 (2): 181–198.

Marriott, S. (2001) 'In Pursuit of the Ineffable: How Television Found the Eclipse but Lost the Plot', *Media, Culture and Society*, 23 (6): 725–742.

Massing, M. (2004) 'Now they tell us', *The New Yorker*, 51: 3, 26 February.

McQuail, D. (2005) *Mass Communication Theory* (Fifth Edition), London: Sage.

McLuhan, M. (1962) 'A Sheet' – 'The TV Image: One of Our Conquerors', in Molinaro Matie et al. (eds) (1987) *Letters of Marshall McLuhan*, Oxford: Oxford University Press.

McLuhan, M. (1964) *Understanding Media – The Extensions of Man*, London: Routledge & Kegan Paul Ltd.

McNair, B. (2006) *Cultural Chaos: Journalism, News and Power in a Globalised World*, London: Routledge.

McSmith, A. (2006) '…and Finally Prescott Appears', *The Independent*, 12 August, p. 7.

McSmith, A. and Judd, T. (2006) 'Extra Checks Are Here to Stay, Air Passengers Warned', *The Independent*, 12 August, p. 6.

Mediamatters (2005) '*Wash. Post's* Criticism of Sensationalist Katrina Coverage Focused on CNN, Ignored Fox', 6 October 2005, http://mediamatters.org/items/200510060009 (accessed 17 November 2006).

Mellencamp, P. (1990) 'TV Time and Catastrophe', in Mellencamp, P. (ed.) *Logics of Television: Essays in Cultural Criticism*, London: BFI, pp. 240–266.

Mellencamp, P. (2006) 'Fearful Thoughts: U.S. Television since 9/11 and the Wars in Iraq', in Martin, A. and Petro, P. (eds) *ReThinking Global Security: Media, Popular Culture, and the 'War on Terror'*, New Brunswick: Rutgers University Press, pp. 117–131.

Mermin, J. (1999) *Debating War and Peace: Media Coverage of U.S. Intervention in the Post-Vietnam Era*, Princeton, NJ: Princeton University Press.

Meštrović, S. G. (ed.) (1995) Genocide *After Emotion: The Postemotional Balkan War*, London: Routledge.

Meštrović, S. G. (1996) 'Introduction', in Meštrović, S. G. (ed.) Genocide *After Emotion: The Postemotional Balkan War*, London: Routledge.

Meštrović, S. G. (1997) *Postemotional Society*, London: Sage.

Mirzoeff, N. (2005) *Watching Babylon: The War in Iraq and Global Visual Culture*, London: Routledge.

Moeller, S. D. (1999) *Compassion Fatigue: How the Media Sell Disease, Famine, War and Death*, London: Routledge.

Moreno, J. D. (2004) 'The Medical Exam as Political Humiliation', *The American Journal of Bioethics*, 4 (2), W20.

Moss, G. and O'Loughlin, B. (Forthcoming). 'Convincing Claims? Representation and Democracy in Post-9/11 Britain', *Political Studies*, Vol. 55.

Nacos, B. L. (2002) *Mass-Mediated Terrorism: The Central Role of the Media in Terrorism and Counterterrorism*, Lanham, Maryland: Rowman & Littlefield Publishers.

Nowotny, H. (1994) *Time – The Modern and Postmodern Experience*, Cambridge: Polity Press.

O'Keefe, E. (2006) 'Bush Accepts Vietnam Comparison', *ABC News*, 18 November 2006, http://abcnews.go.com/WNT/story?id=2583579 (accessed 20 November 2006).

O'Loughlin, B. (2005) 'The Intellectual Antecedents of the Bush Regime', in Colas, A. and Saull, R. (eds) *The War on Terrorism and American Empire after the Cold War*, London: Routledge, pp. 138–174.

Philo, G. and Berry, M. (2004) *Bad News From Israel*, London: Pluto Press.

Postman, N. (1986) *Amusing Ourselves to Death – Public Discourse in the Age of Show Business*, London: Heinemann.

Potter, J. (2004) 'Discourse Analysis as a Way of Analysing Naturally Occurring Talk', in Silverman, D. (ed.) *Qualitative Research: Theory, Method and Practice*, London: Sage.

Phythian, M. (2005) 'Still a Matter of Trust: Post-9/11 British Intelligence and Political Culture', *International Journal of Intelligence and CounterIntelligence*, 18 (4), 653–681.

Preston, P. (2004) 'Writing the Script for Terror', *The Guardian*, 6 September, p. 15.

Qureshi, K. (2006) 'Trans-boundary Spaces: Scottish Pakistanis and trans-local/national Identities', *International Journal of Cultural Studies*, Vol. 9, No. 2, 207–226.

Qureshi, K. (forthcoming, 2007) 'Shifting Proximities: News, Security and Identities', *European Journal of Cultural Studies*, special issue on 'Media, Diasporas and the Politics of Security', 10: 3.

Raban, J. (2006) 'September 11: The Price We've Paid', *The Independent Extra*, 8 September 2006, p. 5.

Reese, S. D. (2001) 'Framing Public Life: A Bridging Model for Media Research', in Reese, Stephen D. et al. (eds) *Framing Public Life: Perspectives on Media and Our Understanding of the Social World*, Mahwah, NJ: Lawrence Erlbaum Associates.

Reid, J. (2003) 'Deleuze's War Machine: Nomadism Against the State', *Millennium*, 32:1, 57–85.

Reid, J. (2006) 'Security, Freedom, and the Protection of our Values', speech to Demos, 9 August, http://www.demos.co.uk/files/johnreidsecurity andfreedom.pdf (accessed 18 November 2006).

Ricchiardi, S. (1996) 'Over the Line', *American Journalism Review*, 18, September, 25–30.

Richardson, J. E. (2004) *(Mis)representing Islam: The Racism and Rhetoric of British Broadsheet Newspapers*, Amsterdam; Philadelphia, PA: John Benjamins.

Robins, K. and Aksoy, A. (2005) 'Whoever Looks Always Finds: Transnational Viewing and Knowledge-Experience', in Chalaby, J. (ed.) *Transnational Television Worldwide: Towards a New Media Order*, London: I.B. Tauris, pp. 14–42.

Robinson, P. (2001a) 'Operation Restore Hope and the Illusion of a News Media Driven Intervention', *Political Studies*, 49, 941–956.

Robinson, P. (2001b) 'Theorizing the Influence of Media on World Politics: Models of Media Influence on Foreign Policy', *European Journal of Communication*, 16: 4, 523–544.

Robinson, P. (2002) T *he CNN Effect: The Myth of News, Foreign Policy and Intervention*, London & New York: Routledge.

Roger, N. (forthcoming) 'From Terry Waite to Kenneth Bigley: How Terrorists Use New Media to Promote Their Cause', in Redmond, S. and Randell, K. (eds) *The War Body on Screen*, London: Continuum.

Schudson, M. (1987) 'When? Deadlines, Datelines, and History', in Schudson, M. and Manoff, R. K. (eds) *Reading the News*, New York: Pantheon Books, pp. 79–108.

Schudson, M. (1990) *Origins of the Ideal of Objectivity in the Professions: Studies in the History of American Journalism and American Law*, New York: Garland.

Sconce, J. (2000) *Haunted Media: Electronic Presence from Telegraphy to Television*, Durham: Duke University.

Seib, P. (2002) *The Global Journalist: News and Conscience in a World of Conflict*, Oxford: Rowman & Littlefield Publishers, Inc.

Seib, P. (2004) *Beyond the Front Lines: How the News Media Cover a World Shaped By War*, Basingstoke: Palgrave Macmillan.

Shandler, J. (1999) *While America Watches: Televising the Holocaust*. New York: Oxford University Press.

Shaw, M. (2005) *The New Western Way of War: Risk-Transfer War and its Crisis in Iraq*, Cambridge: Polity.

Silver, J. (2006) 'Unfriendly Fire from All Sides', *Media Guardian*, 31 July 2006, http://media.guardian.co.uk/pda/avantgo/story/0,,1833642Top+10+media+ stories,00.html (accessed 1 August 2006).

Silverstone, R. (2002) 'Mediating Catastrophe: September 11 and the Crisis of the Other', http://www.lse.ac.uk/collections/media@lse/pdf/mediatingcatastrophe.pdf (accessed 20 January 2006).

Smith, S. B. (2004) 'Famine Reports Show Power of TV', *The New York Times*, 22 November 2004, available at http://query.nytimes.com/gst/fullpage.html?res=9D04EEDF1638F931A15752C1A962948260&sec=&pagewanted=print (accessed 15 January 2005).

Smith, R. (2005) *The Utility of Force*, London: Allen Lane.

Snow, J. (2004) *Shooting History*, London: Harpercollins.

Sontag, S. (1979/1977) *On Photography*, London: Penguin.

Sontag, S. (2002) 'Looking at War', *The New Yorker*, 9 December, available at http://www.newyorker.com/archive/content/articles/050110fr_archive04?050110fr_archive04 (accessed 15 July 2003).

Sontag, S. (2003) *Regarding the Pain of Others*, New York: Farrar, Straus and Giroux.

Soros, G. (2006) 'A Self-Defeating War', available at: http://www.huffingtonpost.com/george-soros/a-selfdefeating-war_b_30591.html. First published in the *Wall Street Journal*, 15 August 2006 (accessed 16 September 2006).

Suskind, R. (2004) 'Without a Doubt', *New York Times Magazine*, 17 October, http://www.ronsuskind.com/articles/000106.html (accessed 17 November 2006).

Suskind, R. (2006) *The One Percent Doctrine: Deep Inside America's Pursuit of Its Enemies since 9/11*, New York: Simon and Schuster.

Taylor, J. (1998) *Body Horror: Photojournalism, Catastrophe and War*, Manchester: Manchester University Press.

Thomson, J. B. (2000) *Political Scandal: Power and Visibility in the Media Age*, Cambridge: Polity Press.

Thrift, N. (2004) 'Intensities of Feeling: Towards a Spatial Politics of Affect', *Geografiska Annaler*, 86 b (1), 57–78.

Thrift, N. (2005) 'Panicsville: Paul Virilio and the Esthetic of Disaster', *Cultural Politics*, 1: 9.

Tomasulo, F. P. (1996) ' "I'll See It When I Believe It": Rodney King and the Prison-house of Video', in Sobchack, V. (ed.) *The Persistence of History: Cinema, Television, and the Modern Event*, London: Routledge, pp. 69–88.

Tumber, H. and Webster, F. (2006) *Journalists under Fire: Information War and Journalistic Practices*, London: Sage.

Urry, J. (2000) *Sociology Beyond Societies: Mobilities for the Twenty-first Century*, London: Routledge.

Urry, J. (2003) *Global Complexity*, Cambridge, UK: Polity.

van Dijk, T. (1997) 'Discourse as Interaction in Society', in van Dijk, T. (ed.) *Discourse as Social Interaction*, London: Sage.

van Zoonen, L. (2005) *Entertaining the Citizen. When Politics and Popular Culture Converge*, Lanham, MD: Rowman & Littlefield Publishers.

Vincent, G. E. (1905) 'A Laboratory Experiment in Journalism', *American Journal of Sociology*, 11 (3), 297–311.

Virilio, P. (1997) *Open Sky*, London: Verso.

Volkmer, I. (1999) *News in the Global Sphere: A Study of CNN and Its Impact on Global Communication*, Luton: University of Luton Press.

Walker, D. 'Who Watches Murder Videos'? BBC News online, 12 October 2004, http://news.bbc.co.uk/1/hi/magazine/3733996.stm (accessed 25 January 2005).

Wark, M. (1994) *Virtual Geography – Living with Global Media Events*, Bloomington: Indiana University Press.

Watson, D. (2005) 'Fox's 24: Propaganda Thinly Disguised as Television Programming', 5 April, www.wsws.org

Weaver, D. et al. (2004) 'Agenda-Setting Research: Issues, Attributes, and Influences', in Kaid, L. L. (ed.) *Handbook of Political Communication Research*, London: Lawrence Erlbaum.

Weber, S. (1996) *Mass Mediauras: Form, Technics, Media*, Stanford: Stanford University Press.

Weiss, G. and Wodak, R. (2003) 'Introduction: Theory, Interdisciplinarity and Critical Discourse Analysis', in Weiss, G. and Wodak, R. (eds) *Critical Discourse Analysis*, London: Palgrave Macmillan.

White, M. and Schwoch, J. (1999) 'History and Television', at http://www.museum.tv/archives/etv/H/htmlH/historyandt/historyandt.htm (accessed 14 May 2006).

Williams, R. (1974) *Television: Technology and Cultural Form*, London: Fontana.

Wittgenstein, L. (2002) *Philosophical Investigations*, Oxford: Blackwell.

Wolfsfeld, G. (2004) *Media and the Path to Peace*, Cambridge: Cambridge University Press.

Wright, E. and Wright, E. (eds) (1999) *The Zizek Reader*, Oxford: Blackwell.

Zelizer, B. and Allan, S. (eds) (2002) *Journalism after September 11*, London: Routledge.

Zizek, S. (ed.) (1994) *Mapping Ideology*, London: Verso.

Zizek, S. (2006) *The Parallax View*, Cambridge, MA: MIT Press.

Index

Page numbers followed by n indicate notes